From
Traders
to **Innovators**

ISEAS – Yusof Ishak Institute (formerly the Institute of Southeast Asian Studies) was established as an autonomous organization in 1968. It is a regional centre dedicated to the study of socio-political, security and economic trends and developments in Southeast Asia and its wider geostrategic and economic environment.

The Institute's research programmes are the Regional Economic Studies (RES, including ASEAN and APEC), Regional Strategic and Political Studies (RSPS), and Regional Social and Cultural Studies (RSCS).

ISEAS Publishing, an established academic press, has issued more than 2,000 books and journals. It is the largest scholarly publisher of research about Southeast Asia from within the region. ISEAS Publishing works with many other academic and trade publishers and distributors to disseminate important research and analyses from and about Southeast Asia to the rest of the world.

From
Traders
to Innovators

*Science and Technology
in Singapore since 1965*

GOH CHOR BOON

ISEAS YUSOF ISHAK INSTITUTE

First published in Singapore in 2016 by
ISEAS Publishing
30 Heng Mui Keng Terrace
Singapore 119614

E-mail: publish@iseas.edu.sg
Website: bookshop.iseas.edu.sg

The responsibility for facts and opinions in this publication rests exclusively with the author and his interpretations do not necessarily reflect the views or the policy of the publisher or its supporters.

ISEAS Library Cataloguing-in-Publication Data

Goh, Chor Boon.
    From Traders to Innovators : Science and Technology in Singapore since 1965.
    1. Technology—Social aspects—Singapore—History.
    2. Entrepôt trade—Singapore—History.
    3. Singapore—Economic conditions.
    I. Title.
    II. Series: Modern economic history of Southeast Asia.
HC445.8 G615   2016

ISBN 978-981-4695-78-7 (soft cover)
ISBN 978-981-4695-79-4 (e-book, PDF)

Typeset by International Typesetters Pte Ltd
Printed in Singapore by Markono Print Media Pte Ltd

CONTENTS

ABBREVIATIONS

A*Star	Agency for Science, Technology and Research
AAS	American Association for the Advancement of Science
APEC	Asia Pacific Economic Cooperation
ASEAN	Association of Southeast Asian Nations
B2C	business-to-consumers
BIM	building information modelling
BMS	biomedical sciences
CADD	computer-aided design and drafting
CIMOS	Computer Integrated Marine Operations System
CITOS	Computer Integrated Terminal Operations System
CPF	Central Provident Fund
DJHS	Division of Biomedical Sciences, John Hopkins in Singapore
DSO	Defence Science Organisation
EAEC	East Asia Economic Caucus
EAEG	East Asia Economic Grouping
EDB	Economic Development Board
EIU	Economist Intelligence Unit
EOI	export-oriented industrialization
ESC	Economic Strategies Committee
EWIPO	Environment and Water Industry Programme Office
FDI	foreign direct investment
FSTI	Financial Sector Technology & Innovation
GCI	Global Creativity Index
GDP	gross domestic product
GERD	gross expenditure on R&D
GIS	Genome Institute of Singapore

ICT	information and communications technologies
IES	Institution of Engineers
IMB	Institute of Medical Biology
IMCB	Institute of Molecular and Cell Biology
IP	intellectual property
IPOS	Intellectual Property Office of Singapore
ISI	import substitution industrialization
JCCI	Japanese Chamber of Commerce and Industry
JHM	Johns Hopkins Medicine
LIUP	Local Industry Upgrading Programme
MAS	Monetary Authority of Singapore
MIT	Massachusetts Institute of Technology
MNC	multinational corporations
MPA	Maritime and Port Authority of Singapore
NAFTA	North American Free Trade Area
NIE	National Institute of Education
NIE	newly industrializing economy
NPI	Nature Publishing Index
NRF	National Research Foundation
NSTB	National Science and Technology Board
NTP	National Technology Plan
NTU	Nanyang Technological University
NUS	National University of Singapore
OECD	Organisation for Economic Cooperation and Development
OHBC	overhead bridge cranes
P&G	Procter & Gamble
PAP	People's Action Party
PCT	Patent Cooperation Treaty
PISA	Programme for International Assessment
PLC	product life cycle
PSA	Port of Singapore Authority
PSC	Public Service Commission
PUB	Public Utilities Board
QCC	quality control circles
R&D	research and development
RCOC	Remote Crane Operations & Control
RIE	Research, Innovation & Enterprise

RSE	research scientists and engineers
S&T	science and technology
SGH	Singapore General Hospital
SISIR	Singapore Institute of Standards and Industrial Research
SIT	Singapore Institute of Technology
STEM	science, technology, engineering and mathematics
STN	Singapore Tissue Network
SUTD	Singapore University of Technology and Design
TEA	Total early-stage Entrepreneurial Activity
TEU	twenty-foot equivalent units
TFP	total factor productivity
WIPO	World Intellectual Property Organisation

INTRODUCTION

In recent years the small island city-state of Singapore has gained the world's attention for its aggressive policies in enticing the international scientific community and corporate entities to relocate and contribute to its agenda of building a world-class research and development (R&D) hub. The Singapore Government has also been making concerted efforts to encourage young Singaporeans to think "science and technology", to motivate science and engineering graduates to pursue their interests in the field of R&D, and to propagate the rise of a critical mass of technopreneurs. At the national policy level, Singapore's science and technology (S&T) policy has shifted from the traditional wholesale adoption of Western technology of the 1970s and 1980s to a policy that aims to promote indigenous technology development through an integral dynamic innovation-systems perspective for stimulating innovation. Singapore is ploughing 2.3 per cent of its gross domestic product (GDP) into R&D, which brings it closer to other countries famed for their focus on research, such as Denmark and Switzerland. Singapore targets to raise R&D spending to 3.5 per cent of GDP by 2015, which would place the small city-state among the top five research-intensive countries, including Israel, Sweden and Japan.

Singapore's determined move to integrate science and technology into its overall economic strategic plan has been largely influenced by many changes. The desire to close the technological gap also reflects the prevalent ideology to survive and to catch up in view of the dynamic changes in economic relations between countries, in which technology has become a dominant competitive force. Singapore's economic growth now centres on an innovation-driven, industrial strategy. Innovation is more than simply new technologies; it involves how business processes are integrated and managed, how services are delivered, how public policies are formulated, how markets are developed and, more broadly, how the society could benefit from creativity and innovation. It is also the case that in a global, knowledge-driven economy, technological innovation — defined as the transformation of new knowledge into products, processes and services of value to society — is critical to competitiveness, long-term productivity growth and an improved quality of life. Among the major factors determining the city-state's global competitive position, a well-planned science and technology policy and technology infrastructure can be considered as important pillars. They serve to provide indigenous firms with opportunities to upgrade, innovate and commercialize their R&D efforts. Whether the country can achieve the successful transition from the imitation of to the creation of technology remains to be seen. One can argue that the availability of an excellent technology infrastructure and a pool of foreign scientists and research engineers alone do not guarantee success. One can also argue that the availability of research funds and monetary incentives is a significant key to achieving technological excellence and self-reliance. However, the creative adaptation of imported technologies and the subsequent transition to the level of indigenous technological innovations — as seen in the case of Japan, South Korea and Taiwan — can only take place within a historical and cultural context of exposure to technological change and transformation. For Singapore, the reality is that it has yet to develop an indigenous, self-reliant technological base capable of producing innovations that can cater to world markets. A major problematic issue is the acknowledged lack of indigenous technological entrepreneurs, research engineers and scientists.

In explaining why some small countries — such as Sweden, Finland, Switzerland, Japan, South Korea and Taiwan — are able to create and commercialize indigenous technological innovations and others are not, the answer seems to lie in the historical traditions, the role of the state, and the sociocultural motivations, attitudes, interests, mindsets and behaviours of the people within a society. Rising from the devastation of the Pacific War, Japan became an economic powerhouse, driven by its technological creativity. But while Japan was successful in its technological leapfrogging strategy, the Chinese (at least during the twentieth century) were not able to meet with the same type of success. This is especially interesting given that the Japanese have borrowed so heavily from Chinese culture in the past. It has been suggested that the Japanese have exhibited a greater willingness to borrow from other cultures and to learn new ways of doing things, whereas in China, where Confucianism was more rampant and respect for the past and one's elders more ingrained, the establishment of science and technology was stifled. In the case of Singapore, viewed from a historical and sociocultural perspective, the book's central argument is that the city-state faces an uphill challenge in generating a self-reliant, indigenous technological base, capable of producing its own scientific and technological products and processes.

As a British colony, Singapore's role was largely to support the trade and commerce of Great Britain in Asia. Scientific explorations and experimentations were the least concern of the colony's British administrators. A scientific and technological culture was never germinated. Instead, entrepôt colonialism in Singapore had successfully transferred and nurtured commercial, financial and brokerage institutions and practices to local entrepreneurs. When full independence was given to the people of Singapore in 1965, Lee Kuan Yew and his political comrades wasted no time in lamenting the bleakness of a newborn nation's ability to survive without an economic hinterland in Malaysia. Neither had they the intention to exploit the situation for their own benefits or, in the words of Lee Kuan Yew, "perpetuate ourselves by renaming streets or buildings or putting our faces on postage stamps or currency notes".[1] The country inherited from an era of British colonialism (close to 150 years) a world-class port infrastructure, a modern city, the use of the English language and an upright civil service. It also inherited an entrenched but viable trading, service-oriented and middleman economy which allows Singaporeans opportunities to accumulate wealth. The political pioneers set about to develop social and economic measures — what many foreign observers would see as draconian and autocratic — that would ensure the survival of a multiracial, multi-religious and multilingual nation. Multinational corporations (MNCs) and their imported technologies were (and are) enticed to set up their manufacturing bases in the strategically located city-state. The constraints facing the government to nurture the growth of a technological culture can be partly attributed to the effective social engineering strategies it employed to achieve political and social stability. While the national ideological obsession with excellence and the accumulation of wealth serve as a motivating force for the people to work hard, it has also created the pragmatic, *kiasu* (a local dialect word which means "afraid to lose out") ethos of the people which has further inhibited technological creativity and innovativeness. However, notwithstanding the lure of the financial, property and services sectors which have provided the best opportunities for Singaporeans to accumulate wealth, there are signs that in recent years an increasing number of Singaporeans are venturing out as technological entrepreneurs (or "technopreneurs", for short).

The "miraculous" growth of Singapore as an Asian newly industrializing economy (NIE) has been analysed from several perspectives, but few, if any, of the existing studies have centred primarily on the technological dimension of its development experience. This study addresses this gap in the literature of Singapore's economic history by examining the processes and problems of the nation's technological development from a historical and contemporary perspective. Notwithstanding the importance of economic considerations, this study attempts to explain technological change in the context of Singapore's historical and sociocultural orientations. This emphasis has been taken for two reasons. First, today's developed and developing nations are often ranked according to the level of their technological development. This narrow view, however, overlooks significant historical, social and cultural differences among nations. These factors must be taken into account when studying the relationship between technology and development. Second, all too often the economic history of Singapore has been seen purely from the economist's point of view. It would be particularly refreshing to document Singapore's economic development from a technological perspective; in this case based on an examination of the relationship between technological change and the country's historical and sociocultural institutions and practices.

This book hopes to contribute to the growing literature on the city-state's bold initiative to make a mark in scientific and technological excellence and creativity. Can a nation of traders, middlemen and shopkeepers be transformed into a nation of scientific and technological innovators? Can an economy with an inherited brokerage culture be transformed into one that thrives on scientific and technological creativity? How can young Singaporeans be enticed to take up careers in research? Admittedly, these are broad questions and it is not easy to speculate on the potential outcome of Singapore's aggressive strategies to develop its research and development capabilities. By tracing the evolution of science and technology and emphasizing the importance of historical and sociocultural factors, this book aims to provide useful insights into the developmental process of how the small city-state has attempted to shake off its traditional comprador-trading image and embark on a pathway of technological and scientific learning.

This study does not purport to any extensive interpretation of existing or new primary sources relating to science and technology in Singapore. Specific references to the subject of science and technology are scarce and the sources here are largely drawn from various official reports, personal interviews conducted by the author, views on science and technology by individuals as reported in printed media such as the *Straits Times*, and the few secondary works done from a "science, technology and society" perspective and centring on the role of science and technology in the development of Singapore since 1950. This book is based on my PhD dissertation entitled *The Role of the State and Society in the Development of Science and Technology in Singapore: A Historical and Socio-cultural Perspective* (1995). Personal interviews with twenty scientists, inventors and R&D managers were conducted in March and April 1994. In addition, a questionnaire survey was administered to 347 engineering undergraduates and 56 professional engineers. Although the fieldwork is dated, interestingly, much of the comments made in the mid-1990s are still very much valid twenty years on, especially when triangulated against the comments made by scientists and entrepreneurs in the media since the start of the new century and in interviews conducted by the author recently.

Chapter 1 anchors the book on the theoretical constructs concerning the process of technological change and development and related issues like "catching-up" and "technological leapfrogging", "creative innovations" and the role of the state and society in bringing about technological change. It examines the changing paradigms from the 1970s and 1980s to the present, which serves to explain how developing countries, particularly the so-called Asian "tigers", have attempted to achieve technological excellence. One of the most pressing problems confronting developing nations today is the fear of the widening technology gap between them and the industrialized economies. One way of catching up is to leapfrog the existing state of the art in the development of a new technology that is still in its pre-standardization stage, or even at a more fundamental exploratory stage when its commercial potential is largely untested. The ultimate objective of such a strategy is to achieve technological self-reliance. For Singapore, implicit in this catching up and technology learning processes are crucial roles of various actors, such as multinational corporations, government agencies that plan and roll out science and technology policies and initiatives, research institutes and universities.

Chapter 2 covers the historical forces that shaped the young nation's industrialization policy from the 1950s to the 1970s. Since the 1950s, industrialization was widely acknowledged by the pro-capitalist, independent states of Southeast Asia as the key to survival and economic growth. But the task was not easy, as long periods of colonialism had produced imbalanced economic structures which confined the rising indigenous capitalist class to comprador trading activities and limited small-scale manufacturing and processing. In the case of Singapore, by the late 1950s it remained primarily an entrepôt, with 70 per cent of its GDP derived from entrepôt activities. The country had a small and limited industrial base. The predominant industry was the shipbuilding and repairing industry, which was largely in the hands of governmental and public bodies such as the Singapore Harbour Board and the British Naval Base. When Singapore gained her independence in August 1965, the newly elected leaders adopted a "catching-up" mandate, emphasizing export-oriented industrialization (EOI) as its growth model in the 1960s and 1970s. Recognizing that the long period of colonialism had produced a trading community, the government adopted an open-door policy and looked to MNCs to provide — and hopefully to transfer — high levels of technology and management skills to local businesses.

While the EOI strategy involved the development of science and technology, Chapter 3 argues that the closing of the technological gap was easier said than done. There were mismatches between Singapore's industrial development and the development of the technological competence of the people. It examines the government's concerted attempt in the 1980s to introduce a "technological trajectory" aimed at helping the city-state enjoy its "second industrial revolution". By the 1980s Singapore had achieved the status of a "newly industrialising economy". Singapore's economic growth purportedly centres on an innovation-driven, industrial strategy. This was done (and continuing the pro-MNC policy of the 1970s) largely through attracting foreign technologies. The desired outcome is to achieve some level of independent capacity for technology absorption and adaption. But Singapore's model of technological leapfrogging through the aegis of MNCs had its limitations. There were also issues relating to the training and development from the 1960s to the 1980s of a scientific and technical manpower base to support the nation's drive towards technological excellence.

Nevertheless, by the 1990s it was obvious to the economic planners that the adoption and assimilation of foreign technology is crucial to achieving sustainable growth pathways. At the same time there is an urgent need to develop the country's indigenous technological base. Given this scenario, a national blueprint for S&T policy in Singapore was formulated. Chapter 4 discusses the role of R&D in achieving national goals and the initiatives towards the construction of a technological infrastructure. Unlike developmental work, pure scientific research could not be placed on a high pedestal within the very pragmatic S&T policy. The general consensus then was to adopt the strategy of tying product development to profits and marketability. It was also clear that the realistic goals of Singapore's R&D strategists were concerned chiefly with the "development" side of the R&D equation.

Chapter 5 documents how the government has introduced measures to cultivate a scientific culture, particularly among the young. At the outset of its attempt to formulate and implement a national science policy in the early 1980s, basic research was not a priority. Within this rather narrow research framework the Singapore scientific community faced problems. It is wrong, however, to assume that the government failed to appreciate such issues. Throughout the 1980s and into the present, Singapore has welcomed visits made by prominent scientists and has taken cognizance of their recommendations of how to establish a suitable climate for basic scientific research. Today, large amounts of resources are set aside for basic research. But the generous availability of funding and pro-research policies does not necessarily mean that the people could now be more ready to "think science" and get involved in R&D. The cultural attributes and mindset have to be considered.

The impressive economic performance of Asian NIEs has gained not only the attention of economists but increasingly social scientists as well. While not rejecting altogether economic explanations, these scholars have attempted to link the macroeconomic dynamism of Asian NIEs with cultural factors inherent in the societal systems of these countries. Chapter 6 examines the cultural context in which science and technology develops in Singapore. Essentially, it sets out to answer the question: Does Singapore's cultural system help or hinder technological creativity? One plausible argument is that within the highly regulated society, capped by the government's constant ideological emphasis on survival, catching-up and excellence, dominant beliefs and behavioural norms of Singapore society are such that much effort will be needed to persuade Singaporeans to delve into research in science and technology and for the society to develop a free-wheeling, non-conforming and Silicon-valley type bohemia.

Nevertheless, by the new millennium Singapore had successfully projected itself with the image of a high-tech city, with its advanced information technology infrastructure, a well-planned science park and technology "corridor", cutting-edge research institutes and foreign multinationals who themselves are technological leaders in their respective fields. Singaporeans have shown their creativity and skill in the planning, development and management of infrastructure construction in areas such as urban renewal; public housing; industrial, science and technology parks; and the transportation network. Certainly, in the provision of financial, trading and sourcing services, Singaporeans have shown great ingenuity and resourcefulness. More significantly, recent years have seen an increasing number of Singaporeans who would actually venture out as technological entrepreneurs. But to sustain this technology climate, more success stories of major innovative breakthroughs that could put Singapore on the R&D map must be forthcoming. Indeed, there are some useful innovative technological projects being developed by Singaporeans. These developments are covered in Chapter 7.

However, despite the rising emergence of technological start-ups, the impact of Singapore's historical role — strongly reinforced by its geographical advantages — as an international commercial transaction and brokerage node is still all-pervasive and provides opportunities for many individuals to accumulate personal wealth.

As a traditional society modernizes it also experiences changes, involving the breaking down of older cultural patterns and usually the adoption of new ones. However, the beliefs, values, traits or behaviours of people within a society are also very resilient to change. As the concluding chapter, Chapter 8, argues, despite the government's agenda to transform the city-state into an R&D hub, Singapore's is still very much a trading and commerce node. Its traditional service-brokerage culture, germinated and nurtured during the colonial era, is still the driving force towards wealth accumulation in the city-state. This was the case particularly in the years when the government's pro-MNCs policy resulted in local entrepreneurs given little guidance or incentive to be involved in advanced manufacturing, and so continued to consolidate their positions in the tertiary sector — in commerce, finance and speculative operations. At the same time, making use of the island's pivotal geographical position, the government adopted measures to strengthen Singapore's traditional roles — as the hub of monetary and brokering activities in Asia and the world at large. One other important factor that contributed strongly to the preservation of its trading and brokerage economic activities is its historical role as a centre of a transnational overseas Chinese business networks. The island's geographical position, its excellent telecommunication infrastructure and a very stable political environment motivated many large Chinese business families to make Singapore one of their bases and to develop profitable commercial and financial activities there.

In the final analysis, this book reiterates that Singapore's quest for the growth and development of an indigenous, innovative and self-reliant scientific and technological base is one of the most challenging tasks facing the government today. There are hurdles to overcome, one of which is creating the mindsets and developing the aptitude of young Singaporeans to take up careers in R&D. There is also the issue of a lack of a critical mass of local R&D personnel with the appropriate postgraduate qualifications. Moreover, there are the historical continuities of a strong service-brokerage culture, with its "comprador mentality", which has produced a large pool of wealthy Singaporeans. It seems remotely possible that the country could produce an individual in the mould of Bill Gates or an enterprise in the mould of Samsung. It is also likely that the country will continue to be dependent on the presence of foreign suppliers of new technologies, scientific knowledge and skills. It is obvious to the government that a culture of technological and scientific innovation cannot be created overnight. But the crucial development is that the government is already making a start — and a forceful one too.

Note

1.   Lee Kuan Yew, *From Third World to First: The Singapore Story 1965–2000* (Singapore: Straits Times Press, 2000), p. 67.

1

FROM DEPENDENCY THEORY TO CREATIVE INNOVATION

During the 1970s and 1980s, perceptions concerning technological advancement changed substantially as a result of the phenomenal post-war rise of Japan, followed by the four Asian NIEs — Hong Kong, Taiwan, Singapore and South Korea. Particularly for South Korea and Taiwan, they have experienced economic growth through their ability not only to manage effectively foreign technology but to also develop a dynamic indigenous base. Hence, for the Asian NIEs, science and technology have become critical catalysts for economic development. Increasingly, attempts to explain the success of rapidly growing economies have involved a technological dimension. In this work, the broad theoretical framework of the relationship between technological change and economic development is seen from two shifting paradigms — from the dependency theory and technological dependence to the theoretical concepts of catching-up and technological leapfrogging and how they are achieved through the role of the state and society.

THE DEPENDENCY THEORY AND
LATE-INDUSTRIALIZATION

The dependency theory, simply stated, maintains that growth and development in the developing countries ("the periphery") is hampered by structural dependence on the advanced, industrialized countries ("the core"), although the degree of such constraints varies widely. The theory was made popular during the 1970s by the pessimistic views of Gunder Franck and Samir Amin, both of whom asserted the impossibility of peripheral development in the so-called Third World because of the ways in which the industrialized countries exploited the resources of the former.[1] In a later work and in response to the emergence of the newly industrializing countries, Frank argues that the popular strategy of export-led growth by these countries did not create genuine development because it was also largely dependent on the flow of international capitalism and foreign technology.[2] Writing in the early 1990s and when the world economy was becoming more competitive, more global and increasingly controlled by information and communication technology, Brazilian political economist Fernando Cardoso reaffirms the dependency position of many poor and developing countries. But now they faced "a crueler phenomenon: either the South (or a portion of it) enters the democratic-technological-scientific race, invests heavily in research and development (R&D), and endures the information economy metamorphosis, or it becomes unimportant, unexploited and unexploitable".[3] Cardoso further argues that even for those former Third World countries, such as the Asian NIEs, India, China and Chile, who have managed to become part of the global economy, there is the urgent task to introduce changes at the societal level. These changes include an appropriate industrial policy, an educational policy to upgrade human resources and to integrate the masses into contemporary culture, a science and technology policy capable of producing a technological leap forward in information technology, new materials and new modes of organization and technological innovation.[4] A similar view on technological dependency was expressed by the historian of technological change, Nathan Rosenberg. He maintains that because developing countries lack an organized domestic capital goods sector, they generally do not possess the indigenous capabilities to make capital-saving innovations.[5] Thus, they have to import capital goods at the expense of not being able to develop their own technological base of skills, knowledge and infrastructure, which are the key elements for further economic progress.

By the late 1970s the dependency perspective came under criticism largely due to the "late industrialization" experienced by a number of East Asian countries. The rapid growth of South Korea, Taiwan, Hong Kong and Singapore confirmed that successful capitalist accumulation and growth of indigenous technological effort in innovation and R&D was possible in "the periphery". More importantly, the dynamic role of the state in promoting industrialization and technological change exposed the structural determinism of the dependency theory as its fundamental flaw. Subsequently, research on the concept of "late industrialization" shifted from issues relating to the cost and benefits of technology transfer to the ways in which these countries adapted and mastered imported technology. In the process, theoretical considerations of the relationship between technological progress and economic development in the developing world gravitated towards explanations of why some nations, like the Asian NIEs, were able to catch up and leapfrog technologically while many others are still struggling to achieve industrial and economic success.

The phenomenal growth of Japan after World War II and the subsequent rise of the Asian NIEs since the 1960s have given rise to a wealth of literature to explain their growth experiences. Most writers hope to provide some answers to two basic questions: Is there a definite pattern or a clear model on which the catching-up process is based? And in view of Japan's economic success, what can emerging economies learn from the Japanese experience? Some observers attribute the industrialization of the Asian NIEs mainly to Japan. This view is expressed in the so-called "flying geese" model of East Asian development.[6] In essence, this model suggests that Japan is looked on as an obvious model of successful economic and technological leapfrogging and provides the force behind the growth of the Asian NIE's. In turn, second-tier NIEs such as Thailand, Vietnam, Indonesia and Malaysia are learning and benefitting from the growth experiences of South Korea, Taiwan, Hong Kong and Singapore. The flying-geese argument gained momentum after 1985 when the appreciated yen forced the outflow of Japanese investments, especially in terms of technology transfer, to the Asian NIEs. It is argued by the proponents of the model that the four "tigers" owe their export achievements largely to Japanese manufacturing subsidiaries operating within their economies. Singapore, for example, benefitted from Japanese companies offering technical assistance, and by the early 1990s received Japanese investment amounting to US$7.5 billion. Some scholars have also made the observation that South Korea, a former colony of Imperial Japan, had modelled its economically powerful *chaebol* on the Japanese *zaibtasu*, generally known as *keiretsu* after World War II. However, critics of the flying-geese analogy have argued that the pattern of late industrialization in South Korea and Taiwan has been dramatically different from that pursued by the original goose, Japan.[7] It also differs from the strategies adopted by countries in Southeast Asia. Export-oriented manufacturing in countries such as Malaysia and Thailand is overwhelmingly dependent on foreign suppliers of new technologies. Japanese investments are not the primary cause for the quantitative changes in the regionalization of production in Southeast Asia. Huge increases in the outflow of foreign direct investment (FDI) from the United States and, increasingly, from Taiwan and South Korea have played a no less important role in driving the process of rapid technological change in the countries of Southeast Asia, including Singapore.

TECHNOLOGICAL LEAPFROGGING

Rapid technological advances in industrialized countries are pressing on developing countries to close the technology gap. Many observers have suggested that the best hope for catching up is to leapfrog existing state of the art in the development of a new technology that is still at a fundamental exploratory stage when its commercial potential is largely untested. Such a strategy aims to achieve technological self-reliance or autonomy. However, to be successful, a country needs to have a pool of research scientists and engineers and the support of a well-planned technology policy and infrastructure.

Moses Abramovitz uses the term "social capability" to explain why some latecomers were able to catch up with the early leaders and even forge ahead while many countries fell behind.[8] Abramovitz indentifies "social capability" with a country's institutional and organizational characteristics which develop or impede its ability to successfully exploit best-practised technology, raise the level of technical competence, promote the diffusion of knowledge and increase the mobility of resources and rate of investment.[9] Using Angus Maddison's new compilation of historical time series of the levels and growth of labour productivity covering sixteen industrialized countries from 1870 to 1979, Abramovitz maintains that "[c]ountries that are technologically backward have a potentiality for generating growth more rapidly than that of more advanced countries provided their social capabilities are sufficiently developed to permit successful exploitation of technologies already employed by the technological leaders".[10] The interaction between social capability and technological leapfrogging in the Asian NIEs was illustrated by Bernhard Heitger.[11] In all of these countries the importation of foreign technology played a strategic role in their attempts to close the technological gap. The process was sustained by favourable socio-economic conditions. Despite some differences, increasing the formation of human capital through improving the level and quality of education and ensuring a high degree of economic openness are the common high priorities for all these countries.[12] Implicit in studies on catching up and technology leapfrogging, such as Heitger's, is the role of the state and society in promoting — or inhibiting — the growth of an innovative technological culture which, in the long run, could determine the success or failure to develop an indigenous and self-reliant technological base.

Takeshi Hayashi's study on the technological development of Japan illustrates the concept of the leapfrogging strategy.[13] Hayashi and his team of 114 researchers rely heavily on the use of historical analysis and case studies of Japan's efforts at adapting and diffusing imported industrial technology over a period of 120 years (since the Meiji era). Hayashi provides a conceptual model by which Japan was able to achieve technological self-reliance. The major components are grouped under "Five-Ms"; namely, raw materials or resources, machinery, manpower, management of new machinery and markets. They are incorporated into five stages of technological development, starting from the initial stage and moving on to the acquisition of operational techniques, the maintenance of new machines and equipment, the repairs and minor modifications of foreign technologies, designing and planning, and finally domestic manufacturing. The "five Ms" exist in different proportions in different countries, but Hayashi and his researchers insist that all components must be present in order for modern technology to be effectively integrated with the five stages of technological development. The Japanese experience has shown that all stages must be passed before a country is able to develop capacities for technological self-reliance. However, Hayashi clarifies two pertinent points related to the model. First, "[a]lthough it proved successful in Japan, it may not elsewhere, especially in countries where the system of technology management is largely based on functionalism and where job-hopping among workers and engineers is common"; and, second, "there is no such thing as a leap in technology" because technological changes are incremental rather than quantal in nature.[14] Hayashi's study highlights two important premises for developing countries aiming to close the technological gap and, in the process, attain some form of technological self-reliance. First, native engineers and technologists must play a key role in decision-making and R&D and, second, the need for a positive cultural attitude and perception of the people, in particular the engineers and creative entrepreneurs, towards technology and development. Post-war Japan, as a latecomer, caught up rapidly with the industrialized West by adapting and bringing into production a large backlog of technological innovations pioneered by the technological leaders such as Britain and the United States.

In the 1990s the literature to explain the success of Japan and the Asian NIEs saw substantial contributions by non-economists hoping to unravel the mystery through their interpretation of sociocultural influences. Their stand is that culture has a profound influence on the innovative capacity of a society. A society's sociocultural beliefs, attitudes and values provide directions to the process of technological change. They may either foster or inhibit technological development. Confucian scholars like Tai Hung-chao and Michio Morishima have postulated an "Oriental model" that stressed "cultural collectivism" and that also allowed Japan and the Asian NIEs to achieve their successful late-industrialization.[15] Another notable contributor to the discussion of the rise of the Asian NIEs is Ezra Vogel. He singles out "industrial neo-Confucianism" as a powerful motivating force.[16] By this term Vogel means a Confucian tradition represented by four clusters of institutions and traditional attitudes adapted to the needs of the industrial society. These four clusters are a meritocratic elite, an entrance-examination system, the importance of the social group, and the goal of self-improvement.[17] The bureaucratic system played a critical role in industrialization. Some of the ablest people in the society were recruited into the civil service and assigned major responsibilities. They came to believe in the need for the government to harness the support of the private sector and to encourage it to prosper, while preserving the overall control of the state. Thus, even in Singapore, "where the old attitude of moral disdain toward the merchant perhaps remain strongest, multinational companies were given considerable leeway and government-financed companies were expected to behave like private profit-maximising corporations".[18]

An explanation of technological catching-up by latecomers is further provided by cultural historian Tessa-Morris Suzuki. Her seminal works on the technological transformation of Japan from the seventeenth century provides an alternative explanation of the country's success in technological catch-up. Notwithstanding the importance of institutional support, government policies and management techniques, Tessa-Morris argues that the most important factor is what she terms the "social networks of innovation", defined as "the network of communications which linked research and production centres in Japanese society".[19] These networks are the conduits facilitating the diffusion of information on the latest technologies developed by large corporations and research laboratories to small production firms and local communities at the periphery. Local governments during the Meiji period promoted technological diffusion through craft and technology exhibitions, by dispatching instructors to towns and villages, and by maintaining research libraries.[20] No period is this social network more significant than during the decades of what is popularly known as the "Japanese economic miracle" — the 1950s to the 1970s. Tessa-Morris writes: "Easy access to foreign technology and vigorous state intervention created a favourable climate for the rapid introduction of new techniques, but neither of these factors would have produced such dramatic results had it not been for an existing system of institutions which allowed new ideas to be readily communicated between companies and put to work in their factories and offices. In this context what matters is not so much the role of the state as a source of financial incentives for technological change, but rather its role in creating nodes in the network, through which knowledge of new techniques could flow to many parts of the industrial system."[21] The key question then is this: Is Japan's social network of innovation uniquely a Japanese model? If not, can it be replicated in the strategies of other latecomers to close the technological gap? Tessa-Morris seems certain that "[f]or other newly-industrialising countries, however, the Japanese model is one which cannot be closely imitated".[22]

For industrialization latecomers like South Korea and Taiwan, during the assimilation-adaptation phase (broadly, during the 1970s to the 1990s) of technology transfer, indigenous engineers and technicians had opportunities to learn and understand the operations of machinery and sophisticated equipment, particularly on the shop floor and, more significantly, to indulge in imitation or reverse engineering, defined as the process of recreating a design by analysing a final product. Reverse engineering is common in both hardware and software. In the process, not just new technologies but also procedures, processes and strategies (of competitors) could be developed and adapted by companies to domestic needs. This accumulation of knowledge and skills is crucial to the growth of indigenous technological capabilities. Steven Schnaars argues that "[i]mitation is not only more abundant than innovation. It is actually a much more prevalent road to business growth and profits."[23] He proposes that "creative adaptions are the most innovative kind of copy [and companies] take an existing product and either improve upon it or adapt it to a new arena of competition".[24] Schnaars' analytical framework is further elaborated in Lim Linsu's documentation of South Korea's dynamic technological transformation in which he highlights the importance of building up indigenous technological capabilities in the country's successful shift from imitation to innovations in technological products and processes.[25]

How have Korea and Korean firms managed to achieve such phenomenal growth in technological learning? What major factors account for their rapid technological growth? Kim highlighted several key factors that influence the direction and speed of technological learning in Korean industries: the role of the government, the *chaebols*, education, export policy, technology transfer strategy, research and development policy, sociocultural systems, and private-sector strategy.[26] In his case study of Hyundai Motor as a successful "Imitation-to-innovation" story of the catching-up process, Kim stressed the importance of "crisis construction" in achieving self-reliance in technological absorptive capability.[27] By "crisis construction", Kim refers to a situation in which workers within the organization (in this case, Hyundai Motors) have to collaborate to solve problems in a critical scenario, which, more often than not, is proactively initiated by the management. The aim is to challenge workers to achieve higher performance goals. Hence, the constructed crisis is more creative rather than destructive. And, by doing so, enhances the absorptive capacity of the workers for innovative change. Hyundai uses constructed crises to shift its learning from duplicative-imitation-oriented, to a more creative-imitation-oriented approach and finally to innovation-oriented.[28] According to Kim, a main strategy for South Korea's successful technology leapfrogging has been the reversal of the research, development and engineering stages. Starting from the years when reverse engineering was actively used to assimilate foreign technology (1960s and 1970s), new, improved products and processes were created and commercialized, and, finally, intensive research efforts were injected for cutting-edge development.[29] Korea's approach to innovation of a reversed product life cycle enabled the country's *chaebols* to leapfrog from being makers of technologically inferior products to producers of technologically superior products achieved through cutting-edge R&D.

ROLE OF THE STATE IN TECHNOLOGICAL CHANGE

Explanations of "developmentalist states" in East Asia in achieving rapid industrial and technological development invariably point to the central role of the state in creating the conditions for exploiting new technological opportunities. In the early 1980s, Hofheinz and Calder attempted to provide a systematic analysis of the complex interaction of economic, political, historical and cultural factors that accounted for the rapid growth of East Asia.[30] After weighing various factors they concluded that the economic success of Asian NIEs was based on political economy systems that seem better geared to competition than those in Western countries, and that an "East Asian development model" exists.[31] Some of the major components of this model included (a) a stable political climate through continuity in the ruling elite or party; (b) a Confucian political culture which stressed a high degree of respect for hierarchy and order; (c) a colonial heritage; (d) heavy investment in education, and (e) export-oriented industrial policies. The importance of the state was given further attention by Chalmers Johnson. In his analysis of the linkage between political institutions and the economic performance of Japan, South Korea and Taiwan, Chalmers stresses that, while a laissez-faire type of political control has allowed countries like Hong Kong attain economic wealth, the "soft authoritarianism" style of highly interventionist and pervasive governments in South Korea and Taiwan (and Singapore) have also been able to achieve economic take-off.[32]

While the role of the state in the process of East Asian development has been noted, how does one explain the preservation of the state structure, autonomy and power vis-à-vis the domestic classes and elite? Hsiao Hsin-Huang attributes the harmonious state–society relationship to two factors. First, the "Four Tigers" shared a common colonial history before the war and colonial legacies have produced a lasting influence on the state structure after independence. Hsiao argues that "the 'over-developed' state bureaucracy that was inherited from the ex-colonial powers (Japan and Britain) and [which] was created to control the indigenous population might be a legacy that led to compliance of the populace with state dominance".[33] Second, East Asian tradition has for long socialized people to respect "authority", which in modern times is represented by the state bureaucracy. The fact that these authoritarian governments did maintain order and provided policies conducive to growth helped reinforce the willingness of the people to accept that order. Hsiao further adds one overarching, common sentiment — that of "national survival" in modern times. Responding to the challenges from the West, people in East Asia view their national survival with great urgency, and "such attitudes may also have some direct and indirect influences on pushing people to work harder under the national ideology toward the goals of national strength and wealth".[34] Such a "national survival" ideology is not uncommon in Japan. The late Akio Morita argued that the Japanese obsession with survival triggered the need to consistently develop technological gadgets that would make life more manageable.[35] Thus, within the general context of the political systems that East Asian governments have adopted and which the people have accepted, the state is able to introduce policies and strategies to produce technological change.

A seminal work on the role of the state in Asia's technological development is the late Alice Amsden's interpretation of South Korea's industrialization. She argued that behind the country's technological transformation has been the ability of the state to plan and stimulate the learning and adapting of foreign technologies.[36] Amsden developed the view that "institutional" rather than "market" factors are at work in South Korea's rapid economic development. The engine of growth was symbolized by the *chaebol*, a Korean conglomeration of modern enterprises largely powered by engineers and managers. As a result of the state's heavy investment in science and technology education since the 1960s, between 1960 and 1980 the number of engineers in Korean industry increased by a factor of ten, and the number of managers by a factor of two.[37] In a later book, *The Rise of 'The Rest': Challenges to the West from Late-Industrializing Economies*, Amsden examined the way Asian countries such as South Korea and Taiwan had helped produce growth through state-promoted industrialization.[38] By contrast, Amsden observed, some Latin American countries had accommodated a greater degree of overseas investment, leaving more economic decisions in the hands of multinational firms, not state actors. Sometime in the 1990s the global technological gadget headquarters had shifted from Tokyo to Seoul. Indeed, the South Koreans themselves voiced their concern about the nation's obsession with technology. Myung Oak Kim and Sam Jaffe have termed the country as a "Technology Nirvana".[39] By the early 2000s, "Silicon Valley and other technology hubs began noticing Korea's position in the digital universe. The country becomes the most popular testing ground for new technologies and products."[40] Again, the Korean government played a crucial role. Its "IT839 Strategy" is anchored on the belief that information technology will bring about qualitative changes in the economic and social paradigm, ultimately aiming to realize a ubiquitous world by forming a virtual cycle of developing new services, infrastructures, and growth engines.

TECHNOLOGICAL CREATIVITY AND INNOVATION

By the 1990s new thinking and new approaches about technological change and technological innovation in developing countries (and also the NIEs in Asia) began to emerge. Particularly in the new century, "creativity and technological creativity", "innovation and technological innovation" and "creative innovations" are inseparable buzzwords in the literature relating to science, technology and economic development. Technological innovation is often referred to as the introduction of a technologically new or significantly improved product (goods or service) to the market, or the implementation of a technologically new or significantly improved process within an establishment. The innovation is based on the results of new technological developments, new combinations of existing technology or the utilization of other knowledge acquired by the establishment arising from in-house or contracted-out R&D activities. However, innovation is not entirely about the development and use of technology. Business establishments can also enhance competitiveness and business performance through implementation of new or significantly improved processes and changes to organization, workplace management and marketing strategy. Organizational innovation is regarded as the implementation of a new organizational method in a business establishment's business practices, workplace organization or external relations.

Michael Porter, in his seminal study of the competitive advantage of nations, clarifies that for a nation to develop its competitive advantage it is important that its indigenous firms are able to create and sustain competitive advantage against the world's best competitors in a particular industry or segment.[41] Central to this creation and sustaining of advantage, argues Porter, is innovation. This is achieved through three main pathways; namely, improvements in technology, better methods or ways of doing things, and product or process changes. Porter maintains that firms gain competitive advantage when the home environment of the nation is the most dynamic and challenging, stimulating firms to upgrade and widen their advantages over time, and when the goals of owners, managers, and employees support intense commitment towards innovation. As an explanation for the rise of the West and a difference between rich nations and poor nations, economic historian Joel Mokyr, in his book on technological creativity through the ages, states the conditions for a society to be regarded as technologically creative. These are the presence of a cadre of ingenious and resourceful innovators willing and able to challenge their environment for their own improvement, economic and social institutions prepared to encourage potential innovators with the right incentive structure, and diversity and tolerance.[42] However, he cautioned that technological creativity has tended to rise and fade away dramatically at various times and places in the history of mankind. It is highly dependent on the social and economic environment and institutions. Using the analogy of a plant, Mokyr argues that "technological progress is like a fragile and vulnerable plant, whose flourishing is not only dependent on the appropriate surroundings and climate, but whose life is almost short. It is highly sensitive to the social and economic environment and can be easily arrested."[43] The medieval Islamic world and China witnessed the spectacular decline of scientific and technological creativity after being leaders in fields from mathematics to mechanical invention. A favourable societal environment, shaped by a variety of social, economic and political factors, is essential for inventions and innovations to take place and to support a high level of technological creativity. Clearly, for firms to be innovative, the role of the government is significant, as are institutional reforms to generate an environment that supports innovation.

Conceptual thinking on innovation in the new millennium shifted towards a more broad-based, dynamic technological strategy that does not depend solely on the importation and assimilation of Western technologies but also concerted initiatives to develop indigenous capabilities for creative innovation with regard to products and processes.[44] The concept of a "national innovation system" became actively debated. The development of innovation for a country is viewed as a result of the integration of a spectrum of agencies, which include enterprises, universities and research institutes. Success in coming up with technologically innovative products and processes depends on strong linkages between these various agencies and the role of the government in bringing them together and in promoting trust and collaboration among them. The strength of a country's innovation system is also shaped by the sociocultural qualities of its national communities. Of particular relevance to public policymakers interested in innovation policy are the works of Henry Etzkowitz. Etzkowitz emphasizes the importance of university–industry–government linkages — what he terms the triple helix — in promoting innovative activities in a country's national innovation system.[45] The triple helix interaction of the three institutional spheres represented by organizations such as the technology transfer office, research institutes, science parks and venture capital firms is a necessary condition for the successful commercialization of innovations and, hence, a vital condition for economic growth. This integration is important because "[i]ncreased knowledge production does not translate readily into increased economic productivity" and the gap between research and development, the so-called "valley of death", has to be bridged.[46] Etzkowitz's "triple helix" approach is actively adopted as a model in Singapore's two main research universities — the National University of Singapore (NUS) and Nanyang Technological University (NTU). In the early stage a single helix university development model in the form of an innovation or technology transfer centre was first created to assist faculty members who were keen to commercialize their ideas. This morphed into a dual helix university–industry symbiotic relationship when the university aggressively established linkages with industry partners; a concerted effort has been in place since the late 1990s to encourage faculty and students to commercialize innovative products and processes through business start-ups. Government funding agencies are now stimulating the triple helix interactions through their convening capabilities, by providing public venture capital and inducing public–private research collaborations. In particular, NUS has started to implement major strategic change to become an "entrepreneurial" university. It has targeted the biomedical sector as a critical focus for technology commercialization.[47]

For economist Daron Acemoglu and political scientist James Robinson, innovation is also seen as the key to economic growth, and inclusive economic institutions are the keys to innovation.[48] Inclusive economic institutions secure private property, encourage entrepreneurship and, in the long-term, produce sustainable growth. The process of innovation is "made possible by economic institutions that encourage private property, uphold contracts, create a level playing field, and encourage and allow the entry of new businesses that can bring new technologies to life. It should therefore be no surprise that it was the U.S. society, not Mexico or Peru, that produced Thomas Edison, and that it was South Korea, not North Korea, that today produces technologically innovative companies such as Samsung and Hyundai."[49] Conversely, extractive political institutions stifle innovation and hence promote underdevelopment and poverty. In brief, Acemoglu and Robinson theorize that the origin of power, prosperity and poverty in the nations of the world today lie in the existence of extractive political institutions: "The growth generated by extractive institutions is very different in nature from growth created under inclusive institutions. By their very nature extractive institutions do not foster creative destruction and generate at best only a limited amount of technological progress. The growth they engender thus lasts for only so long."[50] Extractive political institutions served to benefit the ruling elites, and their persistent presence is the cause of nations — in particular, former colonies of European powers — that were poor in their historical past to still be considered poor today. Using the development differences of North and South Nogales and North Korea and South Korea as explicit examples, Acemoglu and Robinson also dismiss the role of geography (including the environment and the presence of natural resources) in economic development.[51] They also disregard the cultural hypothesis as a valid explanation for differences in the wealth of nations: "there are of course differences in beliefs, cultural attitudes, and values between the United States and Latin America..., these differences are a consequence of [the] two places' different institutions and institutional histories".[52]

However, Acemoglu and Robinson admit that growth can be achieved within a set of extractive political institutions. The elites can simply reallocate resources to temporary highly productive activities under their control (e.g., from agriculture to industry). But the problem is that this growth is unsustainable in the long run. When the economy runs out of steam, so will rapid growth and the country will first be exposed to an economic crisis and ultimately to a political one. The example of the rapid growth of Soviet Russia illustrates this point. It was not driven by innovation, but by Communist state control. And when the foundations for growth were exhausted, nothing came to replace it. The economists predict the same thing happening to Communist China.[53] As to how nations evolved over time, that is, whether they would develop extractive or inclusive institutions, would depend on what Acemoglu and Robinson termed the critical junctures of history that exploited the initial small institutional differences and led to diverging development paths of nations.[54] In their own words, "History is the key, since it is historical processes that, via institutional drift, create the differences that may become consequential during critical junctures. Critical junctures themselves are historical turning points."[55] To Acemoglu and Robinson, political inclusiveness and the distribution of political power within a

society are the key elements that will determine the success or failure
of nations. Jeffrey Sachs, however, argues that such a mono-causal
argument is too simplistic and neglects a host of other crucial factors
— geographical, technological and cultural.[56] A plausible explanation for
the general poverty of sub-Saharan nations is geography. The region
had low population densities prior to the twentieth century, a high
prevalence of disease, a lack of navigable rivers for transportation, scarce
rainfall, and a shortage of coal to be able to take advantage of the age
of steamships.[57] However, in the case of the desert state of Botswana, the
nation is endowed with the Jwaneng diamond mine, regarded by many
as the richest diamond mine in the world, and has one of the highest
per capita incomes in Africa. To Sachs, the major flaw in Acemoglu and
Robinson's *Why Nations Fail* is that their theory "does not accurately
explain why certain countries have experienced growth while others
have not and cannot reliably predict which economies will expand and
which will stagnate in the future".[58] In short, today's economic growth
and development of nations is driven by a complexity of factors which
dynamically interact to produce or hinder inclusive growth that benefits
the society as a whole.

Economists interested in technological change also made a
distinction between invention and innovation. Economist Joseph
Schumpeter, who contributed greatly to the study of innovation, pointed
out that invention does not imply innovation, and that firms must
incessantly revolutionize their economic structure from within; that
is, innovate with better or more effective processes and products.[59]
He asserted that it was innovation that provided capitalism with its
dynamic elements.[60] However, the linkage between invention and
innovation is complementary. The difference between innovation and
invention is that invention involves the creation of new things from
new ideas while innovation is the introduction of new concepts to
improve that which already exists. In the 1970s scholars were in the
process of overthrowing the "Eureka" school of invention. Scholars
now emphasize the evolutionary and collaborative nature of invention
and the importance of failures and false starts.[61] Innovation means
taking an idea through to the point where its applications are put
into practice. The application may be commercial; in that case, success
requires acceptance by the market. Inventions in this case may be
patented, unlike innovations which are meant to be used by the

public to improve existing ideas. Invention is concerned with a specific product while innovation addresses a wide range of concerns, seeking to better them.

Must innovation go hand in hand with research? It was commonly believed that scientific research always precedes innovation. While there are successful companies which were founded by researchers-turned-entrepreneurs, this notion is no longer valid.[62] The history of technological innovations has shown that many ground-breaking innovations were developed by creators who did not have the scientific knowledge to explain why things worked as they did.[63] The steam engine worked well before thermodynamics was known to the inventors. Portnoff argues that many radical innovations are the results of "creative leaps". He explains, "What is needed is the intuition of a poet with a strong technical background combined with the skill of the engineer who can put idea into practice and that of the entrepreneur who can turn it into a viable business."[64] As pointed out by Mokyr on what makes a society technologically creative, Portnoff adds that there must be a critical mass of potential innovators who are willing to challenge the unpredictable environment and establish networks among people of different training and backgrounds.[65] For Mokyr, in the long run, technologically creative societies must be both inventive and innovative. This is because "[w]ithout invention, innovation will eventually slow down and grind to [a] halt [and] without innovation, inventors will lack focus and have little incentive to pursue new ideas."[66]

Last but not least, growth theorists have suggested that the clustering of creative human capital in cities is also a critical driving force for innovation to take place. Writing in 1969, the late urban theorist Jane Jacobs argued that cities humming with productive activities are the key to economic expansion.[67] Jacobs defined a city as "a settlement that consistently generates its economic growth from its own local economy [and] are places where adding new to older work proceeds vigorously".[68] For a city to generate wealth and hence economic development, it has to have an environment where people are encouraged to discover, or to innovate, new ways of doing things, new products and services, and where social stability and economic freedom prevails so that people driven by profit-seeking are incentivized to remain entrepreneurial. Such a city, in turn, will attract an influx of people seeking wealth who will form clusters of social networks. In short, the concentration of creative people using and combining their full talents in urbanized cities is the underlying mechanism producing innovation and driving economic growth. Although not an economist by training, Jane Jacobs and the Jacobsian theory of economic development — how urbanized cities with clusters of talent lead to innovation and subsequent economic expansion — gained strong support from urban economists and sociologists alike.

Economist Edward Glaeser, in his *The Triumph of the City*, paints a brightly positive picture of cities as a powerful driver of wealth and development.[69] He argues that a city's success depends on its ability to innovate and reinvent itself to produce ideas and not things. Hence, it is through a concentration of talent within an urbanized and highly livable environment that cities are able to incubate innovation by connecting their inhabitants and serving as a gateway for ideas. Glaeser points to the success of Singapore in upgrading its human resources through lifelong education as an example to support his human capital theory. The city-state has attracted global talent and capital through a high quality of life and strong urban governance. Richard Florida argues that if cities today wish to rejuvenate themselves, they need to attract creative people.[70] It is what Florida termed the "Creative Class" that cities need to nurture and grow in order to harness their creative capabilities to foster innovation. He theorizes that for sustained innovation and economic growth, cities must possess "Technology", "Talent" and "Tolerance" — collectively, known as the "3Ts".[71] These are interdependent drivers of a creative economy. Florida advocates that countries should invest in developing the full human potential and creative capabilities of all citizens — from the low-wage earners to the top professionals. In the study, Florida pinpoints the rise of the creative class and how creative individuals have transformed American society from the 1950s to 2000. The homo creativus have three outstanding values: a strong preference for individualism and self-expression, a belief in championing the spirit of meritocracy, and respect for diversity and openness. His key finding highlights the pattern of geographic concentrations of the creative class in individual regions. According to his "creative capital theory", the centres of the creative class are "more likely to be economic winners", who succeed in generating high-end jobs and economic growth.

TECHNOLOGICAL LEARNING: THE CASE OF SINGAPORE

The city-state of Singapore's efforts to stimulate technological change and to embark on a technological-based growth trajectory since the 1970s illustrates the various theoretical models mentioned above. Under British rule, as a "peripheral" colony of the British Empire in the East, Singapore's entrepôt economy was highly dependent on the development policies of the "core" administrative centre in London.[72] Economic activities were also mainly controlled by foreign trading houses and supported by local compradors. In the 1960s, entrepôt trade was still the mainstay of the economy. By the 1970s it was apparent to the leaders that to survive and then to catch up, the economy had to shift towards the development of an industrial base. Capital accumulation led to the expansion of labour-intensive industry and, at the same time, a contraction of traditional entrepôt activity. Initially, the pace of industrial catch-up was largely dependent on foreign financial investments. But as Singapore became an exporter of labour-intensive goods, domestic savings rose and the reliance on foreign savings was reduced. From the late 1970s to the 1980s, in response to global trends, Singapore's growth model shifted again, towards gaining comparative advantage through the creation of a more capital-intensive industrial base.[73] Economic restructuring now required the adoption of new technologies.

To climb the technological ladder, the model — popularly known as the FDI-leveraged model — adopted from the 1960s to the 1980s was one that depended on technology transfers by MNCs, especially those who were technological leaders in their respective fields. MNCs were urged to transfer technology and skills through their in-house and joint-venture or licensing agreements with local manufacturers. Inducing advanced technology by encouraging foreign investment had some definite advantages. It was possible to obtain, at one and the same time, both the know-how and the capital. By doing so, MNCs could provide exposure in the latest technologies to local managers and workers. This would help in upgrading the country's technical competence. This traditional pathway in technological leapfrogging was seen as the most effective way for a trading country like Singapore to close the technological gap. The earlier stages of industrial catch-up were made easier because of the large pool of technology that was already in existence. As the economy absorbed the backlog, however, further transfers of technology were made more difficult. Jeffrey Sachs rightly pointed out that while many developing countries have "an easy time adopting technologies that have already been developed elsewhere", few are capable of creating indigenous technological innovations.[74] One negative impact of the MNCs-dependent, technological upgrading pathway is that local small and medium companies tend to become more risk-averse in efforts to develop their own product and process technology. Unlike Japan and South Korea where huge conglomerates accumulate competencies in advanced technologies to build up indigenous capacity and then gear towards developing an innovation-based economy, Singapore (and Taiwan and Hong Kong) businessmen take a more gradual, incremental upgrading of technology capabilities rather than a big leap forward at broad intervals. This approach also simplified the learning process since the same trained staff could be used with minor adjustments in training and re-training. In his analysis of Singapore's electronic sector, Mike Hobday shows that technology was accumulated through a gradual process of learning, rather than by leapfrogging.[75] Local small and medium firms "engaged in a painstaking and cumulative process of technological learning, rather than a leapfrog from one vintage of technology to another."[76] Local firms recruited, trained and promoted employees to senior positions in engineering, management and marketing, building up their technological and organizational capabilities in product design, process adaptation, continuous engineering, selective R&D back-up, management and direct marketing.

By the 1990s a concerted effort was made to shift from an "economy focus" to a "technology focus" as the Singapore Government realized the limitations of tapping on MNCs to develop a self-reliant, indigenous technological base. It was a crucial decision to make the shift towards nurturing indigenous capacity building in science and technology. An R&D policy within a larger S&T framework was actively promoted in the 1990s. This R&D work is carried out in several government-funded research institutes, manned by prominent names in the world of science, technology and medicine. Since the start of the new millennium, the Singapore Government's S&T strategies have been directed towards achieving technological innovations and promoting the spirit of technological creativity, particularly in local small and medium enterprises and start-ups. In this shift towards innovation-led growth, the role of the government is critical. It now places strong emphasis on innovation and creativity, not just in the economic sector but also in schools (and higher institutions of learning), where initiatives such as "Innovation and Enterprise" to instil a spirit of entrepreneurship in young Singaporeans have been introduced.

Economic strategists and planners were reminded that Singapore had to reinvent itself in order to enjoy sustainable growth in the new knowledge-based economy. In the words of Michael Porter, who was frequently consulted by the Singapore Government, "Singapore truly is going to have to step up the pace of innovation, broadly defined, if it is going to have the productivity growth in order to continue to increase its sustainability.... Singapore is at the end of an era of economic strategy that has been very successful and it also is going to face the need to shift the strategy at this point."[77] The Singapore Government responded by putting in place institutional measures aimed at creating an innovative industrial policy and work environment. It promotes creativity and problem solving in the education system, from the schools to the universities. It champions innovation-friendly rules, regulations and legislation to provide better protection of inventions and guarantees of ownership. It rolls out initiatives to attract professional talent from all over the world. It maintains a world-class information and communication infrastructure for individuals and companies to stay connected to the world. In short, the government is attempting to create a "Creative City". Figure 1.1 illustrates the ecosystem for innovation-based growth, encapsulating the critical institutional roles of the Economic Development Board (EDB), the Agency for Science, Technology and Research (A*Star) and the universities, polytechnics and research institutes. Collectively, they plan, implement and drive Singapore's S&T policy.

Figure 1.1
A Conceptual Model of Singapore's Strategy in Technology Learning

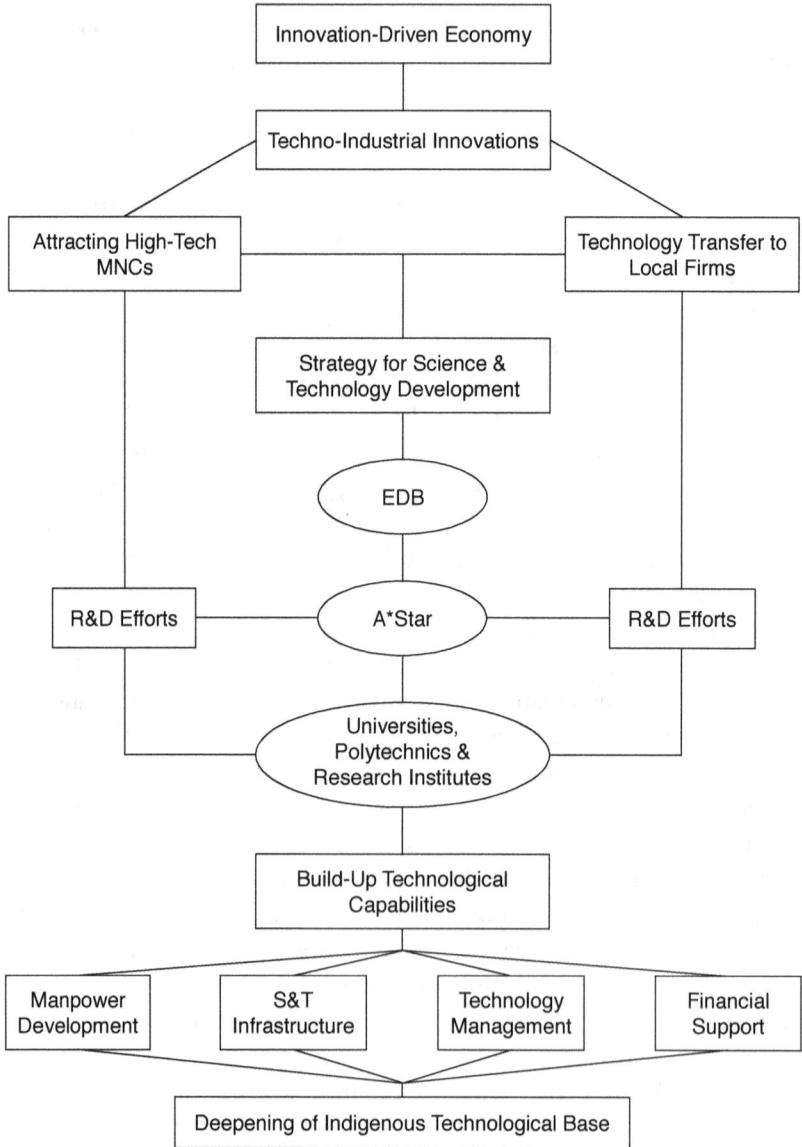

Clearly, Singapore's S&T road map into the twenty-first century centres on the move from an investment-driven strategy to one built on innovation. The question remaining to be answered is, given its historical tradition as a nodal trading centre in the region, would the current heavy investment in research in S&T transform the small island state from a nation of shopkeepers and brokers to a nation of scientific and technological innovators?

Notes

1. A.G. Frank, *Capitalism and Underdevelopment in Latin America* (New York: Monthly Press Review, 1967); S. Amin, *Neo-colonialism in West Africa*, translated from the French by Francis McDonagh (Harmondsworth: Penguin, 1973).
2. A.G. Frank, "Global Crisis and Transformation", in *Development and Change* 14 (1984): 323–46.
3. F.H. Cardoso, "North-South Relations in the Present Context: A New Dependency", in *The New Global Economy in the Information Age: Reflections on our Changing World*, by M. Carnoy, M. Castello, S. Cohen and F.H. Cardoso (Pennsylvania: Pennsylvania State University Press, 1993), p. 156.
4. Ibid., pp. 156–57.
5. N. Rosenberg, *Perspective on Technology* (Cambridge: Cambridge University Press, 1976), pp. 146–47.
6. For a recent reinterpretation of the "flying geese" model, see T. Ozawa, "The (Japan-Born) 'Flying Geese' Theory of Economic Development Revisited – and Reformulated from a Structuralist Perspective", Columbia Business School Working Paper Series, No. 291 (Columbia University in the City of New York, October 2010).
7. See M. Bernard and J. Ravenhill, "Beyond Product Cycles and Flying Geese: Regionalisation, Hierarchy and Industrialisation of East Asia", *World Politics* 47 (1995): 171–209.
8. M. Abramovitz, "Catching Up, Forging Ahead, and Falling Behind", *Journal of Economic History* 46, no. 2 (1986): 385–406.
9. Ibid., pp. 388–90.
10. Ibid., p. 390.
11. B. Heitger, "Comparative Economic Growth: Catching Up in East Asia", *ASEAN Economic Bulletin* 10, no. 1 (1993): 68–74. For an in-depth, comparative analysis of the technological catch-up framework of Korea, Taiwan and Singapore, see Wong Poh Kam, "National Innovation Systems for Rapid Technological Catch–Up: An Analytical Framework and a

Comparative Analysis of Korea, Taiwan and Singapore", paper presented at the DRUID Summer Conference on National Innovation Systems, Industrial Dynamics and Innovation Policy, Rebild, Denmark, 9–12 June 1999.

12. Ibid., pp. 75–78.
13. T. Hayashi, ed. *The Japanese Experience in Technology: From Transfer to Self-Reliance* (Tokyo: United Nations University Press, 1990).
14. Ibid., pp. x and 57.
15. Tai Hung-chao, *Confucianism and Economic Development: An Oriental Alternative?* (Washington, DC: Washington Institute Press, 1989), pp. 26–27. The model provides an alternative, cultural interpretation to the more established Western model of development, popularly known as the Weber-Parson paradigm, or the Rational Model, which emphasized three central characteristics; namely, efficiency, individualism, and dynamism. See also Michio Morishima, *Why has Japan succeeded? Western Technology and the Japanese Ethos* (London: Cambridge University Press, 1982), pp. 14–15.
16. E. Vogel, *The Four Little Dragons: The Spread of Industrialisation in East* Asia (Cambridge: Harvard University Press, 1992).
17. Ibid., p. 101.
18. Ibid., p. 94.
19. Tessa-Morris Suzuki, *The Technological Transformation of Japan from the Seventeenth to the Twenty-first Century* (Cambridge: Cambridge University Press, 1994), p. 7.
20. Ibid., pp. 88–104.
21. Ibid., p. 183.
22. Ibid., p. 244.
23. Steven P. Schnaars, *Managing Imitation Strategies: How Later Entrants Seize Markets from Pioneers* (New York: The Free Press, 1994), p. 1.
24. Ibid., p. 7.
25. Kim Linsu, *Imitation to Innovation: The Dynamics of Korea's Technological Learning* (Boston: Harvard Business School Press, 1997).
26. Ibid., pp. 194–219.
27. Kim Linsu, "Crisis Construction and Organizational Learning: Capability Building in Catching-Up at Hyundai Motor", *Organization Science* 9, no. 4 (1998).
28. Ibid., p. 518.
29. Ibid., 517.
30. R. Hofheinz and K. Calder, *The Eastasia Edge* (New York: Basic Books, 1982).
31. Ibid., p. 248.

32. C. Johnson, "Political Institutions and Economic Performance: The Government-Business Relationship in Japan, South Korea and Taiwan", in *Asian Economic Development: Present and Future*, by R.A. Scalapino et al. (Berkeley: Institute of East Asian Studies, 1985).

33. Hsiao Hsin-Huang, "The Asian Development Model: Empirical Explorations", in *The Asian Development Model and the Carribean Basin Model Institute*, edited by J. Tessitore and S. Woolfson (New York: Council on Religious and International Affairs, 1985), pp. 12–23.

34. Ibid., p. 21.

35. See Akio Morita, *Made in Japan: Ajkio Morita and Sony* (London: Collins, 1987), Chapter 7.

36. Alice M. Amsden, *Asia's Next Giant: South Korea and Late Industrialisation* (New York: Oxford University Press, 1989). See also L. Westphal, E. Kim and C. Dahlman, *Reflections on Korea's Acquisition of Technological Capability*, DRD Discussion Paper 77 (Washington, DC: World Bank, 1984).

37. Ibid., Table 7.4, p. 171 and Chapter 9.

38. Alice M. Amsden, *The Rise of "The Rest": Challenges to the West from Late-Industrializing Economies* (New York: Oxford University Press, 2001).

39. Myung Oak Kim and S. Jaffe, *"The New Korea: An Inside Look at South Korea's Economic Rise* (New York: Amacom, 2010).

40. Ibid., 151–52.

41. Michael Porter, *The Competitive Advantage of Nations* (New York: The Free Press, 1990), pp. 107–17.

42. Joel Mokyr, *The Lever of Riches: Technological Creativity and Economic Progress* (Oxford: Oxford University Press, 1990), pp. 11–12.

43. Ibid., p. 301.

44. See Henny A. Romjin and M.C.J. Caniëls, "Pathways of Technological Change in Developing Countries: Review and New Agenda", *Development Policy Review* 29, no. 3 (2011): 359–80.

45. See Henry Etzkowitz, *The Triple Helix: University-Industry-Government Innovation in Action* (New York: Routledge, 2008); Henry Etzkowitz, "StartX and the Paradox of Success: Filling the Gap in Stanford's Entrepreneurial Culture", *Social Sciences Information* 52, no. 4 (2013): 605–37.

46. Etzkowitz, *Triple Helix*, p. 42.

47. Wong Poh Kam, "Commercialising Biomedical Science in a Rapidly Changing 'Triple Helix' Nexus: The Experience of the National University of Singapore", *Journal of Technology Transfer* 32, no. 4 (2007): 367–95.

48. Daron Acemoglu and James Robinson, *Why Nations Fail: The origin of Power, Prosperity and Poverty* (London: Profile Books, 2013).

49. Ibid., p. 77.

50. Ibid., p. 150.

51. Ibid., p. 50.

52. Ibid., p. 63.

53. Ibid., p. 442.

54. These "critical junctures" are similar to Porter's use of "chance" events as determinants of national advantage. Ezra Vogel, too, makes reference to historical events that influence a country's course of development. He termed them as "situational factors".

55. Ibid., p. 432.

56. Jeffrey D. Sachs, "Government, Geography, and Growth: The True Drivers of Economic Development", *Foreign Affairs* 92, no. 5 (2012).

57. Ibid., p. 145. However, Sachs also recognizes that Africa today "is overcoming these problems one by one, thanks to new energy discoveries, long-awaited agricultural advances, breakthroughs in public health, and greatly improved information, communications, and transportation technologies". See p. 149.

58. Ibid., p. 143.

59. J.A. Schumpeter, *Capitalism, Socialism, and Democracy*, 6th ed. (London: Routledge, [1943] 2010). pp. 81–84.

60. Ibid.

61. For a useful account of the thinking behind the concept of invention, see Susan J. Douglas, "Some Thoughts on the Question: "How Do New Things Happen?", *Technology and Culture* 51, no. 2 (2010): 293–304.

62. Andre-Yves Portnoff, *Pathways to Innovation*, translated by Ann Johnson (Paris: Futuribles Perspectives, 2003), p. 23.

63. See Mokyr, *The Lever of Riches*, Chapters 7–10.

64. Portnoff, *Pathways to Innovations*, p. 29.

65. Ibid, pp. 37–53.

66. Mokyr, *The Lever of Riches*, pp. 10–11.

67. Jane Jacobs, *The Economy of Cities* (New York: Random House, 1969).

68. Ibid., p. 50

69. See Edward Glaeser, *The Triumph of the City: How Our Greatest Invention Makes Us Richer, Smarter, Greener, Healthier and Happier* (New York: Macmillan, 2011).

70. Richard Florida, *Rise of the Creative Class Revisited* (New York: Basic Books, 2013).

71. Ibid., Chapter 12.

72. Economic historians have also debated much on the impact of "developmental colonialism" in former colonies in East and Southeast Asia. It is well documented that the two former Japanese colonies of South Korea and Taiwan have achieved remarkable economic growth post-1945. In her comparative study of the economic performance of colonies in East and

Southeast Asia, Anne Booth concludes that those who argue that "it was post-colonial policies which were crucial in transforming both states [Korea and Taiwan] and in holding back South East Asian countries would still seem to be on stronger ground". See Ramon H. Myers and Mark R. Peattie, eds., *The Japanese Colonial Empire* (Princeton, NJ: Princeton University Press, 1984); Harald Fuess, ed., *The Japanese Empire in East Asia and Its Postwar* Legacy (Munich: Ludicium Verlag, 1988); Stephen Haggard, David Kang and Chung-In Moon, "Japanese Colonialism and Korean Development: A Critique", *World Development* 25, no. 6 (1997): 867–81; Atul kohli, *State-Directed Development: Political Power and Industrialization in the Global Periphery* (Cambridge: Cambridge University Press, 2004); and Anne Booth, "Did It Really Help to Be a Japanese Colony? East Asian Economic Performance in Historical Perspective", Asia Research Institute Working Paper Series, No. 43, June 2005, National University of Singapore.

73. For a summary of the Singapore economy and its growth strategies to 1986, see Lawrence B. Krause, "Thinking about Singapore", in *The Singapore Economy Reconsidered*, by Lawrence B. Krause, A.T. Koh and T.Y. Lee (Singapore: Institute of Southeast Asian Studies, 1987), pp. 1–21.

74. Sach, "Government, Geography, and Growth", p. 144.

75. Hobday, M. "Technological Learning in Singapore: A Test Case of Leapfrogging", *Journal of Development* Studies 30, no. 30 (1994): 831–58. The study was carried out in 1991–92. Thirty-two interviews were conducted with companies in semiconductor manufacturing, disk drive manufacturing, consumer electronics and computers/professional services.

76. Ibid., p. 853.

77. *Sunday Times*, 5 August 2001. The Harvard Business School's professor was invited by the Economic Development Board to brainstorm on how Singapore should prepare itself in the new millennium.

2

SURVIVING AND CATCHING UP IN THE 1960s AND 1970s

The 1950s and 1960s were turbulent decades in Singapore's history. They highlighted the vulnerability of the state and the economy, which was highly dependent on external developments, both regional and worldwide. When Singapore became a sovereign state in August 1965, her leaders were faced with the unenviable task of ensuring the political and economic survival of the small city-state. Colonialism had produced a lopsided economy strongly dependent on entrepôt trade. But the world was changing fast. Increasingly, science and technology became the vital ingredients that would dictate a country's level of competitiveness. Hence, the overriding priority of the Singapore Government in 1965 was to find the quickest and most effective way to develop an industrialized economy. However, it is argued here that historical forces continued to dictate the nature of Singapore's industrialization programme. Moreover, Singapore's industrial strategies adopted during this period had little impact on the growth of the indigenous technological capability of the country.

THE GEOPOLITICAL SCENARIO, 1942–65

On 15 February 1942, the British Commander General E. Percival surrendered the "impregnable fortress" of Singapore to the Japanese. The fall of Singapore "meant not just the end of a campaign; it meant the end of an age".[1] Singapore was renamed "Syonan-to", or "Light of the South", and, together with Malaya, became a part of Japan's Greater East Asia Co-Prosperity Sphere. However, like the British, the Japanese recognized its exceptional geographical advantages, and Singapore became the administrative centre of the Japanese Empire in Southeast Asia.

The economy of Singapore was shattered during the period of Japanese rule. Its infrastructure was badly damaged when the British, while retreating from Malaya, destroyed bridges, machinery and motor workshops, oil depots, railway lines, and other public installations. The island's entrepôt trade and Malaya's export of raw materials such as tin and rubber were severely disrupted as Japanese rule cut off the main European markets. Japanese *zaibatsu* took over most of the economic assets of the British, American and Dutch. The local Chinese, too, lost most of their business concerns. Those suspected of loyalty to the Chungking government in China had their properties confiscated. In short, the Japanese conquest of Singapore exposed the structural weaknesses of the economy — the dependence on entrepôt trade and the virtual absence of an industrial sector.

It is generally said that, in Southeast Asia, the Pacific War brought an end to colonialism and opened the way to a new era of political and economic nationalism. When the British reoccupied Singapore and Malaya in September 1945, they found, as they had seen in Burma, a land devastated by the Japanese. More importantly, they realized that in their absence a native nationalism, previously unheard of, had surfaced. The British now proposed new administrative institutions for Malaya. Singapore was governed as a separate Crown Colony with effect from 1 April 1946. This breakaway from the rest of Malaya, including Penang and Malacca, reflected the desire of the British to keep the island as a viable commercial and military base.

However, Singapore during the 1950s and 1960s was far from quiescent. There was widespread opposition to the presence of the

British. The situation was well expressed in the words of a former
politician:

> The defeat of the British colonial power at the hands of the Japanese
> in the Malayan campaign, followed by three years and eight months of
> Japanese Occupation of Singapore left no doubt that the British were
> not invincible. Their interests in Singapore were pegged to serve the
> wider interests of the British Empire. It was a lesson to Singaporeans
> that Singapore would be abandoned by her colonial master if they
> thought it expedient to do so.[2]

There were also frequent industrial strikes and unrest, which forced
the closure of many British firms and, subsequently, an exodus of
British capital from Singapore. The aftermath of the war had created
severe social and economic dislocations for the people of Singapore.
The population grew from about 960,000 in 1948 to about 1.6 million
by 1954. There was high unemployment and an acute shortage of
public housing. Many squatter colonies sprouted up throughout the
suburban and rural areas. In the 1950s racial integration did
not exist, and within the plural society the main ethnic groups
considered themselves as Chinese, Malays and Indians, rather than as
Singaporeans. Religious differences, if exploited, could also lead to
communal trouble. This was starkly shown in the Maria Hertogh riots
which took place from 11 to 13 December 1950.

In general, the British colonial policies relating to education,
language and citizenship were responsible for stifling the growth of
racial integration and the sharing of a common destiny and identity
by the people of Singapore. In education, for example, the government
did not attempt to regulate and support the number of Chinese schools
and, at the same time, encouraged the growth of the English-stream
schools. The Chinese-educated became an under-privileged group; they
had no opportunities for tertiary education, nor could they hope to
be employed in the civil service. In short, the government failed to
recognize the more dynamic and vocal Chinese-educated group. These
"gaps" were quickly exploited by the Malayan Communist Party in
Singapore. In the 1950s frequent clashes and demonstrations against
the government were held by Communist-infiltrated trade unions
and Chinese schools. The British soon decided that the best political
weapon against the Communist insurgency would be to grant national

independence to Singapore. This would deprive the Communists of their role as the champions of the anti-freedom movement and, hence, the justification for insurrection against the government. Therefore, the stage was set for the first democratic election of a self-governing Singapore in May 1959. The People's Action Party (PAP), under the leadership of Lee Kuan Yew, won convincingly. Lee became the first Prime Minister and, at the same time, the state flag and national anthem *"Majullah Singapura"* were inaugurated. About four years later, in September 1963, Singapore became part of Malaysia. But political differences soon reached an intolerable level. On 9 August 1965, under the leadership of Lee Kuan Yew, the island of Singapore was formally separated from Malaysia and became a sovereign, democratic and independent city-state. Thereafter, Singapore commenced its struggle to survive on its own and to develop a national identity and national consciousness in a disparate population of immigrants.

Singapore's turbulent political history in the 1960s was equally matched with the occurrence of several economic crises which exposed the vulnerability of the small nation completely dependent on her colonial entrepôt status. The first event was known as the "Indonesian Confrontation". Singapore's participation in the formative years of Malaysia had alienated herself from her important traditional trading neighbour, Indonesia. The trade boycott by Indonesia during the years 1963 to 1965 severely damaged Singapore's entrepôt trade and the "whole economy almost grounded to a halt at a growth rate of 0.6 per cent in 1964".[3] Besides the severance of trade, Indonesian saboteurs infiltrated Singapore and exploded a number of bombs. The sudden and forceful separation from Malaysia in 1965 was another crisis which created great anxiety. Singapore, as Malaysia's traditional entrepôt port, was largely bypassed when the latter used her own ports and traded directly with other nations. Furthermore, Malaysia started her own import substitution industrialization policy and this meant the erection of high tariffs which effectively shut Singapore off from her traditional hinterland.[4] Finally, the 1960s ended with the untimely and shocking announcement by Britain in January 1968 of her intention to accelerate the withdrawal of her forces from Singapore and the Far East by 1971. British military expenditure had accounted for an average of about 20 per cent of GDP in the 1960s, and the bases employed about 25,000 Singapore citizens.[5]

The trauma of the 1960s convinced Lee Kuan Yew and his colleagues that two immediate priorities had to be met without delay if the small nation was to survive. To compete as a viable economic entity, the first task was to break away from the long dependency on entrepôt trade and embark on an EOI strategy.[6] The second urgent task was to create its own military capability. The passing of the National Service Act of 1967 marked the beginning of a concerted effort at maintaining a large defence force and, at the same time, of seeking to engender a sense of national loyalty amongst the younger citizens. It is of no coincidence that Singapore's obsession with her own security resulted in an intensive and continual upgrading of the defence force through the direct purchase of advanced weaponry and through indigenous research and development of military technology.

As the Singapore economy progressed into the 1970s, Lady Luck seemed to be constantly on her side. Fortuitous external circumstances, what Ezra Vogel terms as "situational factors", played an important role in ensuring that the island not only survived but enjoyed one of the highest growth rates in the world.[7] As explained by Lee Kuan Yew in his National Day Speech on 17 August 1980:

> It is as well we have made the best of the last 20 years, when external world forces were favourable, to improve our internal conditions. A powerful American economy, with oil in plentiful supply and at low prices, enabled America and Europe to boom throughout the 1950s and 1960s with growth rates of over 6%, and Japan at over 12% per annum respectively. World trade bounced along at 8–10% per annum. So we too bounced along at over 10%.[8]

The Americans' commitment to East Asia, in particular, increased significantly with the country's involvement in the Korean War and the Vietnam War. Though the gain was less direct than in the case of Japan, the wars stimulated the Singapore economy through the provision of support services to the allied troops. Thus, on the whole, due to her extremely positive attitude towards foreign investment and the wide range of attractive incentives to MNCs, Singapore became a favourite site for U.S. investors. During the 1970s, foreign direct investment in manufacturing by U.S. investors averaged 33 per cent per annum.

INDUSTRIALIZATION: THE KEY TO SURVIVAL

For many so-called "Third World" countries, the road to industrialization starts with the adoption of the development strategy strongly recommended by the Argentinian economist Raul Prebisch; that is, import substitution industrialization (ISI) aimed at the reduction of dependence on imported goods.[9] Essentially, it involves the small-scale production of non-durable consumer goods whose production requirements are compatible with conditions existing in countries without previous industrial experience, such as abundant unskilled labour and unsophisticated technology.[10] Comparatively high growth rates were experienced by all countries in Southeast Asia, but by the mid-1960s the limitations and inherent contradictions of the ISI strategy began to be felt.[11] Development strategy gradually shifted towards EOI, and by the early 1970s EOI became the "new orthodoxy" strongly advocated by the Hungarian-born economist Bela Balassa of the World Bank for economic growth in Third World countries.[12]

In the case of Singapore, by the late 1950s it remained primarily an entrepôt, with 70 per cent of its GDP derived from entrepôt activities.[13] The country had a small and limited industrial base. The predominant industry was the shipbuilding and repair industry, which was largely in the hands of public bodies, such as the Singapore Harbour Board and the British Naval Base. The small manufacturing sector consisted mainly of light engineering and processing industries, with shipbuilding, repairing and marine engineering taking up a 43 per cent share.[14] Though employment in the manufacturing sector grew from 22,692 in 1955 to 44,295 by 1961, manufacturing development was slow and stagnated at about 12 per cent of gross domestic production in 1960. In the meantime, population growth was increasing at 4 per cent and unemployment rose to a high of 7 to 8 per cent in the early 1960s.[15] It was clear to the government that solving the rising unemployment problem was a matter of high priority. By the late 1950s the government became more focused on the need to expand the industrial base, though it still advocated that

Singapore continue to "jealously guard its position as an entrepot".[16] But the task of expanding manufacturing activities for a trading port was not expected to be smooth; as noted in a report prepared by the Chief Planning Officer in 1954:

> There is at present a dearth of skilled labour in Singapore, in practically every type of manufacturing industry. This is not because of the fact that natural aptitudes are not present. The recent development of industry in Hong Kong has shown that the labour pool there easily adapted itself to the new conditions, and the experience of industrialists in Singapore shows that a similar state of affairs exists here. It is a well-known fact that adequate facilities are not available at present in Singapore and the encouragement of such facilities is essential if industrialisation is to take place.[17]

It also made the point that "the use of machinery has been kept to a minimum in a large range of industries and, where it exists at all, it is often of a fairly low standard".[18] Local entrepreneurs, too, were not easily geared up to the task. More significantly, it reflected on the extent to which the government had committed itself on the need to develop an industrial base as an integral component of the Singapore economy.

Local entrepreneurs in Singapore had contributed little to the industrial development of the economy before the war. This trend continued in the immediate decades following the end of the war. One explanation relates to the "practice amongst Chinese firms of making the establishment a family concern and restricting the employment of persons outside the family to a minimum".[19] Another factor was the fact that the Malayan (including Singapore) economy was dominated by non-manufacturing European enterprises. These firms were mostly engaged in trade and processing of primary products. They controlled 65 to 75 per cent of the export trade in 1953 and 60 to 70 per cent of the import trade in 1955, and agency houses owned about 75 per cent of the nearly two million acres of land under plantations.[20] The predominating position of rubber and tin and the fluctuations associated with the trade also somehow swayed entrepreneurs in Singapore away from industrial ventures. During boom conditions, they made large profits from speculations in the rubber and tin trade. But when prices were depressed the entrepreneurs, all the more, had no wish to commit liquid reserves to long-term industrial investments which could only reap steady returns in the long run. In addition, political uncertainty and social instability in the form of communal tensions and labour unrest dampened any likely investment, both local and foreign, in industrial ventures. Therefore, by the end of the 1950s the economy of Singapore was still very dependent on the profitable entrepôt trade, a comparative advantage which the island possessed mainly due to its favourable geographical position.

THE WINSEMIUS REPORT, 1961

In 1961 a United Nations Industry Survey Mission, under the leadership of the Dutch economist Albert Winsemius, was commissioned by the Singapore Government, along with other aims, to "advise the necessary economic, organizational and operational measures for promoting sound and speedy development of manufacturing industries".[21] The "Winsemius Report", as it became known, convinced Singapore's leaders that the traditional dependence on entrepôt trade and servicing industries such as banking would not enhance the future economic survival of the small city-state. In the face of increasing unemployment and an expanding workforce, the first priority was the provision of sufficient job opportunities. It was estimated that from 1961 to 1970 some 214,000 additional jobs had to be created.[22] The report highlighted three crucial areas related to the industrialization of the Singapore economy; namely, the state of the manufacturing sector, capital and manpower, and the development of technical competency.

The report highlighted the relatively insignificant, declining and dualistic position of manufacturing industries in the economy; some 70 per cent of the 1,882 establishments in 1960 were small, employing less than ten workers:

> Singapore's manufacturing industry can be divided into two groups. On one side, there are a limited number of usually well managed factories, for the greater part subsidiaries of foreign firms. On the other side, there existed many small establishments characterized by low productivity. The first group pays higher wages, the second group often very low wages. Workers in the two groups are non-competitive.

In view of the limited home market, future manufacturing industry will have to compete in the world markets.[23]

Having no natural resources, the economic development of Singapore would depend to a great extent on developing this competitive position. Furthermore, in the long run only an expansion of manufacturing industry could keep pace with the growing population. To achieve this end, the report recommended a "crashed programme" based on an intensive export-driven expansion of manufacturing industries. The report also stressed that, while Singapore did not lack local entrepreneurs, their main activities were concentrated in entrepôt trade and other commercial transactions that gave them quick returns and high liquidity. Long-term investments in manufacturing industries could not provide them with such advantages. Hence, in many ways, domestically based capital was structurally immobile. However, it was pointed out that "it would be wrong to underestimate the future role which local capital might play in the proposed industrial programme", because "a considerable portion of investment in manufacturing industries is financed by local capital".[24]

The expansion of indigenous manufacturing activities, however, was severely impeded by one factor — the lack of manufacturing, including managerial and technical, "know-how".[25] Most of the entrepreneurs lacked experience in manufacturing ventures, and for those who had gone into manufacturing, "the operational efficiency of their establishments is comparatively low".[26] In many of the smaller industries, machinery and production methods were outdated. Though the entrepreneurs possessed the managerial knowledge in handling trading and commercial activities, the complex operation of a manufacturing industry requires professional managerial and technical personnel. On the quality of labour, the report concluded that "labour is abundant, can be easily trained, and has a high aptitude for work in manufacturing industries".[27] One urgent problem was the level of technical competency of the local workforce involved in manufacturing. The team of economists aptly summarized the situation:

> [Singapore's] greatest asset is the high aptitude of her people to work in manufacturing industries. They rank among the best factory workers in the world.... The crux of the problem is how to transfer a large reservoir of unskilled workers into technicians and skilled workers.

A successful solution to the problem will ensure that the progress
of the industrial programme will not be handicapped in any way
because of the shortage of a particular category of technicians or
skilled workers.[28]

It was pointed out that few manufacturers in Singapore provided
a systematic apprenticeship training scheme. Among 572 firms
surveyed in 1958 that employed 25,000 workers, only 6 per cent
of them employed some form of on-the-job training. To ensure a
continuous supply of skilled workers, the report recommended the
following main measures: (a) the upgrading and expansion of the
Singapore Polytechnic so that the training of professional engineers
could be introduced; (b) the establishment of a prototype production
and training centre for the production of prototypes of tools, machines
and accessories and to make the designs and drawings available to
local manufacturers; (c) the placement of technicians and foremen
in factories in industrialized countries in order to gain practical
training in the various aspects of manufacturing production. Similarly,
foreign technical expertise should be invited to transfer skills and
knowledge; (d) in the long-term, improvements in the level of technical
competency could be ensured through the establishment of a fully
fledged engineering college in one of the two existing universities.
Besides upgrading the skill levels of workers, complementary measures
to ensure consistently high productivity were recommended. These
were aimed at eradicating unstable industrial relations and establishing
cooperative and healthy working relations between the trade unions,
employers and the government.

In short, the Winsemius Report emphasized the need for local
manufacturers to enter joint venture agreements with foreign firms
which could supply them with the necessary initial managerial
personnel and technical "know-how". In this respect, the government
had to play the historical role of a comprador by rendering "all
the necessary assistance to foreign manufacturers in finding the
competent local partners".[29] In early 1961 Singapore's State Development
Plan 1961–64 was announced, based closely on the Winsemius Report.
It adopted a new approach that called for a rapid expansion of the
economic infrastructure and the implementation of specific industrial
promotion measures. At the bottom line, both the Winsemius Report

and the State Development Plan held firmly to the philosophy that the young, independent Singapore had an economic viability of her own.[30]

The journey towards an industrialized state started with the setting up of the Economic Development Board (EDB) in August 1961, specifically to promote and monitor the industrial development of the city-state. In September 1961 the first bulldozer moved into a swampy Jurong, creating in the process the first and largest industrial heartland in Singapore. Most importantly, as pointed out by Garry Rodan, the government "embraced the thesis that positive institutional and financial intervention by the state could form the basis for a fast-growing import-substitution programme led by private investment".[31] A laissez-faire economy, so strongly practised by the British during their rule, could do Singapore no good. To successfully transform Singapore into an attractive investment haven and to compete with other regional countries for such investment, state intervention was essential. The stage was set for the massive influx of foreign investments in the late 1960s and throughout the 1970s.

CATCHING UP THROUGH THE EOI STRATEGY, 1965–79

The State Development Plan of 1961–64 heralded a decade of growth in the 1960s.[32] The notable feature was the more than threefold increase in the number of workers employed in the manufacturing sector. The economic growth during the 1960s also produced beneficial social effects. The rate of population increase fell from 4.1 per cent in 1959 to 1.5 per cent in 1969, infant mortality dropped from 36.0 per thousand in 1959 to 21.0 per thousand in 1969, and school enrolment increased from 305,000 in 1959 to 511,000 in 1969.[33] Economic growth went hand-in-hand with the active promotion of the "ideology of survival" by the ruling PAP. Basically, the ideology propagated the inseparability of economic and political survival.[34] This required the internalization of an entirely new set of social attitudes and beliefs by the people of Singapore. The call was made for the sacrifice of self-interest for the "national interest". Citing the cohesiveness and creativity of Japanese society, Lee Kuan Yew commented:

The non-economic factors, the human factors of the Japanese society — that have made the Japanese economy what it now is. That will not change. The cohesiveness, the industry, the application, the willingness to take over what somebody has discovered and developed and improve upon it — is part of the Japanese make-up. The Japanese will find some way around these difficulties. It is a closely-knit society in which differences in income and status are made tolerable by an embracing and equalising patriotism and national pride.[35]

It was apparent that the leaders of Singapore had deep admiration for the way the Japanese had created their industrialized society through adoption and creative adaptation of Western technology. The cue was well taken that Singapore's economic survival, according to Lee, "depends upon our ability to mobilise the qualities in our population to maximum advantage. It is the one thing to have which makes up for our lack of size and numbers, and it is of utmost importance that, in the field of science and technology, we should lead the field in this part of the world."[36]

As stated earlier, the crucial question facing Singapore in August 1965 was how to produce a viable and expanding industrialization programme in the shortest possible time period. The British had left Singapore with a "colonial economy geared to an imperial system — little industry, some banking and commerce".[37] The PAP reckoned that only government-led industrialization based on export orientation could ensure future economic development. Such a development strategy was made all the more necessary with the announcement by the British Government in 1967 of the intended military pull-out of British forces stationed in Singapore. Essentially, Singapore's EOI programme in the late 1960s and 1970s capitalized on the comparatively low-cost, skilled engineering and technical labour force. During this period, foreign technologies played (and continue to play) a critical role. In 1966, foreign direct investment in Singapore's manufacturing sector amounted to $239 million. As a result of aggressive promotion on the part of the government through a range of tax and investment incentives, the figure increased to $1,575 million in 1971 and $6,349 million in 1979.[38] Some of the major MNCs that set up assembly operations in Singapore during this period were Hewlett-Packard, National Semiconductor, Seiko, Timex, SKF, Sunstrand Pacific, Hitachi, Matsushita, Fujitsu, Sanyo and Asahi. Thus, in the 1970s there was a gradual shift towards higher value-added investments by foreign investors as more sophisticated technology was imported into Singapore.[39] By 1981 the manufacturing sector contributed 24 per cent of GDP.[40]

While the economic performance of Singapore during the late 1960s and 1970s is well documented, not much has been said about the historical forces that shaped the government's industrialization policy and which also affected the government's attempts to develop science and technology during this period. Lee Kuan Yew and his chief economic wizard, Goh Keng Swee, then Deputy Prime Minister, recognized that the long period of colonialism had produced a business community consisting overwhelmingly of small shopkeepers, comprador merchants and financiers who did not possess either the skills in science, technology and modern management or the commitment to play an active part in transforming a trading economy into one based on manufacturing.[41] The trading and commercial culture was too deeply ingrained in the lifestyle of the entrepreneurs. It was an insurmountable task to convert a nation of traders and clerks into a nation of skilled technicians, engineers and scientists overnight. From the outset, therefore, MNCs became the target of the government. They were seen as the surest way not only to provide high levels of technology and management skills but also to ensure accessibility to world markets.[42] At the same time, the government hoped to get "young men and women trained and skilled in the techniques of modern industry, so that the quality and costs of our products are competitive on the export markets".[43] As in some stages of Korea's and Taiwan's economic development, the success of Singapore's EOI strategy also depended strongly on the fact that the government in the 1970s created a number of statutory boards and wholly-owned or semi-owned government companies. Joint ventures were started with both domestic and foreign partners to produce a number of industrial products, such as steel and refined sugar.

A successful EOI programme is also dependent on the willingness of the people to accept change and be flexible enough to adjust and develop themselves. Singapore's adoption of an EOI development strategy was influenced by several favourable historical legacies of

British rule — good transportation, roads, harbours and airports, an honest and effective administration, and reasonably healthy living conditions. By the late 1960s the PAP had tightened its political reins and ensured the stable political climate so eagerly sought by foreign investors in developing countries. Most importantly, however, as stated by Lee Kuan Yew in a National Day speech made on 8 August 1968,

> are the changed attitudes, and the positive outlook of our people. Singapore used to be a conglomeration of migrants, each man for himself. If he cared for anybody else at all, it was his own immediate family. Singaporeans now, particularly those born and educated here, are aware that personal survival is not enough. What we have can be preserved only if we together defend the integrity of our country and secure the interests of the whole community.... They are a different breed, self-reliant, bouncing with confidence, eager to learn, willing to work.[44]

While it is possible that the new breed of Singaporeans possessed new sets of values and attitudes, an underlying and indeed omnipresent cultural trait of the people developed since the days of Raffles has been the driving force behind the "positive outlook". This is the basic instinct of survival; to adapt and to make good according to changing times and societal needs.

In the late 1960s and 1970s, individual survival matched well with the state's ideology of national survival. Collectively, the population was inextricably tied up with Singapore's "catching-up" syndrome — the urgent need to close the gap, to compete, to succeed and to outshine the competitors. The need to survive for the state and the individual did not just stop in the 1970s. More importantly, throughout the decades since independence, the Government of Singapore has created a society which requires the individual to master the skills of survival. Indeed, it is not an exaggeration to say that Singapore is a classic Darwinian example of a modern society where only the fittest survive, emulating in the process what Lee Kuan Yew said of Japanese society — "Japanese society is an illustration in Darwinian evolution, the survival of the more resilient social organism".[45]

EOI AND DEVELOPMENT OF TECHNOLOGICAL COMPETENCE

Singapore's EOI strategy in the late 1960s and 1970s also involved the development of science and technology. But the task of closing the technological gap was easier said than done. British rule had not produced the necessary development in technical and vocational education. Indeed, the long time lag made it difficult for the PAP leaders to work out an effective and systematic plan for the development of technical and engineering education in schools and the two universities. Furthermore, there was a severe shortage of local expertise in the fields of science and technology able to impart knowledge and skills in formal and informal education. The problem was compounded by the drain of the limited pool of engineers into the fast-developing industrial sector during the 1970s.[46] The Winsemius Report had highlighted the deficiency in the number of skilled workers. At the request of the government, Dr Albert Winsemius continued to make regular visits to Singapore. In February 1970 he estimated Singapore would have an annual deficit of between 450 and 500 engineers from 1970 to 1975, despite government efforts to increase the annual output of engineers from the then University of Singapore from 80 to 210 by 1974.[47] The shortage of management personnel and technicians was equally worrisome — the former by about 200 a year over the next three years and the latter by as many as 1,500 to 2,000 each year over the next two years.[48]

Hence, from the outset, the Singapore Government followed an "open-door" policy in an attempt to close the technological gap. MNCs and foreign expertise were attracted into the small city-state to provide the impetus for an industrial take-off.[49] As explained by Goh Keng Swee in his 1970 Budget Speech,

> When foreign corporations bring their expertise, what we experience as a developing nation is a brain-drain in reverse.... It would be wrong for us to resent the inflow of management personnel, engineers and technicians from abroad. On the contrary, we could regard them as blazing the trail for new industries which we do not have the knowledge and technology to set up ourselves.... in the long term the scientific know-how and technological processes which we now borrow from abroad must in course of time develop on an indigenous base at our institutions of higher learning.[50]

These statements reflected the optimism of a young but fast-developing nation. In fact, Goh's comments made in 1970 raised several significant, closely related issues concerning Singapore's quest for technological excellence in the 1980s and 1990s. They are the transfer and diffusion of technology and skills from the MNCs, the lack of a critical mass of local engineers and technicians, brain-drain of local expertise, the weak university–industry linkage, the lack of a well-planned science and technology policy, and the painfully slow development of R&D in Singapore's indigenous firms.

What measures were carried out by the government in the 1960s and 1970s to enhance the role of science and technology in the economic development of the nation? A new ministry, the Ministry of Science and Technology, was established in April 1968 to formulate science policies and to coordinate the deployment of the nation's scientific and technological manpower.[51] There was also an urgent need for a restructuring of the educational system to provide the requisite technical manpower.[52] Radical changes were introduced in the field of technical education, especially in the face of the British military withdrawal from 1971 which created the pressing need for the supply of skilled labour resources to fill the positions formerly occupied by skilled British workers. The yawning gap between the enrolment in academic and technical streams was stressed in a ministerial report in 1968; while in Japan the ratio of academic to vocational students was 3:2, in Singapore the ratio was 7:1, and the ratio of technicians to engineers and scientists was 1:23.[53] To redress the imbalance, the Ministry of Education announced that, from 1969, all secondary school pupils would receive two years of compulsory technical education, after which they would be streamed into technical, commercial or academic education. Several industrial training centres and vocational institutes were built during the 1970s. At the tertiary level, greater emphasis was placed on engineering and technology. Hence, up to the 1970s, concerted efforts were made by the Singapore Government to expand resources in science and technology. How successful were these measures in introducing a culture of technology that could support Singapore's industrialization drive?

As events turned out, Singapore entered into the 1980s still severely hampered by a shortage of labour on three critical levels — skilled labour, qualified technical and engineering personnel, and management trained in modern techniques. As was the case during the colonial period, education during this period also failed to keep pace with the rapid expansion of the Singapore economy.[54] The tight labour market for skilled workers and professionals soon led to crimping and counter-crimping of such personnel, especially in the fast-expanding shipbuilding and repair industry and the petrochemical industry.[55] As a short-term solution, the government encouraged the inflow of skilled personnel by liberalizing "the conditions under which such people can come into Singapore, acquire permanent residence and eventual citizenship".[56] Hence, in this respect, a historical pattern was repeated, since the colonial trading economy and the structural growth of the city itself depended on a consistent influx of migrants — though the British did put up immigration restrictions on the Chinese in the 1930s. But for modern Singapore, right up to the present time, attracting foreign expertise and talent continues to be a matter of high priority and of great urgency.

Clearly, it is not an easy task to reconstruct a trading culture into a manufacturing culture, especially one that has strong underpinnings in science and technology. The government had been too optimistic about the industriousness and adaptability of the people. What factors had acted as barriers to a successful implementation of the various measures to promote science and technology during the early decades of independence? In the first place, education in Singapore has long been characterized by a "white-collar" mentality. The majority of school leavers and university graduates obtained academic and professional qualifications. They gravitated towards clerical and administrative posts in the tertiary sector, mainly in insurance, banking, trade, and in the government service. A useful sociocultural explanation for the continuation of this "colonial" mentality is the perception held by many Chinese families that administrative posts were seen as compatible to the scholar class under the Confucian social hierarchy. They command high prestige, prospects and job security. This "white-collar" complex at this time was considered undesirable and inconsistent with the government's policy shift towards a "blue-collar" workforce. Unfortunately, this historical legacy continued to plague Singapore in the 1980s and beyond.

There is another more important explanation for the government's failure to plant the first seeds of a culture of science and technology in a rapidly changing society. In the midst of catching up to become an industrialized nation, the industrial policy of expanding the manufacturing base through foreign enterprises was a clear mismatch to the government's aim of elevating the general skill level of the workforce. Industrial establishments in Singapore during this period were characterized by their small size, low capital input and the usage of simple technology. In 1969, 70 per cent of manufacturing enterprises employed 10 to 39 workers, while only 10 per cent had more than 100 to 300 workers.[57] Though foreign investors were quick to take advantage of Singapore's open-door policy and the many incentives offered by the government, they were also rational in their technological choice and organization of work. The small domestic market and the scarcity of local managerial and technical "know-how" and expertise also imposed a limit on the size of the foreign firm. Therefore, apart from the shipbuilding and repair industry and the petrochemical industry, industrial firms in Singapore were largely labour-intensive, low wage and low-productivity enterprises, requiring the mere repetition of simple operations along the assembly and production line. With some exceptions, the majority of Singaporeans engaged in the manufacturing sector were low-skilled workers who had to compete in the labour market with the thousands of mainly female, low-skilled "guest workers" from neighbouring countries. In 1978, for example, a rather low estimate of 40,000 foreign workers, out of a total workforce of 950,000, was given by the government. The actual figure could have been much more.[58] This situation also further enhanced the poor image of "blue-collar" occupations and accentuated the trend for the young to deviate from educational pursuits in the technical and vocational streams. Hence, compared to the newly industrializing countries in East Asia and in Japan, Singapore in the 1970s suffered from low labour productivity. Between 1973 and 1978 "real productivity growth in Singapore averaged about 3 per cent per annum, compared to an average of 7 per cent for Hong Kong, Taiwan and South Korea".[59] Nevertheless, the accelerated increase in manufacturing employment greatly contributed to solving the unemployment problem.[60]

Finally, it is interesting to note that, until 1991, the Singapore Government did not have an official blueprint for a science and technology policy. The statements made by Goh Keng Swee in his budget speech in 1970 indicated the parameters within which science and technology would be developed:

> Let us not presume that at the comparative low level of scientific and technological know-how that we find ourselves today, it is our role to train scientists and engineers who will engage in research at the frontiers of knowledge. Ours should be the practical, if more mundane, approach. In the foreseeable future, we are likely to set up those industrial activities which require assiduous application of engineering skills and workmanship in well-developed and well-known industrial processes in which we have a natural advantage by being able to produce or import engineers, technicians, craftsmen and skilled workers capable of performing the most exacting standards of work but at a much lower cost than the advanced countries could.[61]

In many ways, given the institutional and social constraints, the government's stand was sensible and perhaps inspired by the development path taken by Japan. But, seen in the light of Japan's experience, two crucial factors were overlooked in Singapore's strategy. First, Japan had developed a scientific and technological culture dating back to the Meiji Era when technology transfer was carried out by so-called "hired foreigners" and when Japanese students were eagerly seeking knowledge and skills overseas. Second, development of technical education in Japan had kept pace with changes in the nation's industrialization and technological levels.[62]

Although new governmental institutions were set up to deal with science and technology policy problems, quite often the measures recommended did not endure. Instead, there was a bewildering succession of ad hoc committees, councils and agencies, which sometimes sent out different signals. The confusing situation was further reinforced by the existence of a rather inept Ministry of Science and Technology, suffering from a shortage of high-level administrators and having to oversee a wide range of activities, ranging from the coordination of technical education to the promotion of research work.[63] Eventually, on 1 April 1981, twelve years after its formation, the ministry was dissolved. As explained by Goh Chok Tong in June 1981, the defunct Ministry of Science and Technology had only a budget of $100,000 to disburse as research grants. It was hardly enough to sustain a scientific life, leave alone esoteric research.... If a culprit must be found for the sorry state of scientific research and development it must be research and development itself. We did not have a research and development policy until now, because research and development was not critical to our economic growth strategy in the last decade.[64]

Hence, the contradiction in Singapore's industrial policy became quite obvious. On one hand, the call was made as early as 1966 to develop Singapore into a leader in the field of science and technology in Southeast Asia. On the other, the government did not seem all that enthusiastic in promoting research and development in science and technology. Such a paradoxical situation could only serve to retard Singapore's path to develop its own indigenous technological base.

In summary, in spite of the first oil shock in 1973, the Singapore economy performed well throughout the 1970s, registering an average growth rate of 8.7 per cent for the period 1973 to 1979. The nation's open-door policy had also successfully established an industrial base characterized by the dominating power of foreign enterprises. Manufacturing, in the words of Iain Buchanan, "did develop but it developed within an enclave tenuously connected with the rest of the economy".[65] In the meantime, much to the chagrin of the government, domestic capital continued to be structurally immobile and generally remained concentrated in the traditional but secured and profitable tertiary sector. While it continued to expand in the 1970s — earning an unfavourable "sweatshop" image — the share of the manufacturing sector in GDP stagnated around the 22 per cent mark and then declined in the 1980s.[66] On the other hand, the transport and communication sector advanced from 13.5 per cent in 1973 to 18.6 per cent of GDP in 1979, reflecting the traditional strength of Singapore as an entrepôt centre.[67] As far as the development of science and technology is concerned, the 1960s and 1970s added little to its progress and to its role in the industrialization of Singapore. In fact, to achieve the overriding objective of catching-up with the industrialized countries, inconsistencies in government policies, coupled with the continual impact of historical legacies, had "wasted" two useful decades during which a scientific and technological culture could have been properly nurtured and nourished. Recognizing the country's backwardness in the development of science and technology, in the 1980s the Singapore Government adopted strategies designed to push the economy and society higher up the technological ladder.

Notes

1. Paul Kennedy, *The Rise and Fall of British Naval Mastery* (London: Fontana, 1991), p. 377.
2. Fong Sip Chee, *The PAP Story: The Pioneering Years, November 1954 – April 1968* (Singapore: Times Periodical, 1979), p. 9.
3. Lim Chong Yah and Ow Chin Hock, "The Economic Development of Singapore in the Sixties and Beyond", in *The Singapore Economy*, edited by You Poh Seng and Lim Chong Yah (Singapore: Eastern University Press, 1971), p. 28.
4 Ibid.
5 Mary Turnbull, *History of Singapore, 1819–1988* (Singapore: Oxford University Press, 1989), p. 294.
6. The export-oriented industrialization model of industrial development became popular with many Third World countries seeking rapid indus-trialization after World War II. The strategy was actively promoted by the United States and the World Bank. The United States worked hard to create a liberal world economic order based on global free trade. In the 1960s and early 1970s, many U.S. MNCs sought to establish operations in Third World countries possessing low labour costs. At the same time, the World Bank, under Robert McNamara, called on Third World countries to "turn their manufacturing enterprises from the relatively small markets associated with import-substitution toward the much larger opportunities flowing from export promotion". Quoted in Walden Bello, "The Spread and Impact of Export-Oriented Industrialization in the Pacific Rim", *Third World Economics*, 16–18 November 1991, p. 16.
7. See E. Vogel, *The Four Little Dragons: The Spread of Industrialisation in East Asia* (Cambridge: Harvard University Press, 1991), pp. 85–91.
8. Lee Kuan Yew, National Day Rally Speech, 17 August 1980.
9. Chris Dixon, *Southeast Asia in the World Economy* (Cambridge: Cambridge University Press, 1991), p. 152.
10. John Williamson and Chris Milner, *The World Economy: A Textbook in International Economics* (New York: New York University Press, 1991), p. 290.
11. Ibid., p. 293.

12. Ibid., p. 295.
13. Dixon, *Southeast Asia*, p. 158.
14. Colony of Singapore, *Annual Report* (Singapore, 1965).
15. Dixon, *Southeast Asia*, p. 158.
16. *The Malaya Tribune*, 13 March 1953.
17. Colony of Singapore, "Report of the Industrial Resources Study Groups, September 1954", in Andrew Gilmour, *Official Letters, 1931– 1956*, Mss. Ind. Ocn. s. 154, para. 86, p. 13.
18. Ibid., para 37, p. 8.
19. Ibid., para 36, p. 8.
20. J.J. Puthucheary, *Ownership and Control in the Malayan Economy* (Singapore: Eastern Universities Press, 1960; repr. Kuala Lumpur: University of Malaya Co-Operative Bookshop, 1979), pp. xiii–xiv.
21. *The United Nations Report on Singapore, 1961*, p. i.
22. Ibid., p. ii.
23. Ibid., pp. ii and v–vi.
24. Ibid., pp 57–58.
25. Ibid., pp. 57 and 60.
26. Ibid., p. 57.
27. Ibid., pp. 48 and 55.
28. Ibid., pp. xxiii and 48.
29. Ibid., p. 74.
30. Lee Soo Ann, *Industrialization in Singapore* (Camberwell, Australia: Longman, 1973), p. 112.
31. Gary Rodan, *The Political Economy of Singapore's Industrialization* (Kuala Lumpur: Forum Press, 1991), p. 64.
32. Budget Statement presented to Parliament on 9 March 1970 by Dr Goh Keng Swee.
33. Goh Keng Swee, *The Economics of Modernization* (Singapore: Asia Pacific Press, 1972), p. 257.
34. Chan Heng Chee, *Singapore: The Politics of Survival 1965–67* (Singapore: Oxford University Press, 1971), pp. 32–36.
35. Lee Kuan Yew, speech at the Second International Alumni Night, Shangri-la Hotel, 11 September 1971.
36. Lee Kuan Yew, speech at the University of Singapore, 1 July 1966.
37. Lee Kuan Yew, speech made on 15 July 1972.
38. Economic Development Board, *Annual Report, 1972* and *Annual Report, 1980*.
39 Rodan, *Political Economy of Singapore*, p. 123.
40. Ting Wen-lee, *Business and Technological Dynamics in Newly Industrializing Asia* (Westport: Quorum Books, 1985), p. 6. As a matter of comparison, for South Korea and Taiwan, manufacturing contributed 32.8 per cent and 42.7 per

cent of GDP in 1981, respectively. This could reflect the impact of Japanese colonialism on both countries where the Japanese had developed heavy industries and infrastructure to exploit the resources therein.

41. Vogel, *Four Little Dragons*, p. 77.
42. Ibid., pp. 77–78.
43. Lee Kuan Yew, speech made in Parliament on 15 July 1968.
44. Lee Kuan Yew, speech made on the eve of National Day, 8 August 1968.
45. Lee Kuan Yew, speech made at the National Day Rally on 17 August 1980.
46. Goh, *Economics of Modernization*, p. 275.
47. Ibid., p. 273.
48. Ibid., p. 274.
49. The role of Singapore's Economic Development Board in pioneering the industrialization of Singapore by engaging MNCs is well documented in Chan Chin Bock, *Heart Work* (Singapore: Economic Development Board, 2002).
50. *Parliamentary Debates*, Singapore, Annual Budget Statement, 9 March 1970.
51. David Chew, "Investment in Human Capital", in *Singapore Economy*, edited by You and Lim, p. 303.
52. *Singapore Year Book 1969* (Government Printing Office), p. 181.
53. Ministry of Culture, *The Mirror*, 22 April 1968, pp. 6–7.
54. Goh, *Economics of Modernization*, p. 277.
55. Chia Siow Yue, "Growth and Pattern of Industrialization", in *Singapore Economy*, edited by You and Lim, p. 219.
56. Goh, *Economics of Modernization*, p. 274.
57. Singapore, *Census of Industrial Production, 1959 to 1969*.
58. *Far Eastern Economic Review, Asia Year Book 1979*, p. 292.
59. Speech by the Minister of Trade and Industry, quoted in Lim Joo-Jock, "Bold Internal Decisions, Emphatic External Outlook", in *Southeast Asian Affairs 1980*, edited by Leo Suryadinata (Singapore: Institute of Southeast Asian Studies, 1980), p. 279.
60. Chia, in *Singapore Economy*, edited by You and Lim, p. 201.
61. Goh, *Economics of Modernization*, pp. 275–76.
62. Takeaki Shimizu, "Technology Transfer and Dynamism in Technology Education in Japan", in *Technology Culture and Development*, edited by Ungku A. Aziz (International Symposium at the University of Malaya, December 1983), pp. 507–8.
63. *Straits Times*, 18 February 1981.
64. *Straits Times*, 8 June 1981.
65. Iain Buchanan, *Singapore in Southeast Asia: An Economic and Political Appraisal* (London: Bell, 1972). p. 136.
66. Lawrence Krause, Koh A.T. and Lee T.Y., *The Singapore Economy Reconsidered* (Singapore: Institute of Southeast Asian Studies, 1987), p. 8.
67. Ibid., p. 9.å

3

DEVELOPING A TECHNOLOGICAL GROWTH TRAJECTORY IN THE 1980s

One key aspect to the development of Singapore's industrialization in the 1960s and 1970s was the recognition by the Singapore Government of the importance of science and technology in economic development. However, its liberal economic philosophy of attracting a mainly product-assembly type of foreign enterprise was a mismatch for meeting the objective of raising the level of technological competence of the workforce. By the end of the 1970s, realizing that low-technology and low-skill types of industries would not maintain a strong competitive edge over her neighbours, Singapore moved into the 1980s with the introduction of a new industrial policy package aimed at shifting the economy into a "Second Industrial Revolution".

As a key component of Singapore's industrialization and with the aim of enhancing the country's economic competitiveness, a technological trajectory plan was developed during the 1980s. This was the first official blue print of the government's strategy to tap on science and technology. But the central role of MNCs in spearheading

51

the country's progress in techno-industrial innovations reinforces technological dependency on external sources and, because of the "pro-MNCs" industrial policy, indigenous firms, as in the 1970s, were left behind. The overall impact of Singapore's industrialization during this period was to stifle the growth of a technological culture and, hence, slowed the drive towards deepening the indigenous technological base. Singapore achieved "fame" as the most competitive NIE in the Far East, but in reality achieved few "gains" in terms of developing its indigenous technological capability or self-reliance. The government's haste in leapfrogging towards achieving an advanced industrial status for the country created contradictions that could narrow rather than widen the road to this end.

THE SECOND INDUSTRIAL REVOLUTION

The 1980s saw the implementation of an aggressive development strategy, probably not undertaken by any other developing country — and the Singapore Government designated it as the "Second Industrial Revolution".[1] Presumably, Singapore had its "first" industrial revolution during the 1970s when the industrial policy of transforming the economy from a labour-intensive to a capital-intensive one was launched. Did Singapore actually experience an "industrial revolution"? Interestingly, the literature on the Singapore economy has so far failed to address this issue. Perhaps it was just a title with no significant implications. But the use of the term "industrial revolution" in the context of an economic history generally denotes a sustained and accelerated growth of indigenous technological innovation and scientific inquiry.

In 1980, after two decades of intensive expansion of the manufacturing sector largely through the aegis of foreign MNCs, the manufacturing sector contributed 28 per cent of GDP, compared with 12 per cent in 1960. However, its annual growth rate slowed to 6.4 per cent for the period 1970–79, compared with 10.2 per cent for the period 1960–69. In the late 1970s it became clear that as countries in Southeast Asia began to compete effectively for foreign investments in low-skilled, labour-intensive industries, Singapore's previous comparative advantage in labour-intensive manufactured products was gradually being eroded. The emphasis now shifted to a strategy which could accelerate Singapore's transition from a "third-league" labour-intensive industrializing country to a "second-league" capital-intensive economy. According to Donald Dore's accurate observation, this obsession with the need to move quickly towards higher value-added production was partly "a matter of retaining export market share in the face of competition from countries with even greater low-wage cost advantages" and partly "a matter of national pride".[2]

By the end of the 1970s, comparative social and economic indicators pointed to a relatively rich and progressive Singapore in the midst of developing countries still battling with the problem of poverty. Together with its historical but invaluable comprador role between Association of Southeast Asian Nations (ASEAN) countries and the industrialized countries, the city-state tended to adopt an exploitative role within ASEAN. Moreover, as stated by Dore, "in an increasingly technology-conscious world, how close a country can claim to be to the high-tech frontiers comes to be an ever-stronger element in determining its 'international standing'".[3] It is safe to conclude that Singapore fitted this judgment then and does now. In his 1981 Budget Speech, then Finance Minister Goh Chok Tong optimistically stated that the Singapore economy was to be "developed into a modern industrial economy based on science, technology, skills and knowledge".[4] Thus, the "Second Industrial Revolution" was launched under the Ten-Year Plan, which aimed to increase the manufacturing sector's share of GDP from 22 per cent in 1979 to 31 per cent in 1990. The two main strategies of the restructuring programme were, firstly, the continual task of attracting MNCs to invest in high-technology types of operations and, secondly, the promotion of science and technology, such as activities in research and development.

To break away as quickly as possible from the labour-intensive type of industrialization, a bold and unprecedented move was made by the government to introduce a dirigist wage policy, with the aim of raising wage costs in order to discourage low-skilled, labour-intensive operations by foreign investors. At the same time, generous tax and fiscal incentives were given to attract capital-intensive and technologically sophisticated foreign investments. Indigenous enterprises, however, were left much to themselves. Herein lies the most significant negative impact and a paradox of the new strategy; that is, economic restructuring to achieve a high-technology industrial base was done not by encouraging indigenous technological development but by continuing to be fully dependent on foreign technology.

The high-technology motor of Singapore's industrial development in the 1980s was the export-oriented electronics sector. Its share in manufacturing value-added increased from 11.7 per cent in 1975 to 26.2 per cent in 1984.[5] Some new projects — in areas such as integrated circuit design, production of microprocessor development systems and high-density disk drives — were started during this period. In particular, a vital role was played by U.S. disk drive companies, propelling Singapore to become a major world disk drive exporter within a few years. However, it should be noted that these investments were made for the assembly and testing of disk drives rather than any sophisticated manufacturing process. Singapore's development of its aeronautical industry was also boosted by the entry of multinationals such as Sunstrand, Hawker Pacific, TRW and General Electric. Other industries targeted for development during the 1980s, and which also attracted reputable MNCs, included automotive components, machine tools and machinery, medical and surgery apparatus and instruments, speciality chemicals and pharmaceuticals, optical instruments and equipment, precision engineering products, and hydraulic and pneumatic control systems. These industries were selected on the premise that they would enhance Singapore's export capability to the markets of the developed countries.

THE CENTRAL ROLE OF FOREIGN TECHNOLOGY

Theoretical considerations behind the technology transfers by MNCs to developing countries have often been based on the product life cycle (PLC) framework. Briefly, in the first innovative phase of the PLC a relatively large number of engineers and skilled workers are involved. In the second intermediate phase of the cycle the production process becomes effectively streamlined and routine so that mass production techniques are being incorporated. In the final product-standardization stage, as the industry becomes fully mature, much of the production is taken over by specialized machines which require only unskilled workers. At this point, consideration of cost effectiveness induces the industry to shift production to peripheral areas with a surplus of cheap labour. The electronic and textile industries in developed countries are illustrative of the PLC paradigm. Thus, during the 1960s and 1970s, MNCs in these industries faced with the prospects of rising costs — especially labour — and market saturation at the maturity stage of the product life were pressurized to transfer part or the whole productive as well as technological resources to low-cost locations in Southeast Asia. This interest was eagerly reciprocated by the receptiveness of ASEAN countries, including Singapore.

There are three common traits in ASEAN countries which contributed to a favourable climate for investments by MNCs.[6] First is the abundant natural resources in countries like Malaysia, Indonesia and Thailand. The second is that the countries' economic philosophies, albeit with some differences in approaches and techniques, are basically the same; that is, they believe in and practise pragmatic, market-oriented economic systems, with minimum governmental interference in the private sector. The task of the government is to provide a stable, predictable set of investment regulations and policies. The third common factor is the young, forward-looking population of the ASEAN countries. Of all the ASEAN countries, Singapore is perhaps the most internationalized in terms of its openness to the inflow of MNCs into the country.[7] It is not an exaggeration to state that, collectively, the MNCs formed the "backbone" of the Singapore manufacturing sector.

The role of foreign MNCs in Singapore's quest for technological excellence is seen in two ways. Firstly, they are critical channels through which Singapore could acquire updated scientific and technological knowledge. Essentially, foreign technology was perceived by the government as an effective means to overcome domestic limitations, such as the lack of an indigenous technological base. Thus, the advantage of MNCs to a country like Singapore, which does not possess a high level of indigenous technological or industrial management capability, is the potential transfer of at least some of the multinationals' special assets to local manufacturers. Dahlman and Westphal have referred to this as a process of technological accumulation. As in the case of Singapore, the eventual objective is to achieve some degree of technological mastery, defined by the authors as "the effective use of technological knowledge through continuing effort to assimilate, adapt, and/or create technology".[8] Even if the multinationals decide to tighten control over specific technologies, managerial capability and worker skills would theoretically have to be transferred through in-house training and backward linkages, such as in local sourcing. Thus, the more willing the MNC is to recruit local managers and to source locally, the more learning-by-doing opportunities will be made available. The transfer and diffusion of such knowledge is seen to be crucial for Singapore's economic development.

Secondly, and perhaps the one feature that is almost uniquely Singaporean, the MNCs, and not the indigenous industries, were expected to spearhead the country's push towards high technology in the 1980s and beyond. In this way, Singapore hoped to leapfrog and close the technological gap. In the words of A.E. Pannenborg, a former science adviser to the Singapore Government, MNCs are the "most conspicuous asset of Singapore".[9] Indeed, Singapore became an "export platform" for MNCs, which, by the mid-1980s, conducted more than 70 per cent of all direct exports. To a large extent MNCs control the type of technology and the timing of technology transfer into Singapore. The rationale here is that it is much cheaper and faster to get access to new technologies through the aegis of high-tech MNCs than by developing across-the-board R&D activities. However, in retrospect, it must be emphasized that the central role of foreign MNCs and technology importation under the main development strategy of the Singapore Government was very much an "economic focus" rather than a "technological focus".

ASSIMILATING FOREIGN TECHNOLOGY

Although the literature on the extent of technology transfer and diffusion to Singapore by MNCs in the 1970s and 1980s is limited, a few notable studies were conducted by local and foreign scholars. In a comprehensive survey involving 65 firms (47 were wholly foreign-owned, 5 were wholly local, and 13 were joint ventures; all incorporated in Singapore during the 1970s and early 1980s) from the industrial machinery, precision equipment, electrical and electronics industries by Chng and others, significant conclusions on the effectiveness of technology transfers by MNCs in Singapore were reached.[10] One common observation was that expatriates invariably occupied the top management posts in all the MNCs.[11] They were mainly senior managers who had gained considerable experience at the company headquarters and at other overseas manufacturing facilities. Management positions which were indigenized were usually those related to personnel, accounts and general administration. In order to maintain the company's prestige and reputation, the expatriate staff made all the key decisions and carried out inspections, especially those concerned with the quality of finished products.[12] This was clearly the case for Japanese MNCs in the precision instrument industry. In general, MNCs (especially Japanese firms) in Singapore and the other ASEAN countries exercised a relatively high degree of control over their subsidiaries, especially in the diffusion of management practices in marketing and finance.[13] This limitation in the degree of indigenization and decentralization had important implications for the transfer of technology and R&D activities.

In the 1980s, contrary to the expectations of the government, MNCs in Singapore failed to generate the much-desired R&D in areas like product design, product development, process development and innovation technology.[14] A similar observation was made by Edward Chen K.Y. in Hong Kong. In his study of 529 foreign MNCs and local firms in the textiles, garments, plastics and toys, and electronics industries, it was found that "foreign firms do not have a higher tendency to take up R&D activities than local firms, though they tend to spend proportionately more on R&D if they do".[15] However, foreign MNCs did stimulate the rate of technical progress because of the training facilities offered and the technologies transferred. Foreign MNCs in Malaysia, too, show "a reluctance on their part to allocate funds for R&D activities in their local subsidiaries".[16] In any case, MNCs tend to preserve their control over "key" elements of technical knowledge by conducting crucial R&D, including basic research, in home countries, by putting expatriates in decision-making positions, and by including "secrecy" clauses in agreements.[17] Consequently, the linkage between the MNCs and local research and technological institutions was also "conspicuously unimportant".[18] The observation here matched the results of a 1978 survey conducted by the Ministry of Science and Technology. It was found that only 51 manufacturing establishments, or 2 per cent of the total, were engaged in some R&D activities. These were undertaken more for product or process adaption, quality control, or marketing strategies and not in fundamental or applied research geared towards the development of new products.[19]

Forward and backward economic linkages of MNCs' operations on the Singapore domestic economy were also low, since industrial production was export-oriented and no mandatory domestic sourcing rules were in force.[20] A majority of the firms depended on less than 25 per cent of inputs sourced from indigenous subcontracting companies, indicating the low level of technological capability of the local subcontractors. Several MNCs also pointed out the poor quality of domestically manufactured components and the unreliability of local suppliers. Japanese firms, in particular, sourced from Japanese subcontracting firms, citing additional factors such as similar cultural background, work attitudes and management styles for establishing internal backwards integration.[21] Finally, it was found that MNCs did not fully exploit their capabilities in imparting a wide range of skills to local workers and firms. In a study of the transfer of managerial and technological skills by foreign-owned electronic companies in Malaysia, Mark Lester highlighted three inhibitive factors; namely, the predominance of an assembly line type of operation and a lack of complex production processes, the control over the transfer of new technology, and minimal linkages with domestic firms because of the outward orientation of MNCs.[22] The situation was no different in the case of Singapore. The study by Lim in 1978 on foreign-owned "footloose" electronics firms in Malaysia and Singapore confirmed that any skills development of the production staff was limited.[23] Production line employees were mostly female, local and guest workers with either primary or lower-secondary education. In addition, the nature of assembly jobs was task specific, such as soldering, bonding and wiring, and thus required minimal technical skills to perform. Some MNCs also encountered difficulties in implementing in-house training programmes due to factors such as a high labour turnover, a lack of commitment from workers, and poaching of trained workers by other firms.[24]

Generally, while little skill development took place at the lower hierarchy of the workforce in MNCs, "training of skilled and professional workers appears to be considerably greater than that of the unskilled".[25] The task, as in the case of Japanese MNCs, was to first familiarize all professional and management personnel with the production process and then to train technical staff in different aspects of the production process so that they could ensure the smooth operation of the whole system.[26] This mechanism was complemented by the transfer of expatriate engineers stationed in Singapore and by visits of foreign experts.[27] In their study of 20 MNCs (16 wholly foreign-owned, 3 joint ventures, and 1 fully locally owned) in the electronics and computer industry, Hakam and Chang also made the same observation that the diffusion of technology took place in the form of trained young professional and managerial personnel leaving their MNCs to be either hired by other firms or even to start their own high-tech companies.[28] They concluded that, through the MNCs, "the combination of good human resource infrastructure and the government institutional set-up in the provision of technological upgrading incentives is working well in the transferring of skills to Singapore".[29]

Though no data are available, the spin-off effect mentioned by Hakam and Chang was, at best, minimal because the learning-by-doing skill transfer did not include product design or process development.[30] Only a few individuals actually "made it", in the sense of utilizing knowledge and skills learned to develop their own high-technology enterprises.[31] Moreover, as mentioned above, top professional and management posts remained in the hands of foreign expatriates. Similarly, American MNCs were "reluctant to hire local nationals because they are concerned with the competence and loyalty of potential candidates".[32] Even within a joint venture between an American multinational and a local firm, for proprietary reasons, locals were not trained to replace the expatriates.[33] Unlike other ASEAN governments which pressurized MNCs to replace expatriate personnel with local workers, Singapore's laissez-faire policy towards MNCs during the 1980s perpetuated an increase in the inflow of foreign expertise to the city-state. In 1980 the increase was about 15 per cent; it climbed to between 35 and 50 per cent in 1981.[34] This dependency on foreign expertise continues till today.

The limitation of Singapore's experiment to create a high-technology industrial base during the 1980s was shown by the decision of Japan's electronics giant Sony Corporation in 1986 to hold back its expansion plan in Singapore.[35] It was pointed out that Singapore did not yet have the "right soil to nurture high technology industries", and this reality was compounded by the prevalence of job-hopping, the lack of indigenous suppliers of sophisticated, high technology materials and the general shortage of workers with engineering skills.[36] Japanese MNCs were known for their unwillingness to site their state-of-the-art R&D in host countries. Malaysia's then Prime Minister Dr Mahathir, for example, openly criticized Mitsubishi for not transferring the latest technology in car manufacturing to the local partner in their joint effort in producing the country's home-grown car model, the Proton Saga.[37] Interestingly, as Japan becomes the world's leading manufacturer, pressure groups within the country, such as the "Japan's Choices" Study Group, headed by Kyoto University professor Masataka Kosaka, are becoming active in exhorting Japanese MNCs to "contribute to world economic expansion and progress by actively moving to release technical information (such as patent information) to the world community".[38]

While the independent studies indicated that MNCs were not fully committed to play a key role in shaping Singapore's strategies to leapfrog up the technological ladder, government sources, on the other hand, provided a rosier picture of success. To help local companies that were used by MNCs as supporting industries, the Local Industry Upgrading Programme (LIUP) was set up in 1986. Through this mechanism, local companies were upgraded via the hands-on support of an LIUP manager seconded from the MNC partner. They also gained in-depth understanding of clients' procurement needs, while the MNCs benefitted from better quality and more reliable parts. By 1993 LIUP had garnered 28 MNC-partners and more than 140 local companies working closely together.[39] However, it is a matter of speculation as to the actual success of the partnership programme, especially in the development of new processes or products, because no official data in this respect was publicly released. In any case, one can generalize that for firms from Japan, technical cooperation was a useful channel to expand the extent of Japanese vertical integration in the country and to "tie-up" local firms by requiring them to buy components or raw materials from Japanese technology suppliers. American manufacturers, on the other hand, were more willing to transfer "know-how" rather than just to "show-how". Thus, companies such as Motorola and Hewlett Packard were key players in conducting R&D projects aimed at developing new innovative products in Singapore.

BUILDING A SCIENTIFIC AND TECHNICAL MANPOWER

One of the first urgent tasks of the Singapore Government in 1965 was to implement a national education system to support the country's export-oriented industrialization strategy. Ironically, while the British as the colonial rulers failed to do enough, the Singapore Government tried to do too much and too quickly. Up to the late 1980s, education in Singapore was subject to the "roller-coaster" effect. Numerous reforms and changes were abolished even before they could be consolidated and new ones introduced hastily, only to be replaced in a matter of time. Despite heavy governmental expenditure on education during the 1960s to the 1980s, educational wastage was high during this period.[40] Another problem area which gained little attention from the government during this period was the lack of commitment and investment in ongoing in-house training by local firms. While in Japan and Germany successful firms consider such programmes a form of continuing education, hence enhancing the skills of their workers, Singapore firms generally do not accept this. Another critical issue which did not receive much governmental attention was the failure of the education system to inculcate positive values and attitudes towards technical training and "blue-collar" jobs. Until the early 1990s, little effort was made in improving vocational or technical education. Vocational training was specifically aimed at providing a form of continual education for the less academically inclined pupils. Those who failed their Primary Schools Leaving Examinations and the exam at the end of their Secondary Two education were channelled into vocational institutes. Unlike in South Korea and Germany, where vocational and technical training is held in high esteem, Singapore's system failed to project the same image. Vocational institutes became "dumping grounds" or "catch-nets" for those who failed to meet the required academic rigour.

The unpopularity of vocational training was further stained by many cases of crime and vandalism committed by students of the institutes. There were even cases in which students purposely committed petty crimes so that they could be forced out of the institutes, much against the wishes of their parents. As the young continued to show an aversion towards blue-collar jobs, the danger of the country not possessing a sufficient pool of technically skilled local workers became obvious. This scenario prompted a serious warning from Lee Yock Suan, then Minister of Education (1992–97): "Singapore will be the poorer if everyone aspires to and gets only academic qualifications but nobody knows how to fix a TV set, a machine tool or a process plant. We need a world-class workforce with a wide variety of knowledge of skills to achieve a world-class standard of living."[41]

What is the impact of the frequent and often confusing educational changes on the development of scientific and technical manpower in Singapore? In an attempt to identify the country with the Confucian traditions of East Asia, the government emphasized competitive examinations and respect for learning, and discouraged the habit of questioning authority. The end result was an education system — from pre-primary right up to university level — that was strictly exam-oriented and flawed with rigidities. What mattered most were good examination results. Consequently, parents and children were caught in the rat race to achieve academic excellence. Ideologically, such a system is effective in instilling a common level of knowledge and skills and in getting students to endure a pressurized learning environment. It will also produce social harmony and a well-trained, educated and obedient workforce. However, a strictly exam-oriented system tends to promote dependency on rote-learning which, in turn, stifles independent, creative and analytical thinking. Moreover, traditional and uninspiring methods of teaching had also blocked the path to creative thinking among students at the school and tertiary level. Such an orientation towards learning did not pair well with the government's attempt to create a scientifically and technologically innovative society. In short, up to the early 1990s the education system produced a stereotyped Singapore student who lacked several qualities essential to scientific and technological innovativeness, such as a broad-based knowledge of the world; an inquisitiveness to seek new perspectives on problems and issues; the patience, persistence and endurance to complete challenging tasks; a positive orientation to planning for the future; and the general desire to create or "tinker with the fingers".

Another critical issue associated with the development of the Singaporean workforce is the attitude towards pride in their work and skills upgrading. Although training and retraining is now an urgent issue on the national agenda, up to the early 1990s many of Singapore's unskilled and semi-skilled workers remained reluctant to receive any form of formal upgrading programme. As early as August 1980 the problem of the Singapore worker was highlighted by Lee Kuan Yew:

> They lack quality consciousness. Instead of detecting and preventing defective products as Japanese workers do, our workers leave quality controllers to discover and reject defective work ... they were not interested in what happens outside their immediate area of job responsibility and take no initiative to safeguard the company's interests or property.... They will discourage management from bringing in expensive high technology equipment that they must install to increase productivity and reduce the workforce.[42]

What barriers did workers face in picking up new skills? One explanation for the workers' resistance to skills upgrading through retraining is both historical and circumstantial. Colonialism had inhibited the rise of a manufacturing culture. The situation remained largely unchanged in the 1970s and 1980s when local industries were marginalized because of the government's pro-MNC policy. Thus, for many years the majority of low-skilled workers performed routine operations in small, family-owned manufacturing firms which were slow to keep up with technological change, to replace obsolete machinery, or to upgrade workers' skills. Consequently, a negative attitude towards retraining is strongly ingrained in older workers. The negative attitude of workers in turn discouraged local industrialists from upgrading their technology. While skills can be acquired or upgraded through training courses, without the right attitude the productivity of workers will suffer even if they have the right skills.[43]

In the 1980s, as Singapore continued its attempt to become a technologically advanced city-state, it faced one crucial problem: A low supply of indigenous scientists and engineers. The unmistakable situation, however, is that, even today, Singapore is experiencing a severe shortage of scientists and engineers capable of leading the country through an innovative phase of technological change. In 1990, for example, out of every 10,000 Singapore workers, 114 were qualified engineers, but only 29 were research scientists or engineers. Paradoxically, the number of students enrolled in science and engineering studies in the local universities and polytechnics increased from 20,305 in 1980 to 92,683 in 1992.[44] Thus, in line with the government's policy to transform Singapore into a developed country, total enrolment in local degree and diploma courses increased by more than 300 per cent during the period 1980 to 1992.[45] There was also an increase in the number of university graduates in science and engineering throughout the 1980s, with a doubling of the number of engineering graduates between 1980–85 and 1986–89.[46] Given the heavy support from the government to upgrade tertiary education and the increasing intake of students in science and engineering courses in the two local universities, how does one explain the shortage of scientists and engineers in Singapore? In the Singapore Parliament, the issue was debated and it was stated that,

> the major constraint on the expansion of technical education has been the number of qualified trainees, not the demand for graduates or the availability of places.... the Engineering faculty at the University, which expanded rapidly, had difficulty in filling its places, and admitted some marginal students, and then suffered high failure rates in its five year examinations.... Similarly at polytechnics, even last year [1987], courses like Mechanical Engineering, by no means a discipline in the doldrums, had places still unfilled.[47]

The shortage of able students doing engineering was compounded by the fact that "[t]he biggest misallocation in our tertiary education is the very low proportion of girls doing engineering".[48] Girls were more interested in courses like Accountancy and Business Administration. As explained by Lee Hsien Loong,

> There is a strong cultural bias. Girls do not do Engineering because they think they may get their hands dirty. But in electrical engineering, you do not get your hands dirty. That has not sunk in. If we can shift that bias, we will have a more optimal allocation of University undergraduates.[49]

It can be assumed that the supply of science and engineering graduates and technologists needed to meet the demands of the manufacturing sector is a priority objective of the two local universities — the National University of Singapore (NUS) and Nanyang Technological University (NTU) — and the polytechnics. To satisfy the upgrading aspirations of technical diploma holders, then Prime Minister Lee Kuan Yew advocated that the then Nanyang Technological Institute (now NTU) reserve 10 per cent of its enrolment for polytechnic-trained students into engineering or the hard sciences.[50] Today, this policy continues and many of the best polytechnic graduates have the opportunity to receive their university education, some even acquiring doctorates. The pool of engineers is also expanding by the addition of returning engineering graduates from overseas universities. Though the number of these graduates is not known, it can be assumed to be high because engineering, besides business management, is a popular course for Singaporean polytechnic graduates pursuing overseas education, mainly in the United States, Australia and the United Kingdom.[51] In 1991, for example, 4,760 headed for universities in the United States, and in 1992 some 4,392 Singaporeans went to universities in Australia and 3,411 to the United Kingdom.[52] The increase in the supply of science and engineering graduates also coincided with an increase in the manpower involved in R&D during the 1990s — from 4,329 research scientists and engineers in 1990 to 8,340 in 1995.[53] This remarkable expansion was also due to a more open immigration policy initiated by the government. Singapore's structural dependence on foreign talent, in particular in the high-skilled segment, has significant implications for the government's planned transition to a knowledge economy. The government sees its challenges as low productivity growth and a lack of both innovation and entrepreneurship.[54]

LIMITATIONS ON TECHNOLOGY TRANSFER

Multinationals were (and are) looked upon as vital components of the engine of economic development in Singapore and other countries in Southeast Asia. In the words of Martin Carnoy, "if multinationals are willing to train and educate and transfer knowledge as part of the 'deal,' whereby they will gain access to local markets or other local

resources, then the location of an MNC in a particular country could
be a rapid and efficient way of stimulating new types of production
and facilitating the acquisition of new methods locally".[55] Though
basically profit-oriented enterprises, MNCs do help a small trading
nation like Singapore to achieve her socio-economic objectives —
broadly defined in terms of employment creation and the transfer of
technology and management skill. Then Education Minister Tony Tan
provided the official view in 1980:

> A large part of Singapore's economic success is attributable to
> the contribution of multinational enterprises in the fields of
> manufacturing, commerce, banking and finance. Through their
> international network, these corporations assure for Singapore-
> manufactured foods ready access to world markets. There are other
> benefits. Many Singaporeans are now occupying key management
> and technical positions in these corporations. Local industrialists and
> businessmen have found that the presence of MNCs has created new
> business opportunities, contributed to the enlargement of the market,
> and paved the way for joint ventures between foreign and local
> partners. It has been a very fruitful relationship and MNCs will have
> an even greater role to play as Singapore enters the next stage of its
> economic development.[56]

Obviously, these benefits have been bought at considerable cost. The
few but useful studies on the impact of the operations of MNCs
have shown that there has been little by way of technology transfer,
especially in the area of development and design of new products. The
high technology and R&D are more often than not kept in the home
country, and largely only the labour-intensive production processes
are located locally. But why should MNCs be concerned about
transferring the "know-how" — and perhaps more importantly, the
"know-why" — of high technology, when their primary objective for
coming to Singapore is profitability? The basic, profit-making motive
for the arrival of a large number of MNCs in Singapore was echoed
by Goh Keng Swee when he said "this is an acceptable fact of life
since they are not charitable organisations".[57] Although some "new
business opportunities" were created between MNCs and local firms,
most of the linkages appear to be "cross-industrial", with the indigenous
firms supplying supporting services like port facilities, warehousing,

distribution operations, business and technical assistance.[58] Therefore, these linkages aside, MNCs and indigenous enterprises essentially "co-exist in their respective niches, reducing the likelihood of either group producing a competitive stimulus on the other".[59]

Moreover, the government's total reliance on MNCs to spearhead the nation's push towards high technology contradicts the country's long-term plan to become technologically self-reliant, and any move towards this goal is now likely to be slow because of the crucial role of MNCs in the economy. Hence, as long as they could make profits, remit the money home freely and import product components from wherever they wished, MNCs could actually choose to operate within their own enclave. In any case, MNCs are wary of the "boomerang" phenomenon; that is, widespread transfer and diffusion of high technology will strengthen economies like Singapore to become proficient enough to export and compete against them. When Singapore was plunged into a severe recession in the mid-1980s, major MNCs "relocated at least a part of their operations elsewhere.... some have closed their Singapore plants and consolidated their activities back to their home countries".[60] Although it was claimed that "most of them have retained or diversified into higher value operations", the danger they posed in hollowing out the manufacturing sector is real and worrisome. It is also clear that the gap, in terms of market control and technology upgrading, between MNCs and local firms is not going to be narrowed as long as the former decide to have minimal business and social contacts with the latter. Progress in high technology requires the development and integration of three elements — high-quality scientific skill, bold entrepreneurship and large amounts of venture capital.[61] Unfortunately, during the 1970s and 1980s there was a severe lack of R&D and aspirations on the part of local businesses, coupled with fear in their encounters with high technology, and the government did not effectively attend to these.

Although the government does not often admit the situation, the question of national sovereignty remains critical. The fear, especially among developing countries, that the capacity to introduce or implement public policy is lessened by a large MNC presence, cannot be dismissed lightly. An example would be unwarranted intervention by foreign governments or by foreign MNCs in political activity. Though the evidence is scanty and not well publicised, the government actually rejected the entry of several foreign enterprises that insisted on guarantees that their subsidiary plants would not be unionized.[62] In any case, given the authoritarian nature of the government, foreign investors are well aware that they are to keep clear of domestic politics. The Singapore bureaucracy's priority to maintain a corruption-free society "does sometimes frighten foreign investors away" and "into the arms of the more easygoing Malaysians".[63] And, because Singapore's economic performance hinges to a large extent on their presence, the economic power and technological prowess of MNCs could seriously create, in the words of local economist Lim Joo Jock, "the impression that local enterprise is cast in a subordinate role".[64] The weakness of Singapore's export-led industrialization with foreign MNCs in the vanguard was frankly acknowledged by the government in "The New Strategic Plan" of 1991:

> Many of the MNCs in Singapore have activities which are largely production based. The rest of the business functions from R&D to marketing are generally carried out elsewhere. Recognising the need for greater innovation, serious attempts have been made to promote R&D with some companies coming up with innovative products in Singapore. However, the extent to which this is happening today is quite limited, and major progress needs to be made here in the next phase of economic development.[65]

Increasing degrees of protectionism in the world market and continuous heavy dependence on MNCs to spearhead export manufacturing and high technology transfer could also severely inhibit the nurturing of domestic industrial entrepreneurs and an expansion of the indigenous technology base.[66] By the end of the 1980s there were still few signs of the local manufacturing sector developing any independence of foreign technology. Moreover, the lack of an R&D tradition in Singapore increased the country's technological dependence on MNCs. Therefore, to many observers Singapore remains "little more than a sub-contractor of the rich countries".[67]

The central role of foreign technology and its impact on Singapore's attempt to develop its own indigenous technology base was also actively discussed during the case interviews in the mid-1990s.[68] A team leader with Du Pont Singapore pointed out that the manufacturing culture in Singapore is "very orderly, very disciplined" and these are traits which foreign MNCs like. Hence, the EDB model of attracting foreign investments into the manufacturing sector was adjusted to tap the inflow of new technologies so that these could be diffused to local firms. An academic don felt that MNCs are the best source of local technological entrepreneurs because of the training and business contacts they have established. In most cases, bigger MNCs like Philips Singapore and Hewlett Packard can transfer and diffuse technology and skills to local engineers because they have their own in-house R&D centres employing a large pool of researchers. More significantly, these companies have attempted to lure their top industrial researchers to remain in the organization by providing them incentives such as rapid promotions within the R&D department. A Taiwanese scientist in the semiconductor industry explained that Singapore needs to be technologically dependent on the MNCs "because they can widen the technology base ... which can eventually spawn more entrepreneurship and indigenous technology competition". However, as cautioned by the Du Pont scientist, Singapore's model of technological leapfrogging is essentially aimed at "attracting intellectual property, the intellectual capital, into Singapore.... Your goal is very noble but have you created the right environment; that's the issue, the real debate."

The question of how effectively Singapore's indigenous technological base has developed as a result of the presence of high-tech MNCs was also eagerly tackled by the interviewees. For a Singaporean scientist with National Semiconductor, an American MNC, the level of indigenous technological innovations achievable in Singapore would depend "on the willingness of high-tech companies to develop more design groups" which consist not only of design engineers but also non-technical personnel providing essential support services. He emphasized that teamwork, corporate culture and the working environment are critical factors for the successful diffusion of technology and skills. The scientist also pointed out that it is not uncommon for the parent companies of MNCs to keep the latest R&D projects in the headquarters. Citing the case of his own company, although Singapore engineers have the opportunity to be attached to the parent company in the United States, it is very unlikely that they will be directly involved with cutting-edge research projects. At the most, the Singapore plant will work on a "small portion" of a major project. A research manager too had the same experience. Despite the opportunity to collaborate with the company's Swedish partners in some research projects, she hardly received the latest on methods and technology through formal channels. It was only through informal, social interactions at the engineers' level that she managed to learn more about the "know-how" and "know-why". One of the two innovators interviewed was more critical of MNCs' contributions to the upgrading of Singapore's indigenous technological base. He said that MNCs, in line with the objectives of the country's technology policy, would always welcome the extra monetary sources — and publicity — from the National Science and Technology Board (the predecessor of A*Star) to indulge in some "piggy-backed" technology and repackaging of existing products which looked high-tech. In actual fact there is nothing high-tech about these products and local firms; the Taiwanese, especially, could also produce the same products. Unfortunately, he added, the Singapore Government only gave lip service to rather than full support for the growth and development of home-grown high-tech industries. A principal R&D manager with Hewlett Packard, however, maintained that MNCs do establish close consultations with local firms that are producing component parts. Technical knowledge and skill are also transferred to these local firms in order for them to meet technical specifications and standards.

Closely associated with the role of MNCs in technology transfer is the utilization and contributions of foreign scientists and professional engineers. These foreign imports could make up for the lack of a critical mass of research personnel in science and technology. However, there was the general perception that, while they were seen as useful sources of knowledge and skills, the government should not place a heavy reliance on their presence. The scientist at Du Pont Singapore explained that "[i]f Singapore cannot offer a competitive environment to satisfy their [the expatriates] needs[,] not just material but also intellectual, freedom of expression of their scientific findings and recognition of their work, they will leave" for greener pastures, such as Malaysia, if the country offers a better environment. There is also the common fallacy that there is a direct link between financial outlays and scientific-technological advance. Singapore cannot produce an "instant" scientific or research culture by enticing foreign expertise with monetary rewards. Singapore's aggressive move to attract scientists and researchers from all over the world — especially from China — has its own limitations because, in the words of an academic don in Chemistry, "if you don't have the scientific culture it is hard to get good people.... And money is not everything. You will never be able to get top-ranked scientists because they just think that when they come to Singapore they are not going to progress very much in their scientific achievements. So I don't think salary is the real issue." In the 1990s, scholarships for graduate studies in science and technology and for research positions in Singapore's two main universities attracted a constant stream of applicants from China. But Singapore is not getting the cream because the best tend to head for the United States and Britain. An R&D manager of Creative Technology, then the home-grown company frequently cited by the government for its technological creativity, added that a foreign industrial researcher tends to give only a portion of his best; otherwise, the recipient of his knowledge and skill would turn out to be his competitor. The majority of these foreign researchers are highly paid and, after some time, their contributions tend to slacken because they are pressurized to produce results within a given time frame. They have also gotten acquainted with Singapore's "9 to 5" working culture and thus follow suit. But scientific and technological research requires patience, determination and, above all, the willingness to sacrifice personal time. The manager neatly summarized the situation — "what we get is not the best; what is the best do not come to Singapore".

AN INDUSTRIAL REVOLUTION OR A "TECHNOLOGYLESS" INDUSTRIALIZATION?

Singapore's economic growth under the so-called "Second Industrial Revolution" restructuring programme was dented by a severe recession in the mid-1980s.[69] In 1985 the economy, after more than a decade of high growth, declined in real terms by 1.8 per cent and grew by only

1.9 per cent in 1986.[70] To pull the economy out of the doldrums and restore the country's international competitiveness, a high-powered economic committee was formed in 1985 by the Ministry of Trade and Industry. The 1986 *Report of the Economic Committee* recommended a shift from a strong industrial base to a much more diversified, mostly tertiary economy. Subsequently, "The Strategic Economic Plan" was launched in 1991.

The Singapore Government learned one important lesson — that it was a mistake to "put all its development eggs in one basket".[71] The technological upgrading of the manufacturing sector was too rapidly enforced and, at the same time, not enough attention was paid to the traditional services sector.[72] A warning of this flaw in the industrial policy had already been given in 1981 when a group of U.S. consultants on the government's plan to scale the technology ladder concluded that the strategy was too ambitious and that attempts to move into high technology had been attempted too swiftly and within too short a time frame.[73] It also recommended that the government should focus on the development of the quality of manpower by setting up laboratories and research departments within NUS.[74]

During the first half of the 1980s the government had actually forced foreign and local investors to quickly upgrade from labour-intensive operations to capital-intensive and high technology operations. In 1986, backed by ministerial-led promotion missions to major foreign investor countries as well as advertisements in international publications, the EDB embarked on an aggressive, high-pitched programme to attract new investments with high technical content.[75] High-tech projects were sought because these presumably would mean a higher usage of local professional and skilled manpower resources.[76] At the same time, the EDB called on local firms to support industries to upgrade their range and quality of operations to cater for the incoming new technologies.[77] Unfortunately, this pragmatic industrial policy did not match up with the reality of Singapore's technological competencies. The pool of skilled manpower was already very limited and the government's open invitation to new foreign investors would mean greater competition with local firms for these skilled workers. In the process, it was not the MNCs but indigenous entrepreneurs who faced the prospect of being left behind because they did not have the necessary capital, the "know-how", or the governmental support to improve themselves. Therefore, domestic industrial entrepreneurs who had found it difficult to thrive during the labour-intensive phase of industrialization were further handicapped by the rapid shift towards high-technology industrialization.[78] The plight of small private enterprises was made known to the government early in 1985 in a Chinese press editorial:

> Government participation in private economic activities and monopoly of public undertakings is indeed a great contribution to Singapore's economic growth and social construction. However, the private sector has often complained of unfair competition in circumstances in which government bodies participate in private economic activities. In addition, active government interference has more or less hampered the growth of Singapore entrepreneurs. Dr Winsemius, our economic advisor, now retired, frankly pointed out during his visit to Singapore early last year that Singapore should in future encourage the growth of entrepreneurs and allow them to give fuller play to their enterprising spirit.[79]

It went on to argue that — as in the case of Japan, South Korea, Taiwan and Hong Kong — in order for local private establishments to upgrade into new areas of high technology and to grow into multinational corporations, "it is essential for the government to create more favourable conditions".[80] Moreover, the government's high technology policy also created confusion among local businessmen, who requested that the industrial strategy be reviewed.[81] In particular, the local entrepreneurs wanted clearer guidelines on what was meant by "high tech" and "high value-added" industries. They also requested that the nation's drive towards technology upgrading be slowed down and the government establish closer rapport with indigenous firms so that more could participate in the high-tech programmes.[82]

As stated in his report to the government, the chairman of an ad hoc committee on local businesses reiterated that "as far as the private sector is concerned, we know about hotel, banking, trading, pig farming ... but we do not know what is high-tech", and that the use of pressure to hasten the high-tech programme would not work.[83] The report further stressed that the rate of decline of indigenous, labour-intensive businesses had far exceeded the growth level of high-tech industries. The local businesses that could not integrate with the government's high-technology policy were encouraged to relocate to other countries. Clearly, the government had failed to consider carefully "the practical problems arising from relocations such as the industrialisation and economic policies of other countries, loss of jobs for those affected and problems with foreign exchange".[84] Hence, once again, the aggressiveness shown in the attempted transformation of the manufacturing sector brought to mind the ideology of survival in a Darwinian-type of society. The *Business Times* put it succinctly: "it is a shove made together with the blunt warning that those unable to swim or at least afloat with this new tide of policy will have to sink".[85] Statistically speaking, the mid-1980s recession resulted in the closure of 10,044 businesses in 1984 and 9,992 in 1985.[86]

What then was so "revolutionary" about Singapore's Second Industrial Revolution? The Singapore economy did not experience anything near to an "industrial revolution". There is no evidence of a sustained and accelerated development of indigenous techno-industrial innovations. Indeed, Yoshihara Kunio has boldly claimed that Singapore could not be categorized as a newly industrialized country because it does not have an indigenous technological base and its growth is heavily dependent on services; Singapore's industrialization can best be described as "technologyless".[87] Unlike Japanese capitalists, domestic manufacturing capitalists, argues Yoshihara, could simply import wholesale sophisticated machinery for immediate production and,

> if his staff do not know how to operate it, he can enlist a foreign engineering company to give the necessary training before the plant is completed; and if this is not enough, he can hire its technicians to stay on at plant. Even if this is unnecessary, he may later have to depend on the engineering company or the supplier of the machines when something goes wrong, for his technical staff may lack the ability to make complicated repairs.[88]

To a certain extent Yoshihara was correct in his observation of Singapore's industrialization. Historically developed as a trading entrepôt port, Singapore never possessed an effective domestic capital-goods industry, in terms of both the capacity to make equipment and the motivation to do so. There is a linkage between establishing a capital goods sector and the development of indigenous technological capabilities. Nathan Rosenberg explained the importance of this linkage for a developing country:

> It is the producer[s] of capital goods who have the financial incentive and therefore provide the pressures to adopt the innovation. Creating a capital goods industry is, in effect, a major way of institutionalizing internal pressures for the adoption of new technology.[89]

Manufacturing's contribution to Singapore's GDP rose from less than 10 per cent prior to 1959 to an average of around 25 per cent in the 1980s, with a corresponding emphasis on non-traditional areas such as machinery and transportation. However, as argued by Salahuddin Ahmed, Singapore has failed to develop a genuine capital, that is, an engineering industry, or an indigenous invention sector.[90] Firstly, although machinery and transport equipment accounted for an estimated 48 per cent share of domestic exports in 1990, this category of manufactures consists mainly of office machines, electric generators, telecommunications accessories, refrigerators, air-conditioners and ventilating machinery rather than traditional producer goods. Secondly, output is dominated by parts and components of machinery and transport equipment rather than complete production. Thirdly, the limited success of Singapore's "Second Industrial Revolution" was evidenced by the unwillingness of multinationals to introduce sophisticated engineering and design processes into Singapore.[91] Moreover, local manufacturers tend to only import machinery and made little attempts to design and build them because they were "formerly traders so that they have neither technical training nor interest in technical matters — all they are interested in is quick profit".[92] Thus, Singapore had failed to develop a critical pool of technological entrepreneurs committed to manufacture locally designed capital goods. However, the reality of a small core of domestic industrial entrepreneurs does not imply that they are not innovative. Innovation can also take the form of the desire and eagerness of these entrepreneurs to upgrade technologically by constantly sourcing and purchasing the latest technologies in order to stay competitive. Nevertheless, added to this general lack of interest in technological entrepreneurship, Singapore also possessed in the 1990s a limited supply of local scientists, engineers and technicians. More often than not they are being lured by the technologically superior foreign MNCs with their conducive working environment.

However, one can argue that Yoshihara's interpretation of Singapore's industrialization is biased and heavily influenced by the Japanese experience, to the extent that he stereotyped capitalism. Some recent research, especially the work of Garry Rodan on Singapore's industrialization, has shown that ASEAN economies are thriving precisely because they possess a dynamic, capitalistic system (as opposed to capitalism being equated to a form of "economic activity", in Yoshihara's view). Nevertheless, Yoshihara's remarks on the role of Singapore's domestic industrialists provide a useful point for a brief reference to their counterparts in South Korea and Taiwan. Like Singapore, the two NIEs were also labelled by Yoshihara as "Japanese compradors", depending to a large extent on Japanese technology and linkages.[93]

For South Korea and Taiwan, whose sources of growth are already geared towards the knowledge-based industries, indigenous entrepreneurs in the private sector have become the spearhead of economic development. By the 1990s both countries were moving rapidly towards achieving technological innovations through R&D. South Koreans are transforming themselves, in the words of Alice Amsden, "from learner, or borrower of foreign technology, to creator of new products and processes".[94] Both countries have also stepped up formal linkages with foreign high-tech industries. Taiwan Aerospace Corp, for example, tied up with British Aerospace to push the country into the leading edge of aeronautical technology.[95] And since 1987, Korea's top two *chaebol* — the Samsung and the Lucky-Goldstar groups — have established design or research operations overseas, thus strengthening their technological base.[96] South Korea edged one up in ranking to become the world's fifth largest carmaker in 1994, with production of 2.4 million vehicles.[97]

Though on a much smaller scope and scale and with close technical assistance from the Japanese in the beginning, Singapore, too, has been successful in developing its own shipbuilding and marine industry.[98] Led by its local shipbuilding and engineering firms, Singapore developed its technological capability in the construction and repair of commercial and naval vessels as well as the design and fabrication of military engineering equipment.[99] At the same time, the port of Singapore is rapidly automating its facilities in order to transform itself into a new mega port suitable to serve the city-state into the twenty-first century.[100] However, the fact that during the recessionary years of 1985–86 Singapore experienced a heavier negative impact than its East Asian rivals — South Korea and Taiwan — is indicative of the tremendous importance of developing a home-grown high-tech capital-goods industry that can compete globally.

Finally, in a study on the total factor productivity (TFP) growth of Hong Kong and Singapore, Alwyn Young of Massachusetts Institute of Technology showed while 56 per cent of Hong Kong's increase in output per worker over the two decades after 1970 came from a rise in TFP, Singapore's TFP fell by 6 per cent in the same period.[101] Overall, between 1970 and 1990, TFP growth contributed to −1 per cent of output growth in Singapore. This meant that, firstly, Singapore's growth in output came mainly from capital accumulation and, secondly, "while technical change has contributed substantially to economic growth in Hong Kong, its contribution to growth in Singapore is next to nil".[102] Young suggested that, although Singapore's "industrial targeting" policy is not wrong per se, the government should slow the speed at which it selects new industries to promote. Local businesses did not have the time to really master a technology before moving on to a more sophisticated one, as the country is targeting the development of new industries all the time.

Young's study reveals explicitly that, while the Singapore economy grew at a remarkable 8.5 per cent per annum (three times as fast as the United States) between 1966 and 1990, the "miraculous" growth was due more to increases in measured inputs rather than increased efficiency due to technological advances. In other words, economic development was achieved through mobilization of resources, especially in capital stock and education. This is to say that, unlike competitive industries in the United States or Japan which increase their efficiency by being technologically innovative, Singapore firms largely depend on the purchase of new technology to increase productivity. And, over a few decades, using domestic savings, the government had made a heavy

investment in physical capital, which according to Young's estimates
rose from 9 per cent of the country's GDP in 1960 to a high of 43 per
cent in 1984.[103] The worrying point is that mere increases in inputs,
without an increase in the efficiency of those inputs being used, must
run into diminishing returns. In the words of economist Paul Krugman
of Stanford University:

> Even without going through the formal exercise of growth accounting
> ... Singapore's growth has been based largely on one-time changes
> in behavior that cannot be repeated. Over the past generation the
> percentage of people employed has almost doubled; it cannot double
> again. A half-educated work force has been replaced by one in which
> the bulk of workers has high school diplomas; it is unlikely that a
> generation from now most Singaporeans will have PhDs. And an
> investment share of 40 per cent is amazingly high by any standard;
> a share of 70 per cent would be ridiculous. So one can immediately
> conclude that Singapore is unlikely to achieve future growth rates
> comparable to those of the past.[104]

In summary, it was a fortuitous coincidence that, since the late 1960s,
Singapore's export-oriented manufacturing was strongly supported
by the arrival of multinationals in their search for cheaper offshore
production bases. Thus, in the 1970s, growth spurts were fuelled
mainly by the diffusion of labour-intensive technologies. By the
1980s, in line with the government's industrial restructuring strategy,
manufacturing development efforts were concentrated on the adoption
of more sophisticated industrial technology. Although sustained
industrial expansion was achieved largely through the pro-MNC policy,
rapid economic growth was gained at the expense of developing an
indigenous technological base. The transfer and diffusion of technology
through the auspices of the foreign MNCs were, at best, limited. Being
a very open economy, heavily dependent on external forces, and
facing increasing competition from her ASEAN neighbours, Singapore
continued to rely on foreign corporations for the transfer of more
sophisticated industrial technology and must ensure that the
investment climate is conducive to foreign investors, including those
who are already active in the country.[105] Mirza Hafiz was more
direct in his comments when he stated that "it is such worries, of
course, which always make the PAP rush, pell-mell, into the arms

of the multinationals".[106] However, to be an effective player in the game of high-technology and globalized competition, Singapore must possess an abundance of skilled and scientific manpower, an excellent technology infrastructure and a competitive and rewarding investment climate for indigenous technology entrepreneurs. Recognizing that its MNC-driven industrialization had failed to nurture an indigenous technological base, in the 1990s Singapore's economic planners actively initiated strategies towards institutionalizing an R&D culture.

Notes

1. Interestingly, the term "Second Industrial Revolution" is popularly used by academics to denote the 1930s in Japan's economic history (after the Manchurian Incident in 1931). The period was marked by the take off of Japan's heavy and chemical industries. Technological advances made during this period allowed Japan to develop state-of-the-art military technologies which surprised the Americans in the Pacific War. See John Dower, *Ways of Forgetting, Ways of Remembering: Japan in the Modern World* (New York: The New Press, 2012), pp. 86–92; and Paul Kennedy, *Engineers of Victory: The Problem Solvers Who Turned the Tide in the Second World War* (New York: Random House, 2013).
2. Ronald Dore, "Reflections on Culture and Social Change", in *Manufacturing Miracles: Paths of Industrialization in Latin America and East Asia*, edited by Gary Gereffi and Donald L. Wyman, (Princeton, NJ: Princeton University Press, 1990), p. 366.
3. Ibid.
4. Goh Chok Tong, *Budget Speech*, 6 March 1981.
5. *Yearbook of Statistics 1985–86*, Singapore.
6. Tony Tan K.Y., "MNCs as Engines of Economic Growth", *Speech* 4, no. 4 (1980): 59.
7. Mirza Hafiz, *Multinationals and the Growth of the Singapore Economy* (London: Croom Helm, 1986), p. 2.
8. Carl J. Dahlman and Larry E. Westphal, "The Meaning of Technological Mastery in Relation to Transfer of Technology", *Annals of the American Academy of Political and Social Sciences* 458 (November 1981): 80.
9. *Straits Times*, 3 October 1987. For a first-hand account of how MNCs played their roles in transferring skills and knowledge to Singapore firms, see Chua Soo Tian, "How MNCs Helped Start-Up SMEs", in *Heart Work*, by Chan Chin Bock (Singapore: Economic Development Board, 2002), pp. 54–59.

10. Chng M.K., ed., *Effective Mechanisms for the Enhancement of Technology and Skills in Singapore* (Singapore: Institute of Southeast Asian Studies 1986), Chapter 5. The Singapore study was conducted under the ASEAN Regional Studies Promotion Programme. Country research teams from the five ASEAN countries and Japan were required to identify and examine the problems in their respective countries in technology transfer and skills enhancement. Collectively, the papers were published in Ng C.Y., R. Hirono and Robert Y. Siy, Jr., eds., *Effective Mechanisms for the Enhancement of Technology and Skills in ASEAN: An Overview* (Singapore: Institute of Southeast Asian Studies), 1986.

11. Ibid., p. 69.

12. Ibid.

13. Ibid., pp. 78 and 40.

14. Ibid., p. 82 and Rodan, *Political Economy of Singapore*, p. 179.

15. Edward Chen K.Y., *Multinational Corporations, Technology and Employment* (Hong Kong: MacMillan, 1983), pp. 60–61 and 207.

16. Anuwar Ali, *Malaysia Industrialization: The Quest for Technology* (Singapore: Oxford University Press, 1992), pp. 79–80.

17. Norman Clark, "The Multinational Corporation: The Transfer of Technology and Dependence", *Development and Change* 6, no. 1 (1975): 15; Charles W. Linsey, "Transfer of Technology to the ASEAN Region by U.S. Transnational Corporations", *ASEAN Economic Bulletin* 3, no. 2 (1986): 226.

18. Chng, *Effective Mechanisms*, p. 78.

19. *Business Times*, 28 April 1980.

20. Ibid.

21. Ibid.

22. Mark Lester, "The Transfer of Managerial and Technological Skills by Electronic-Assembly Companies in Export-Processing Zone in Malaysia", in *The Transfer and Utilization of Technical Knowledge*, edited by Devendra Sahal (Lexington, MA: Lexington Books, 1980), pp. 211–12.

23. Linda Lim Yuen Ching, "Multinational Firms and Manufacturing for Export in Less Developed Countries: The Case of Malaysia and Singapore" (PhD dissertation, University of Michigan, 1978), pp. 439 and 514.

24. Chng, *Effective Mechanisms*, p. 73.

25. C.W. Lindsey, "Transfer of Technology to the ASEAN Region by U.S. Transnational Corporations", ASEAN Economic Bulletin 3, no. 2 (1986), p. 228.

26. Chng, *Effective Mechanisms*, p. 70.

27. Ibid.

28. A.N. Hakam and Zeph-Yun Chang, "Patterns of Technology Transfer in Singapore: The Case of the Electronics and Computer Industry", *International Journal of Technology Management* 13, nos. 1–2 (1988): 187.

29. Ibid.

30. Hafiz, *Multinationals and the Growth*, p. 258.

31. Two such rare entrepreneurs are Wong Tai and Robin Lau, former employees of Hewlett Packard and a Japanese MNC, respectively. After six years in Hewlett Packard, Wong Tai left and established Informatics Holdings Limited. Besides being one of the largest chains of computer schools in the region, the company is also involved in software development, computer consultancy and computer distribution. Robin Lau started Excel Machine Tools Private Limited in 1986. See the *Straits Times*, 17 July 1993.

32. Lindsey, p. 230.

33. Ibid., p. 227.

34. Ibid., p. 231.

35. *Straits Times*, 9 October 1986.

36. Ibid.

37. *Straits Times*, 7 November 94.

38. Masataka Kosaka, ed., *Japan's Choices: New Globalism and Cultural Orientations in an Industrial State* (London: Pinter, 1989), p. 78.

39. *Growing With Enterprise: A National Effort* (Singapore: Economic Development Board, 1993), p. 36.

40. For a more detailed discussion on the evolution of Singapore's education system, see Goh Chor Boon and S. Gopinathan, "The Development of Education in Singapore since 1965", in *Toward a Better Future: Education and Training for Economic Development in Singapore since 1965*, by Lee Sing Kong, Goh Chor Boon, Birger Fredriksen and Tan Jee Peng (Washington, DC: World Bank, 2008), Chapter 1.

41. *Straits Times*, 14 June 1994. Several institutional changes were introduced to enhance the image of technical education in Singapore. In 1992 the Vocational and Industrial Training Board was totally revamped and renamed the Institute of Technical Education (ITE). See Law Song Seng, "Vocational Technical Education and Economic Development", in Lee et al., *Toward a Better Future*, Chapter 5.

42 Lee Kuan Yew, speech at Tanjong Pagar National Day Celebrations, 15 August 1980.

43. *Straits Times*, 12 February 1994.

44. Ministry of Education, *Annual Report*, various years.

45. As a matter of comparison with some OECD countries, enrolments in the Netherlands' higher education sector increased by 13 per cent from 1980 to 1988; in Japan, university undergraduate enrolments rose by about 9 per cent between 1978 and 1989; and in Norway, the corresponding figure was 10 per cent between 1979 and 1986. The main reason for increased enrolments was the stronger presence of women in the student population. See *Technology and the Economy: The Key Relationships* (OECD, 1992), p. 137.

46. Calculated from *Yearbook of Statistics*, Singapore, 1989, Tables 15.12 and 15.13, pp. 304–5.
47. Lee Hsien Loong, Parliamentary Debates, Official Reports, 28 March 1988, vol. 50, col. 1503–5
48. Ibid., col. 1505
49. Ibid., col. 1505. Encouraging females to take up engineering studies and work continues to be an issue today, as highlighted by Lee Hsien Loong in his 2014 National Day Rally speech. See <http://www.pmo.gov.sg/mediacentre/prime-minister-lee-hsien-loongs-national-day-rally-2014-speech-english>.
50. *Straits Times*, 22 February 1982.
51. Ibid.
52. *Straits Times*, 20 September 1993.
53. National Science and Technology Board, *National Survey of R&D in Singapore*, 1995, p. 18.
54. *New Challenges, Fresh Goal – Towards a Dynamic Global City*. Economic Review Committee (Singapore: Ministry of Trade and Industry, 2003).
55. Martin Carnoy, "Multinationals in a Changing World Economy: Whither the Nation-State?", in *The New Global Economy in the Information Age: Reflections on Our World*, by M. Carnoy, M. Castells, S. Cohen and F.H. Cardoso (Pennsylvania: Pennsylvania State University Press), 1993, p. 96.
56. Tony Tan, "MNCs and ASEAN Development in the 1980s", speech, 7 September 1980.
57. *Straits Times Overseas Edition*, 29 August 1992.
58. Hafiz, *Multinationals and the Growth*, p. 261.
59. Ibid.
60. Lee Hsien Loong, Parliamentary Debates, Republic of Singapore, Official Reports, 25 March 1986, vol. 47, col. 1117.
61. Krause, L.B., Koh Ai Tee and Lee (Tsao) Yuan, *The Singapore Economy Reconsidered* (Singapore: Institute of Southeast Asian Studies, 1987), p. 61.
62. Pang Eng Fong, "Foreign Investment and the State in a Newly-Industrializing Country: The Experience of Singapore", *East Asia*, vol. 3 (Frankfurt: Campus Verlag, 1985), p. 89.
63. Dore, in *Manufacturing Miracles*, edited by Gereffi and Wayne, p. 361.
64. Quoted in Hafiz, *Multinationals and the Growth,* p. 262.
65. The Economic Planning Committee, *The Strategic Plan: Towards a Developed Nation* (Ministry of Trade and Industry, Singapore, 1991), pp. 27–28.
66. A.H. Hakam, "Deliberate Restructuring in the Newly Industrializing Countries of Asia – The Case of Singapore", *East Asia*, vol. 3 (Frankfurt: Campus Verlag, 1985), p. 106; Chia Siow-Yue, "Direct Foreign Investment and the Industrialization Process in Singapore", in *Singapore Resources and*

Growth, edited by Lim C.Y. and Peter J. Lloyd (Singapore: Oxford University Press, 1986). p. 112.

67. *Far Eastern Economic Review*, 16 July 1987, p. 60.

68. These one-to-one, in-depth interviews were conducted in March and April 1994.

69. According to the report by the Economic Committee, both demand and supply factors were responsible for Singapore's first severe recession. Externally, the worsening fortunes of the oil, marine and electronics industry worldwide severely affected the demand for Singapore's services and components. Internally, businesses were hit by rising labour costs, which rose faster than productivity. Domestic demand was weakened by increases in domestic savings, which in turn were not matched by a rise in productive domestic investment.

70. *Yearbook of Statistics 1986*, p. 3.

71. G. Rodan, *The Political Economy of Singapore's Industrialization* (Kuala Lumpur: Forum Press, 1991), p. 183.

72. Ibid.

73. *Business Times*, 5 August 1981.

74. Ibid.

75. *Business Times*, 17 December 1986.

76. Ibid.

77. Ibid.

78. Chia, "Direct Foreign Investment and the Industrialization Process in Singapore" in C.Y. Lim and P.J. Lloyds (eds.), *Singapore Resources and Growth* (Singapore: Oxford University Press, 1986), p. 113.

79. *Lianhe Zaobao*, 19 January 1985.

80. Ibid.

81. *Straits Times*, 31 December 1985.

82. Ibid.

83. Ibid.

84. Ibid.

85. *Business Times*, 27 June 1979.

86. Lee Hsien Loong, Parliamentary Debates, Republic of Singapore, Official Reports, 7 March 1986, vol. 47, col. 439.

87. Yoshihara Kunio, *The Rise of Ersatz Capitalism in South-East Asia* (Singapore: Oxford University Press, 1988), Chapter 5. Yoshihara maintained that development in Southeast Asia has produced an "ersatz" capitalism, one which is "inefficient and lacklustre" compared to "real" capitalism. This is because countries in this region are heavily dependent on foreign capital and technology and, as such, are incapable of indigenous production

of manufactured goods to sustain industrialization ("real" capitalism in Yoshihara's interpretation).

88. Ibid., pp. 112–13.

89. Rosenberg, *Perspective on Technology*, p. 164.

90. Aby Taher Salahuddin Ahmed, "The Role of the Capital Goods Sector in Small, Open Economies", *Journal of Contemporary Asia* 24, no. 3 (1994): 327–29.

91. Rodan, *Singapore's Industrialisation*, p. 179.

92. Yoshihara, *Ersatz Capitalism*, p. 113.

93. Notwithstanding the point that both countries were former colonies of Japan, Yoshihara's comment beckons a sense of nationalistic pride and prejudice. In recent years, both countries have carved for themselves a respectable niche in their respective paths towards technological self-reliance.

94. A.M. Amsden, *Asia's Next Giant: South Korea and Late Industrialisation* (New York: Oxford University Press, 1989), p. 328.

95. *Straits Times*, 5 July 1993.

96. Martin H. Bloom, "Globalization and the Korean Electronics Industry", *Pacific Review* 6, no. 2 (1993): 124.

97. *Straits Times*, 4 March 1994.

98. Hal Hill and Pang Eng Fong, "Technology Exports from a Small, Very Open NIC: The Case of Singapore", in *Working Papers in Trade and Development* (Australian National University, August 1989), p. 14. According to Hill and Pang, a few locally owned firms have also pioneered "early-stage" technology exports, particularly in the modification and adaption of products and processes. Ibid., p. 35.

99. *Straits Times*, 5 February 1993.

100. *Straits Times*, 24 October 1992.

101. Alwyn Young, "A Tale of Two Cities: Factor Accumulation and Technical Change in Hong Kong and Singapore", in *NBER Macroeconomics Annual 1992* (Massachusetts Institute of Technology Press, 1992). Growth accounting brings into consideration two sources of growth. On one side are increases in "inputs"; that is, growth in employment, educational standards of workers, and stock of physical capital. On the other side are increases in output per unit of input, and such gains are the result of greater efficiency due to better management, increases in knowledge and technological advances. Thus, growth accounting provides an indication of how much growth is due to each input and how much is due to increased efficiency by producing an index, or "total factor productivity", that combines all measurable inputs.

102. Ibid., p. 5.

103. Ibid., p. 2.
104. Paul Krugman, "The Myth of Asia's Miracle", *Foreign Affairs* 73, no. 6 (1994): 71. Krugman made an interesting point that the growth of Lee Kuan Yew's Singapore is an "economic twin" of the growth of Stalin's Soviet Union.
105. *Straits Times*, 28 June 1993.
106. Hafiz, *Multinationals and the Growth*, p. 263.

4

STATE INTERVENTION AND TECHNOLOGICAL CHANGE

As the world economy develops, markets and nations alike have become more global and competitive. Technology has become a dominant competitive force. Unlike the older form of mass production technologies, by the late 1990s the emphasis had shifted to such strategies as productivity, quality, speed in getting new custom or semi-custom products to the market and after-sale technical services. These changes have created tremendous pressures on nations to respond quickly. Equally important, the vastness of these changes have exposed weaknesses and imbalances in the socio-economic structures of nations, such as inadequacies in education systems, poor government–industry–university linkages, the inappropriateness of R&D policies, inefficiencies of the technology infrastructure, and the incompatibility of existing sociocultural orientations towards technological change. These trends and their repercussions not only affect nations like the United States and Japan, they also exert demands on latecomers like Singapore. How has the small, trading city-state fared? This chapter examines the attempts made by the Singapore Government to establish a scientific and technological environment since 1980 and analyses the policies and problems associated with this development. The discussion is seen against the context of changing global scenarios.

INTERNATIONAL AND REGIONAL SCENARIOS IN THE 1980s

Undoubtedly, in terms of per capita GDP growth during the 1980s, East Asian countries were well ahead of the developed countries, with the former achieving a growth rate of 9.3 per cent in 1988 and the latter achieving 3.5 per cent.[1] As the major economic power in Asia, Japan's success also produced what has been called the "flying geese" pattern, with the implication that ASEAN countries (except Singapore) and China are catching up with the East Asian NIEs, or the "little dragons", in labour-intensive, low-technology industries, while the East Asian NIEs are, in turn, catching up with Japan in high-technology and knowledge-intensive industries. By the early 1990s the East Asian NIEs — South Korea, Taiwan, Hong Kong and Singapore — had graduated as major exporters of more mature consumer products in microelectronics, computers and telecommunications equipment, and this trend created a new dimension to the relationship between East Asian NIEs and the developing countries, particularly those in Southeast Asia.

Equally significant is the fact that the expansion of exports in consumer products indicates the aspirations and deep commitment of the East Asian NIEs to achieving leadership status in research and development. The American writer Daniel Greenberg commented on this growing strength in science and technology:

Asia (specifically, Japan, China, India, South Korea, Taiwan and Singapore) is plunging into science and engineering with resources and enthusiasm that portend even fiercer battles for world markets in the post–Cold War era of global competition [and] there is a common thread in their attempts to step up from low-cost production to home-based design capability for "knowledge-based innovative products and processes". The build-up is often accompanied by increased imports of advanced equipment from the United States, thus masking the long-range prospects of intensified competition.[2]

This commitment to science and engineering and export-led growth was pursued with certain advantages in Asia (outside of Japan) — lower labour costs (at least in the 1980s and early 1990s) than in North America, Europe and Japan and an open international trading order protected by the military strength of the United States. But, by the late 1990s, these advantages were diminishing in the face of two developing trends — increasing difficulty in gaining access to new technologies and the likely formation of trading blocs in international trade. The increasing restrictions on market and technology access is due in part to the rapid shortening of life cycles of new technologies and in part to the strategies and policies of firms and governments of the developed nations to cope with the competitive pressures from the East Asian NIEs.[3]

At the same time, the international trade environment was becoming much more protectionist, particularly when developed countries like the United States have large foreign debts and substantial trade deficits. Two main factors account for this growing protectionism in world trade. They are, first, the serious trade imbalances between Organisation for Economic Cooperation and Development (OECD) countries, especially between the United States and Japan, and second, the desire to prevent further "dumping" of technology-intensive products from the East Asian NIEs.[4] Uncertainties in the global economy have been reflected in the protracted Uruguay Round of GATT (launched in September 1986) negotiations and the intensification of the movements towards the building of economic trading blocs, such as the Asia Pacific Economic Cooperation (APEC), the East Asia Economic Grouping (EAEG), the North American Free Trade Area (NAFTA), and the Malaysian concept of an East Asia Economic Caucus (EAEC) covering Japan, China, the East Asian NIEs and ASEAN. The end of the Cold War had also led to Eastern Europe joining the economic race. The countries of the region may be able to adopt the proven strategies of the East Asian NIEs at the initial stage of development and become significant players in the world economic scene in time to come.[5]

In Asia itself, one major development since the mid-1980s has been in the form of a relocation of Japanese small and medium enterprises to the East Asian NIEs and ASEAN countries. Japan has reached the stage of economic development where it no longer has an advantage in labour costs or worker motivation. Propelled by the sharp rise of the yen since the late 1980s, Japanese firms had been shifting production out of the country in order to remain competitive. The outflow, in the opinion of the late Sony Chairman, Akio Morita, marked an "unprecedented challenge" to the Japanese competitive spirit and, if not met, "could lead to the shrinking of Japan's domestic manufacturing base".[6] Another factor for this capital flight is the desire of Japanese firms to be closer to their fast-expanding markets in Asia, including China.[7] Such changes influenced the pace of growth in Southeast Asia in the 1990s. The countries in the region, including Singapore, rapidly upgraded their technology infrastructure in order to integrate closely with the rising Japanese investment, presumably in areas of new technologies.

Finally, developments in the 1980s were pointing to increasing competition from Singapore's neighbours in Southeast Asia. The Indonesian Government had been introducing, within the limits of preserving her national interests, new packages of deregulation measures to improve the country's investment climate and, at the same time, encouraging local and foreign enterprises to upgrade to middle and high-tech industrial production.[8] To reduce the 70 per cent of Indonesian exports which went through Singapore during this period, Indonesia developed a port on Batam Island so that "exports can gradually be handled directly without going through Singapore".[9] Malaysia, too, was rapidly joining the rank and file of Asian NIEs with the aspiration to become a developed nation by 2020.[10] The launching of the Industrial Master Plan 1986–1995 marked the start of a national effort to accelerate the growth of the manufacturing sector by, besides other measures, an upgrading of the country's indigenous technological capability.[11] The state of Penang seemed to be showing the way. Its astounding progress in transforming itself from a "little brother" and a "sleepy hollow" into a thriving manufacturing haven prompted Singapore's Goh Chok Tong to issue a warning of an up and coming "tiger", catching up quickly with Singapore.[12] His observation that "many of the activities in Singapore can also be done in Penang" was demonstrated when the U.S. disk drive maker Quantum Corporation decided to join the other major U.S. disk drive makers Seagate and Connor Peripherals to build its worldwide "re-manufacturing" facility in Penang.[13] The island's skilled but relatively cheap labour has also attracted Singapore manufacturers to either relocate or expand their low-tech manufacturing activities there.[14]

These new challenges from ASEAN countries were compounded by another significant domestic trend — the "hollowing out" of Singapore's manufacturing sector. Although the government seemed to think otherwise, capital flight has been occurring with local and foreign investors moving their manufacturing operations off the island.[15] In a survey of 148 Japanese manufacturers (out of the total of 400 Japanese manufacturers in Singapore) carried out by the Japanese Chamber of Commerce and Industry (JCCI), more than one third were planning to relocate their labour-intensive operations to the neighbouring state of Johor and the Indonesian Riau Islands between 1993 and 1996.[16] Out of the companies that decided to remain in Singapore, only about 20 per cent had plans to upgrade their operations by investing in more sophisticated equipment for high-tech production.[17] As explained by the JCCI's secretary-general, the main reason for this capital flight is that "Singapore can no longer maintain low-tech manufacturing because of labour shortages and wage increases."[18] A final point to note is that, besides the economic challenges, Singapore's survival and prosperity is also highly dependent on its geostrategic circumstances. Philippe Regnier correctly emphasized the fact that "It is ... imperative for the city-state never to forget that every break in relations with the regional environment, whether brought about by its own action or by one of its neighbours, could spoil the geopolitical conditions which have governed its brilliant development."[19] Thus, the successful management of Singapore's relations with its immediate neighbours has always received the highest consideration by its leaders.

For Singapore, the race against the other East Asian NIEs and the dynamic economies in ASEAN intensified in the 1990s. Using the analogy of danger posed by deadly tigers, Singapore's then Prime Minister Goh Chok Tong commented: "At this stage of our development, we are like someone being chased by tigers with a cliff in front. The tigers are closing in fast but the cliff is difficult to climb." [20] Goh's concern for the future was echoed by Lee Kuan Yew when he added: "It is not a static world. The fact is that you have won the race last year, doesn't mean you are going to win the race this year. Every day you start a new race."[21] As mentioned in the previous chapter, South

Korea and Taiwan have been quick to respond to the global changes. South Korea's two leading business groups — Samsung and Lucky-Goldstar — were propelled on their rapid internationalization by a government policy that stressed export-led growth and R&D.[22] External pressures also spurred them to set up or acquire overseas research facilities and "listening posts" in the United States and Japan. With its very open economy, the success of Singapore's industrial policy to attract international capital is highly contingent on the changing world scene — no matter how meticulous the economic growth blueprint has been planned and no matter how well the whole society is controlled by a paternalistic and dirigiste government. This realization is even more acute when Singapore hopes to become technologically self-reliant under the aegis of international capital. In the 1990s the pace of Singapore's industrialization arrived at a crossroads where careful planning and decisions had to be made. It became vital for the city-state to develop an internationally competitive manufacturing sector as the cornerstone of long-term national development and sustainable economic growth. But success in international trade and production of high value-added goods is heavily dependent on product or process uniqueness or differentiation. This comes mainly from research and development and the use of advanced manufacturing technologies.

R&D AND NATIONAL GOALS

It is now widely accepted that the state plays a central role in shaping various forms of technical change and that a national R&D effort is a matter of great importance to its citizens. It is expected to play a leading role in stimulating techno-industrial innovations through such channels as organizing academic research to meet the needs of innovation, organizing markets and innovative indigenous industries for new science-based products, creating a conducive environment that can foster the innovative potential of industries, and creating incentives for industries to engage in fields that have high commercial returns.[23] The pathway taken or the style in technology policy adopted by the state is clearly dependent on the country's history and the people's inherited attitudes towards science and technology.

In the case of Singapore, science and technology were never a part of its history, at least till the 1990s. Even by the 1970s, the state's overriding political agenda was national survival in a highly volatile region. This lack of traditional experience in science and technology has serious implications for Singapore's technology policy culture.

In view of the assumption that national governments recognize the importance of science and technology in meeting national goals and their indispensable role in promoting industrial R&D, why did the Singapore Government decide to pay great attention to R&D only in the late 1980s, and not earlier? What motivated the leaders? On the surface the answer seems obvious; that is, technological progress will enhance the competitive position of Singapore in the face of changes in the world economy. However, the answer may be more complicated than expected.

From the various studies conducted on the spin-off effects of MNCs, it has been determined that little by the way of high-tech knowledge and skills in R&D has been diffused to local firms. It has also been emphasized that Singapore's industrialization was not based on the expansion of an indigenous manufacturing sector. Although Singapore became a major centre for the operation of MNCs, local entrepreneurs were slow in moving into the manufacturing sector, not to mention investment in R&D. The government was conscious of the realities of its restructuring programme, especially in its perception of how the MNCs could be used to spearhead the nation's path to technological excellence. Indeed, the government admitted that "some innovative approaches" in its industrial strategy were urgently required.[24] The economic planners also recognized that the Singapore economy had undergone significant stages of development. As reported in the *Straits Times*, "Having grown from the traditional role as a regional port and distribution centre in the 1960s, and an international manufacturing and service centre in the 1970s, Singapore has now set its sight on developing into a centre of science-based manufacturing and knowledge-intensive technical activities."[25]

Externally, rapid globalization of the world economy has produced a totally new kind of economic contest, characterized by new sources of strategic advantage. In the words of Lester Thurow, the twentieth century was "a century of niche competition" and the twenty-first is "a century of head-to-head competition".[26] A nation's comparative advantage, hitherto based on factor endowments, is now gradually becoming man-made, and the key lies in the nation's spending on R&D, with an emphasis, in Thurow's opinion, on process technologies.[27] Singapore's EOI strategy became a victim of this new economic game when the country's low labour cost comparative advantage was eroded by technology itself. Automation and robotics, for example, could easily cancel out the cost advantage of cheaper labour. As the then Prime Minister Goh Chok Tong himself admitted, technological innovation which pushed MNCs to set up offshore production also served to undermine the EOI model in the long run.[28] To meet the new challenges, Singapore had to shift towards "high technology" industrialization and the promotion of R&D.

The pressure on the Singapore Government to pursue a clearly defined national science and technology policy also came in the form of the rapid technological transformation of the rival East Asian NIEs, especially South Korea, producing catalytic effects on the city-state. Moreover, by the mid-1980s, ASEAN countries like Thailand and Malaysia had already established their national blueprints to utilize science and technology for national growth. Hence, one can say that Singapore's spurt in science and technology development in the late 1980s was to a certain extent politically motivated. The pressure to sustain the country's economic competitiveness was reinforced by ideological considerations. It has to do with the nation's deep desire to survive, to catch up, to excel and stay ahead. This obsession is, however, more real than apparent, as evident by the constant political rhetoric stressing the need to adapt and to compete in the face of new challenges. As Lee Kuan Yew himself commented, "By being complacent, unable, or unwilling to change with time or change with technology, and staying put — believing that the world has recognised that we are number one and will always be number one — then the world will pass us by."[29]

Having achieved not only a "newly industrialising economy" status, but one which is only behind Japan in terms of per capita income in Asia, the government is constantly monitoring the performance of the city-state vis-à-vis the other "little dragons". Since 1979, Singapore has been in the leading position in terms of the average annual growth of real GDP and real GDP per capita.[30] The severe recession in

1985–86 was a tremendous blow to the state, but the other East Asian NIEs, especially South Korea and Taiwan, continued to enjoy buoyant growth during this recessionary period. Why was this the case? Facing a substantial rise in labour costs and a higher rate of currency appreciation, South Korea and Taiwan were spurred to upgrade their economic capabilities through comprehensive, state-supported R&D programmes. The Korean Government stimulated a technological upgrading of the economy since an amendment was made to the Foreign Capital Inducement Law in 1962 to regulate both foreign direct investment and the acquisition of foreign technology.[31] More importantly, the government has also used its technology policy to restructure the manufacturing sector and reap the economic benefits.[32] Singapore, on the other hand, was plagued by a manufacturing sector consisting mainly of foreign-owned, "footloose", low-tech industries and was painfully lacking "home-grown" industries.

International comparisons of statistics relating to R&D also indicate that Singapore is behind South Korea and Taiwan.[33] In terms of gross expenditure on R&D (GERD), in 1990 Singapore spent 0.9 per cent of GDP compared to 1.8 per cent for Korea and 1.4 per cent for Taiwan. In terms of the number of research scientists and engineers (RSE), Singapore had 34 RSEs per 10,000 labour force in 1991; the figures for Korea and Taiwan in 1990 were 37 and 55 RSEs per 10,000 labour force, respectively. The reason behind this gap is obvious — both Korea and Taiwan had made a much earlier commitment to tailor a science and technology policy for its industrialization drive. Thus, it is not surprising that in terms of productivity per worker, Singapore too lags behind her rivals. In the first half of 1990 the productivity growth rate for Singapore was 3.6 per cent. For the same period, South Korea and Taiwan registered 14 per cent and 7 per cent, respectively.[34] This relatively poor productivity growth rate has been a major cause of concern for the Singapore Government to this day.

Finally, after nearly two decades of loose and fragmented commitment, the government's decision to inject a substantial amount of its national savings into R&D was reached in the face of a changing internal political situation. The National Technology Plan (NTP) was drawn up in 1991, following the recommendations of the *Economic Committee Report* in 1986. It was seen by some observers as yet another instrument to legitimize and strengthen the political leadership of the ruling PAP. Unexpected circumstantial changes within Singapore, compounded by the external scenario mentioned above, exerted considerable pressure on the PAP. There was the urgent task for the PAP to re-examine its policy and to introduce measures which, directly or indirectly, could restore and strengthen its reputation in the eyes of the electorate. Since the early 1980s the traditional hegemony of the PAP has been severely jolted by an unexpected decline in electoral support. In the 1984 general election the two main opposition parties — the Singapore Democratic Party and the Worker's Party — succeeded not only in attracting voters but in gaining two seats in Parliament. The apparent invincibility of the PAP was shattered. At the economic level, the rapid growth of the city-state was punctured by the recession of 1985 and 1986. Singapore registered a negative growth rate for the first time since 1965. Also, the nation's successful "export-oriented industrialisation strategy appear[ed] to have peaked".[35] Socially, several policy decisions made by the leaders did not go down well with the populace. These included the raising of the age at which withdrawal of the Central Provident Fund savings could be made, the unpopular procreation measure targeted at female graduates, and a series of unsettling changes to the education system. Moreover, the government's pro-MNC policy and their domination of the economy alienated local entrepreneurs. Finally, the money-driven society had eventually produced a middle class that not only enjoys a quality lifestyle and a pattern of conspicuous consumption, but also one strong and vocal enough to pressure the government for policy changes. In short, the 1980s was a decade of dramatic change and adjustment.

Thus, there was every incentive for the PAP and Singapore to try to regain the competitive edge, both politically and economically. Indeed, technological backwardness could be seen as a threatening factor to the political supremacy of a ruling government.[36] Historical examples — as in the cases of Peter the Great's Russia and post-1867 Japan — have shown that ruling regimes sometimes may intentionally and successfully support technological change in order to preserve their hegemony.[37] The Singapore Government took it upon itself to create the educational and research environment that would be needed to bring about technological change. However, after the debacle of the 1984 election it became necessary for the PAP to adopt a more consultative style when formulating policies. Thus, the concerted effort towards the planning of a national science and technology policy, involving a wide range of expertise from the public and private sector and documented under the 1991 National Technology Plan, was seen as one of the many exercises aimed at more "consultative and participatory representation".[38] More significantly, it reminded the people that due to rapid domestic and international change, the government "must increasingly be a team player for the realisation of the full potential of the private sector, both foreign and local, in the development process".[39] In this respect, the state has to campaign continuously for an increase in political commitment and public awareness of developments in science and technology.[40] There is also the need to monitor the technological gap between Singapore and the East Asian NIEs and the industrialized countries.

DEVELOPING A SCIENCE AND TECHNOLOGY FRAMEWORK IN THE 1990s

Historically, from 1965 to 1979 there were efforts to create an awareness of science and technology, but most of them were ad hoc in nature and thus provided little focus or sense of direction. The poorly developed state of R&D in Singapore was revealed by a national survey carried out in 1978. The government spent $37.2 million on R&D, or about 0.23 per cent of GDP. The figure was below the 0.5 per cent level set by the United Nations for less developed countries, and was certainly well behind the average spending level of 2 per cent for developed countries. Of the total R&D spending in 1978, about 33 per cent was incurred by the public sector, and the private sector accounted for about 67 per cent.[41] In terms of manpower deployment in R&D, only 2.5 per cent of the eight thousand scientists and engineers were engaged in some form of R&D in 1979.[42] Most of these held positions in the universities and government laboratories and carried out research projects directed towards basic research.[43]

Arising from the 1978 survey, several factors were diagnosed as responsible for the poor state of R&D in Singapore. These included the shortage of trained personnel, a lack of research funds, inaccessibility of research information, the dominance of foreign investment in the manufacturing sector, the small size of the locally owned industrial plants and the absence of a favourable research climate. The survey also indicated a growing tension between the development work and applied research conducted by the private sector and the more fundamental and applied research carried out by the public sector.[44] Adding to the picture was the disbanding of the weak and unproductive Ministry of Science and Technology in 1981; though, as claimed by the government, "there were no tears, not even crocodile tears".[45] During the 1970s the government paid scant attention to the development of industrial technology and failed to initiate policy guidelines to nurture a science and technological culture. The single-minded economic objective then was to create employment for national survival, essentially through the attraction of foreign direct investments.

In June 1979 Goh Chok Tong, then Minister for Trade and Industry, spelt out the objectives and strategies of what was probably the first positive signal of the establishment of a national programme to help Singapore develop and enlarge its technological capability:

> The key issue that will confront us in our formulation of a national research and development programme are what technologies to develop, what industries to specialise in, what manpower we can harness and what role we can earmark for the local and foreign companies.... Research and development efforts in Singapore must serve our political, social and economic needs — the ultimate goal being to develop technological capability in areas strategic to our national development. R&D in Singapore should be based on the needs of the markets — both present and perceived. A national effort to develop and enlarge technological self-reliance must also include the training of engineers and technicians to move beyond operational roles and into management, design and engineering functions.... Investors who are prepared to share technology with us or invest in high technology industries will be encouraged through fiscal incentives to set up operations here. Indigenous enterprises will be encouraged to develop linkages with them and with others who are already operating in Singapore — linkages with equipment manufacturers, design and engineering organisations and industrial research bodies like SISIR (Singapore Institute of Standards and Industrial Research).[46]

Hence, from the very beginning of what might be considered a serious effort towards the implementation of a national science and technology policy, three related issues were given priority. First, R&D in Singapore should be "market-pulled" instead of "science-pushed"; second, the country hoped to achieve technological self-reliance through, among other measures, necessary changes in education; and, finally, high-tech foreign investors were seen as indispensable channels to transfer and diffuse technology and skills. One significant institutional change was made in January 1991, when the National Science and Technology Board (NSTB) was formed, specifically to promote research and development in Singapore. Its strategies were documented in the NTP, which sets out that it was "to develop Singapore into a centre of excellence in selected fields of Science and Technology so as to enhance our national competitiveness in the industrial and services sectors".[47] The NTP outlined Singapore's R&D policy in the 1990s.

The main strategy adopted to meet these objectives was the "targeted industry", or "picking winners", strategy in which a few technologies were singled out as priorities or core capabilities and given intensive government support to accelerate their development. Within the broad framework of Singapore's Strategic Economic Plan, the core capabilities are grouped into clusters, each cluster selected having some features common to most industries. Such an approach is well suited to a small, industrialized economy like Singapore where a multinational infrastructure had been well developed. Thus, under the NTP, incentive programmes and fiscal measures were drawn up to encourage the private sector to invest in R&D in nine priority areas; namely, information technology, microelectronics, manufacturing technology, materials technology, energy, water environment and resources, biotechnology, food and agro-technology, and medical sciences. The state had also committed S$2 billion as public sector support for industry-driven R&D between 1991 and 1995.

Statistically, Singapore's GERD has been increasing since 1978, reaching S$756.8 million in 1991, representing 1.1 per cent of GDP.[48] The private sector accounted for 58 per cent of the total amount. Similarly, in terms of manpower, there were 8,631 personnel engaged in either full- or part-time R&D work in 1991, representing a fourfold increase since 1978. Of these, 5,239 were RSEs, representing 34 RSEs per 10,000 of the labour force. Fifty-five per cent of the R&D manpower was employed in the private sector. Despite an increasing R&D budget, by the 1990s Singapore faced a shortage of skilled R&D professionals. A number of large local firms have embarked on employment drives to recruit Singaporeans working overseas and foreign graduates in engineering, information technology, telecommunications, design engineering and instrumentation engineering. Britain, North America, Australia, New Zealand, the former Soviet Union, South India and China are popular countries for the recruitment drives.[49] Through its International Manpower Division, the EDB helped recruit more than 3,300 foreign professionals and skilled workers, including 230 researchers and scientists.[50] In the opinion of the government, Singapore needs to attract more foreign researchers and scientists if it is to realize its ambition to become a centre for scientific research and development. As explained by Lee Hsien Loong, then Deputy Prime Minister in June 1992, the main constraint was not so much a lack of funds, as lack of a critical mass of talent to form a scientific community where ideas and collaborative research projects can be fertilized.[51]

Statistical evidence also indicates a dearth of local RSEs. Out of a total of 10,611 personnel involved in R&D activities in 1992, only 6,454 were RSEs — the rest were technicians and support staff. However, native RSEs only account for 60 per cent, and the rest were permanent residents and foreign citizens.[52] Another pertinent trend to note is that the annual growth of R&D manpower with PhDs as a percentage of the total number of RSEs has been insignificant for the last few years. Unfortunately, there are no official figures on the number of Singaporeans comprising this section of the RSE population. But it is likely that the majority of them are foreign citizens working in the universities and research institutes.[53] And out of a total of 1,424 researchers in 1992, 1,085 (76.2 per cent) were in the higher education sector, 89 (6.3 per cent) in the government sector and 143 (10.0 per cent) in the public research institutes.[54] Thus, only 107 (7.5 per cent) conducted their R&D in the private sector.

Finally, in the 1993 survey conducted by the National Science and Technology Board, 74 per cent of the private firms rated "Shortage of R&D Personnel" as the top factor limiting R&D in Singapore. It must not be assumed, however, that this reflects a rising demand for research personnel in Singapore, more particularly in the private sector, as a result of more companies willing to invest in R&D. Factors such as high risk, a lack of R&D management know-how and a shortage of risk capital acted as barriers to the growth and development of R&D activities in the private sector. Moreover, corporate attitudes and perceptions towards R&D also determine to a certain extent the demand for scientists and engineers.

CONSTRUCTING THE TECHNOLOGY INFRASTRUCTURE

One of the most critical issues in technology-based competition is the creation of a technology infrastructure consisting of a range of technology-related elements mainly developed by the government to facilitate proprietary technology development and use.[55] A highly integrated and modernized technology infrastructure is now considered an indispensable component of an overall systems approach to economic strategy. This is especially the case when the emphasis is on flexible and adaptable manufacturing systems to produce "small but rapid and precise product changes".[56] Hence, a technology-based infrastructure is needed to disseminate scientific and engineering information. For many developed nations today, this has become a major determinant of a country's global competitiveness. Within a short span of time the Singapore Government had developed a technology infrastructure which, as stated in the NTP, "includes a high concentration of high technology industries, research centres and higher education establishments integrated within an attractive living environment".[57] The eventual objective is the creation of a technopolis.

In the 1990s, Singapore's R&D infrastructure development was planned under the concept of a "technology corridor" — a site located at the southwestern portion of the island which houses the Science Parks, NUS, NTU, Singapore Polytechnic, the National University Hospital and the Business Park. It also offers excellent social amenities in order to achieve an ideal work and living environment for the scientific community. This "hard" infrastructure is complimented by the upgrading of the "soft" infrastructure to support R&D and to ensure successful commercialization of R&D. In January 1992, Technet, a S$3.53 million electronic network, was launched, linking the local R&D community in Singapore with the world scientific community via the Internet.[58] In the 1990s the patent system in Singapore also underwent changes. Under the revised system, Singapore acceded to the Paris Convention and the Patent Cooperation Treaty (PCT).[59] Patents filed in Singapore could thus be examined by any of the PCT offices worldwide and could be recognized in specific countries at the time of application. All these measures reduced costs and time and worked towards encouraging a greater spirit of entrepreneurship and innovation among Singapore firms and inventors.

The establishment of the Science Park at Kent Ridge in 1984 was the first positive indication of the government's recognition of the need to link up R&D activities with its overall economic policy. Modelled along the lines of British science parks, such as the Heriot-Watt research park in Edinburgh, the Science Park is the focal point for all industrial R&D activities and "brain services" in Singapore.[60] Its proximity to NUS is to foster closer interaction and exchange of knowledge and ideas between university staff and industrial researchers. By the mid-1990s, work on Science Park 2, covering twenty hectares, had started. Besides the Science Park, several other research centres and institutes were established during the 1980s and early 1990s.[61] These public sector research institutes and centres formed the nucleus of R&D in Singapore, providing the source of manpower, skills, technology, knowledge, products and processes for the private sector. Collectively, in 1991 they housed 452 RSEs, or 9 per cent of Singapore's total RSEs, and their R&D expenditure accounted for 9.4 per cent of the country's gross R&D expenditure.[62]

In industrialized countries such as the United States, the whole technology infrastructure system is a complex web of functions and organizations. In the case of Singapore the situation is much simpler. Generally, the tertiary institutions concentrate more on basic research for educational purposes, though some applied research in generic technologies is also undertaken. For the research centres the main focus is on R&D in generic and proprietary technologies. Although manufacturing and management practices are usually carried out in the private sector, they are also adopted in the government agencies whenever the need arises. The SISIR is the main agency providing the supporting infratechnologies. Generic technology or pre-competitive technology research is the first phase in technology R&D. Its objective is to show that a product or process concept with a potential market application "works" in a laboratory environment, and thus reduces the technical uncertainties before channelling the laboratory prototype to a series of proprietary phases of R&D, eventually leading to commercialization. All phases of R&D are supported by a set of infratechnologies. These are practices and techniques, basic data, test and measurement methods aimed at increasing productivity or efficiency from the early phase of generic technology research to the development and commercialization stage. Manufacturing or management practices enable the product and process technologies as well as the infratechnologies to be efficiently developed. Within this "technology corridor", the government hopes to stimulate the creativity and innovative processes of its citizens. However, having the science and technology hardware does not necessarily lead to a more technologically driven economy. There is also the people's perception towards automation and skills upgrading through training.

AUTOMATION, SKILL ACQUISITION AND RE-TRAINING

Like the steam engine, which revolutionized industrial production in the nineteenth century, robotics is also creating a technology-driven revolution in how industrial goods are made. The use of robots in the automation of manufacturing processes has rapidly established itself as a key competitive edge in the high-value-added markets. Many countries have recognized the inevitability of automation in maintaining their competitiveness. Japan has become the world leader in robotics. And developed nations like Germany and Sweden — each with traditional strengths in machine tools, electrical engineering and high-quality automobiles — are also investing heavily in automation. In these countries a strong "engineering culture", high per capita living standards, high labour costs, and a large supply of scientists and engineers are the main conditions which favour the use of robots in industrial production. In the case of Singapore, swift progress was made towards automation in the electronics and computer industries. However, the problem is that these industries are dominated by foreign MNCs. Most of these companies are willing to automate their production processes because Singapore has a skilled workforce, excellent infrastructure and an advanced telecommunications network.

Nevertheless, although automation is becoming a key component, a huge workforce of unskilled and semi-skilled workers is still required. Another point to note is that, according to borderless-world theories, MNCs will switch production from one country to another by determining whether wages in the developing countries are greater or less than the robot's "costs" in the automated factory back home. Thus, governments in these countries must reckon that, due to the intensification of the use of robots which resulted in lower production costs, the possibility of MNCs transferring their operations back to the home base is always a strong possibility.

To what extent has robotics or automation technology in general become an integral feature of the manufacturing sector in Singapore? In the 1992/92 National Automation Survey, an indication of a weak attitude towards automation was reflected in the responses of participating firms to statements regarding automation culture.[63] There was a relatively high level of uncertainty with regards to "Automation improves product quality" (43.0 per cent), "We will retrain our people when we automate" (25.7 per cent), "We have people directly responsible for automation" (39.7 per cent), and "Robots are essential to the successful implementation of automation" (44.8 per cent). These responses indicated a general lack of information and understanding, as confirmed by the fact that 71.2 per cent of the participating firms said that they do not participate in technical activities organized by professional bodies.[64] When firms were asked what factors hindered their progress in automation, the highest three responding firms felt that heavy investment and uncertainties (56.4 per cent), inadequate in-house knowledge/expertise/skills (39.0 per cent) and initial high operating costs (35.8 per cent) were the main obstacles.[65] Overall, the survey concluded that "manufacturing firms studied largely have yet to adopt a focussed approach towards automation. 39.9 per cent do not have any budget for automation over the next three years and half the firms do not have any advanced planning for automation."[66] In the absence of a national automation plan, efforts to promote factory automation, particularly in small and medium enterprises, have not been focused. It has also been suggested that the implementation of automation may at times be in conflict with the training and educational upgrading policy of workers, and may be accompanied by increasing labour turnover due to the demands of new working hours associated with automation. However, in the 1990s the high level of demand for labour within Singapore, and the ready availability of alternative sources of supply from outside, meant that this was not a serious problem. In general, workers considered that their levels of skills had been enhanced as a result of automation, but also that the intensity of their effort had been increased.[67]

The cultural attitudes of these workers, especially those aged over forty, is perhaps the most important factor influencing their motivation with respect to adapting to new technologies. While skills can be acquired or upgraded through training courses, without the right attitude the productivity of workers will suffer. Many do not see the need to retrain because they firmly believe that what they do is a cursory kind of work requiring minimal skills. Instead of spending time attending upgrading courses, these workers would rather choose to spend the time moonlighting in other jobs in order to supplement their income.[68] From the workers' perspective such attitudes are pragmatic and economically rational. One observer concluded that "Singaporean workers are hardworking, but the Malaysians are more willing workers [and] more open to training and willing to put in extra effort to improve."[69] Malaysia's "Vision 2020", the government's target year for the country to reach developed status, has given the people a collective will to improve themselves and the economy of the country. This perception of the Malaysian worker is one contributing factor motivating large MNCs to increasingly turn to Malaysian states like Penang for the production of their high-end electronic products.

Moreover, it was generally felt that management's perception of training does not help to alleviate the problem facing Singapore's unskilled and semi-skilled workers. Many local small- and medium-sized companies are too production-oriented and tend to place production costs above staff training needs. And if they do not upgrade to high-technology operations, no retraining will be required. This is not surprising since, historically, local firms have not considered training to be part of the working culture. In South Korea the Japanese in-house training concept was accepted with great enthusiasm. From the management viewpoint, such an investment in human capital only made sense in companies with a relatively stable workforce.

Unfortunately, in many of Singapore's small and medium Chinese companies, the phenomenon of job-hopping, particularly among the younger workers, is so prevalent that it does not pay to upgrade workers' skills. Furthermore, there is a tendency for local manufacturers to adopt a more gradual and even upgrading of technology, and each incremental change merely uses a bit more capital and a bit less labour. This strategy also inhibits a learning and retraining culture, since the chances of breakdown of new, imported machinery is slim and they do not need higher or specialized skills to operate. In short, the bottom line is still the issue of economic survival and profit. The time devoted to training is often seen in terms of opportunity cost loss. The government was realistic about the situation when it confirmed that "there is still a long way to go before training becomes a tradition as it has in many other developed countries, especially in Japan and also in America and the European countries".[70] This is despite the fact that there was a "21–fold increase in the number of workers who are involved in QCCs (Quality-Control Circles) over the last six years from 2,000 odd in 1982 to 56,000 odd in 1988".[71]

Singapore's S&T policy aims to propel the economy to an innovation-driven phase of industrialization. This means that product and process R&D will receive special attention. In the context of the NTP, applied research, defined as "the discovery of new scientific knowledge having specific commercial objectives with respect to products or processes", and developmental research, defined as the "systematic use of the knowledge or understanding gained from research directed toward the production of useful materials, devices, systems, or methods, including design and development of prototypes and processes" are the key categories of R&D.[72] What, then, is the role of science or basic research, defined as "the experimental or theoretical work undertaken primarily to acquire new knowledge of the underlying foundation of phenomena and observable facts, without any particular application of use in mind", in Singapore's S&T framework? After all, "basic research creates fundamental discoveries which become the source of thousands of downstream new products, process and services".[73] The government's attempts at cultivating a scientific culture through an emphasis on science education and other initiatives will be discussed in the next chapter.

Notes

1. World Bank, *World Development Report 1989*, quoted in A. Ali, *Malaysia's Industrialisation: The Quest for Technology* (Singapore: Oxford University Press, 1992), Table 4.1, p. 57.
2. Greenberg, D.S., "R&D in Asia Signals Battle for Markets", *Straits Times*, 30 August 1993.
3. Dieter Ernst and David O'Connor, *Technology and Global Competition: The Challenge for Newly-Industrialising Economies* (OECD, 1989), p. 57.
4. Ibid.
5. The degree of participation in the world economy of the former Communist states of Eastern Europe will, of course, depend on many factors. It is difficult to envisage them catching up to the current level of the East Asian NIEs and playing a dominant role in the near future, even though they have a rich historical tradition in science and technology.
6. Quoted in Andre Pollack, "Rising Yen Forcing Firms to Move Out of Japan", *Straits Times*, 30 August 1993. As pointed out by Pollack, this threat to Japan's manufacturing base should not be exaggerated since, according to a survey by MITI, only about 6 per cent of the total production of those firms surveyed was outside Japan in 1991. Moreover, another positive signal is that "while Japan is shifting the manufacturing of less expensive and simpler products offshore, it is retaining the manufacturing of products and key components that are more technologically advanced and more expensive."
7. Ibid.
8. *Straits Times Overseas Edition*, 8 May 1993. Despite these developments, there are still many sticky problems and obstacles for both local and foreign enterprises. Indonesia's economic structure is quite complicated and its manufacturing sector is heavily concentrated and protected. The country is still grappling with a severe shortage of trained, skilled and experienced engineers and managers.
9. *Straits Times Overseas Edition*, 29 May 1993.
10. *Straits Times Overseas Edition*, 5 September 1992.
11. Ali, *Malaysia's Industrialisation*, p. 34; *Straits Times*, 25 August 1993.
12. *Straits Times Overseas Edition*, 17 April 1993.
13. *Straits Times*, 18 September 1993.
14. Ibid.
15. *Straits Times*, 14 July 1991.
16. Ibid.
17. Ibid.
18. Ibid.

19. Philippe Regnier, *Singapore: City-State in South-East Asia*, translated by Christopher Hurst (Honolulu: University of Hawai'i Press, 1987), p. 98.
20. *Straits Times Overseas Edition*, 17 October 1992.
21. *Straits Times*, 10 June 1993
22. M.H. Bloom, "Globalization and the Korean Electronics Industry", *Pacific Review* 6, no. 2 (1993): 123–25.
23. Ulrich Hilpert, ed., *State Policies and Techno-Industrial Innovation* (London: Routledge, 1991), p. 3.
24. Economic Planning Committee, *Strategic Economic Plan* (Singapore: Ministry of Trade and Industry, 1991), p. 28.
25. *Straits Times*, 1 October 1987.
26. Lester Thurow, *Head to Head: The Coming Economic Battle among Japan, Europe, and America* (New York: Morrow, 1992), p. 29.
27. Ibid., p.45.
28. *Straits Times*, 27 February 1986.
29. *Straits Times*, 10 June 1993.
30. L.B. Krause, A.T. Koh and T.Y Lee, *The Singapore Economy Reconsidered* (Singapore: Institute of Southeast Asian Studies, 1987), p. 6. Singapore's average annual growth of real GDP and GDP per capita for the years 1979 to 1984 were 8.6 and 7.3 per cent, respectively; ahead of Hong Kong (7.4 and 5.5 per cent), South Korea (5.1 and 3.4 per cent) and Taiwan (6.8 and 4.9 per cent). In 2013 the International Monetary Fund estimated Singapore's per capita at $64,584 and that of Japan at $36,899.
31. A.M. Amsden, *Asia's Next Giant: South Korea and Late Industrialisation* (New York: Oxford University Press, 1989), p. 73.
32. Martin Fransman, *Technology and Economic Development* (Brighton: Wheatsheaf, 1986), p. 97.
33. *National Survey of R&D in Singapore 1991* (Singapore: National Science and Technology Board, 1992), pp. 50–51.
34. *Far Eastern Economic Review Yearbook 1991*, p. 208.
35. G. Rodan, ed., *Singapore Changes Guard: Social, Political and Economic Directions in the 1990s* (New York: St Martin's Press, 1993) p. xii.
36. J. Mokyr, *The Lever of Riches: Technological Creativity and Economic Progress* (Oxford: Oxford University Press, 1990), p. 181.
37. Ibid.
38. Linda Low, "The Public Sector in Contemporary Singapore: In Retreat?", in Rodan, *Singapore Changes Guard*, p. 179.
39. Ibid., p .180.
40. Since 1987, a "Technology Month" has been set aside each year to promote and highlight the development of science and technology in the republic.
41. *Business Times*, 28 April 1980.

42. *Straits Times*, 7 June 1979.
43. Ibid.
44. *Business Times*, 28 April 1980.
45. *Straits Times*, 8 June 1981.
46. *Business Times*, 8 June 1979.
47. *National Technology Plan 1991* (Singapore: National Science and Technology Board, 1992), p. ii. The NTP has the following aims and strategies: Science and technology research must be driven by the need to enhance national competitiveness; Excellence in science and technology must be sought in selected niches relevant to the country's strengths; Government must work in close collaboration with industry; The build-up of science and technology infrastructure must be result-driven, namely, that it produces results eventually relevant to economic competitiveness; and government's research institutes must support and complement industry efforts, by emphasizing generic pre-competitive research and process development.
48. *National Survey of R&D in Singapore 1991*, pp. 6–7.
49. *Sunday Times*, 7 February 1993; *Straits Times*, 8 February 1993. One measure strongly adopted by the Singapore Government to meet the critical shortage of skilled professionals in R&D is immigration. Enrolment in the doctoral programmes and recruitment of post-doctoral teaching assistants in science and engineering at the two main local universities consists mainly of Chinese nationals. Due to relaxed immigration laws, many would eventually be offered permanent residence status. However, two points must be noted here. First, although official figures are not published, the number of foreign imports might not be sufficient to replace the number of skilled Singaporeans leaving their homeland for greener pasture overseas. Second, the benefits of having imported talents, in terms of, say, transfer and diffusion of knowledge and skills to locals, is still very much an open question.
50. *Straits Times*, 6 January 1993.
51. *Straits Times*, 16 June 1992.
52. *National Survey of R&D in Singapore 1992*.
53. *National Survey of R&D in Singapore 1991* and *National Survey of R&D in Singapore 1992*. The number of researchers with PhDs and who are Singapore citizens is strictly confidential.
54. *National Survey of R&D in Singapore 1992*, Table III.8, p. 30.
55. George Tassey, *Technology Infrastructure and Competitive Position* (Norwell, MA: Kluwer Academic, 1996), p. 105. Proprietary technologies are any type of system, tool or technical process that is developed by and for a specific business entity. Technologies of this type are often developed as part of the ongoing research efforts of a business.
56. Ibid., p. 6–7.

57. *National Technology Plan 1991*, p. 71.
58. *The First Year 1991* (Singapore: National Science and Technology Board), p. 14.
59. Ibid.
60. *The Mirror*, 1 November 1986, pp. 1–3.
61. *National Technology Plan 1991*, pp. 50–53. By the early 1990s, six of these research institutes had been set up; namely, Institute of Molecular and Cell Biology (IMCB), Information Technology Institute (ITI), Grumman International/Nanyang Technological University Institute of Computer Integrated Manufacturing (GINTIC), Institute of System Science (ISS), Institute of Manufacturing Technology (IMT), and Institute of Micro-electronics (IME).
62. *National Survey of R&D in Singapore 1991*, p. 11.
63. *Automation Survey 1992/92* (Singapore: Singapore Industrial Automation Association, n.d.) pp. 64–66. A total of 770 of the 2,591 users of automation in the manufacturing sector (29.7 per cent) completed the questionnaire and 63.2 per cent of the respondents were locally owned firms.
64. Ibid., pp. 70–71.
65. Ibid., p. 47.
66. Ibid., p. 77.
67. See Hing Ai Yun, "Automation and New Work Patterns: Cases from Singapore's Electronics Industry Work", *Employment & Society* 9 (June 1995): 309–27.
68. Interview with acting executive secretary, Singapore Labour Foundation, 11 August 1994.
69. This point was made by the first secretary for industrial relations of the National Trade Union Congress, as reported in the *Straits Times*, 6 June 1994.
70. Mah Bow Tan, Parliamentary Debates, Republic of Singapore, Official Report, 21 March 1989, vol. 53, col. 613.
71. Ibid.
72. Definitions of basic research, applied research and developmental research are provided by the National Science Foundation of the United States, as quoted in the NTP, p. 19.
73. Bruce Merrifield, "Research Consortia: The Concurrent Management of Innovation", in *Innovative Models for University Research*, edited by C.R. Haden and J.R. Brink (Amsterdam: North-Holland, 1992), p. 51.

5

NURTURING A SCIENTIFIC CULTURE

When Singapore gained its independence in 1965, the government recognized that the acquisition of scientific knowledge was of paramount importance to the survival of the young nation. The learning of science had to be actively promoted in the school and higher education systems. Scientists and particularly engineers were needed to meet the needs of the influx of MNCs with their R&D facilities and manufacturing plants. At the outset of its attempts to formulate a national science policy in the early 1980s, the country's policymakers grappled with an important issue: Was the government in favour of a "policy for science" or "science for policy"? Was basic or "upstream" research strongly encouraged? Official remarks on the issue of state support for many areas of modern science were scant. An indication of the government's stance that R&D in Singapore must be tuned to the needs of the market was given in 1978 by S. Dhanabalan, then Senior Minister of State for National Development:

> [P]ure or basic research to enlarge the frontiers of knowledge without conscious applicable goals is not wasteful. Seemingly esoteric research has led to very practical applications affecting our daily life, but a

developing nation like Singapore has neither the financial nor human resources to indulge in it. Our efforts have to be primarily in that area of research more properly termed development, which works on bringing out new or modified products and processes based on established findings and technology.... Such an approach is precisely one reason for Japan's success.[1]

It is true that the Japanese had been very successful in the practical application of new technology.[2] But one has to note that Western science and technology had taken root in Japan since the seventeenth century. *Rangaku*, or "Dutch Learning", was already making inroads into Japan during the *sakoku* period (1641–1853), during which the country was closed to foreigners. As the Dutch trading post at Dejima was effectively an enclave of the Netherlands, for 212 years it was just about Japan's only way to keep tabs on European scientific progress. *Rangaku* has influenced Japanese medicine, anatomy, engineering, meteorology and chemistry, among other fields. Western science continued to be assimilated during the Meiji era (1868–1912) and the imperial government actively promoted the learning of scientific principles and application right up to the end of the Pacific War in 1945.[3] Indeed, the country had its first Nobel Prize winner just after the war — Hideki Yukawa, in physics in 1949 — and since then there have been eighteen other winners (including two in 2012).[4] Another important point to note is that Japanese "industry leaders realize they must cultivate more creative scientists and researchers, not just creative product designers, if Japan is to gain full acceptance in the world".[5] Japan is working towards the pursuit of creative basic research while still retaining its strength in process and product innovation.[6] In the case of Singapore, there is no such scientific tradition that the country can build on.

SCIENCE POLICY BEFORE 2000

In the 1960s and 1970s, science and science education did not receive full monetary or manpower support from the government because the national agenda during these years was shrouded in the ideology of survival and the need to stay politically and economically viable as a young independent nation. Scientific research in those days was not something that interested the general public, nor was it well covered by the media. Thus, the limited pool of scientists was left very much on their own in their ivory tower. When the idea of building the Singapore Science Centre was first mooted in the Singapore Parliament in 1970, one Member of Parliament commented:

> [T]his Bill will not arouse the interest of the people because it concerns science and tec]nology. It seems to have nothing to do with the workaday life of the people. However, for the nation it is a very important Bill. This is because it will help to promote technology and science in the country.[7]

Within the science discipline and fraternity there was a dichotomy and snobbishness between the "hard" sciences, such as chemistry and physics, and the "soft" sciences, such as biology. The scientists and the science educators had created a "false image" of science, that it was a discipline reserved only for the very brightest. There was a clear division between the science and the arts or humanities students. The dire consequence of this form of science education was the production of a generation of people who had no interest in or understanding of science, especially its impact on and role in society.

While commercialization of developmental research is perceived to meet national goals, the Singapore Government also needs to tackle the obstacles accounting for the lack of a scientific culture. In the 1980s, anecdotal evidence — in reports, interviews with local and foreign scientists and speeches of decision makers — seemed to indicate some tension and uncertainties behind the formulation of a science policy able to treat the whole spectrum of scientific and technological activities in Singapore. In 1983 four eminent physicists from the United States were in Singapore to share their views on the country's potential for developing frontier science and technology.[8] But despite making several accurate observations, they were too sanguine about Singapore's "readiness" to embark on frontier science R&D. As reported in the *Straits Times*, this optimism was based on their understanding that "the republic's approach to science is maturing, its young students' interest in scientific research growing and most important of all, the country can afford to spend on the advanced study of science".[9] Perhaps it was a gesture of kind comments, since there is no conclusive evidence to show that in the 1980s there was an increasing level of students' interest in the study of pure sciences. Also, it was certainly not the case that the science scene in Singapore was "maturing", since the formulation and implementation of its official policy in science and technology was still in its infancy. Finally, the recommendation that Singapore could move in the direction of frontier science R&D and compete with industrialized nations because, among other factors, the country could afford to spend on advanced scientific research was too idealistic or even futuristic to be considered seriously by the pragmatic government at the time.

Unlike developmental work, pure scientific research could not be placed on a high pedestal within the very pragmatic S&T policy. Nevertheless, throughout the 1980s there were recommendations made by prominent visiting scientists on how to establish a suitable climate for basic scientific research in Singapore. For example, the need for a good institute of technology was conveyed by MIT scientist Samuel Ting.[10] He made it clear that a policy of recruiting foreign scientists would not guarantee an indigenous scientific base. Only the establishment of a technical school, similar to the Zurich Institute of Technology, could initiate the establishment and growth of such a base. He also disputed the argument that basic research is expensive and thus a luxury for a developing country.[11] World-renowned physicist Abdul Salam urged the Singapore Government to place an emphasis on basic scientific research because "Technology stems from science".[12] It was, he stressed, as essential for Singaporeans — and leaders in Third World countries — to recognize the importance of understanding the knowledge of nature; that is, the "know-why", before they could master technology.[13] Another Nobel Prize physicist and scientific adviser to the Singapore Government, Yang Chen Ning, suggested that greater emphasis on inexpensive, pure research activities such as theoretical physics and mathematics should be encouraged.[14] By broadening the field of pure research, a climate conducive to research could be established.[15]

These visits by world-renowned scientists were indicative of the government's serious desire to listen to the experts. But, in most instances, that was about as far as the government would go. Singapore's "high tech" or R&D policy in the 1980s was a "down-to-earth" one based on developing a technological capability strategic to the country's national development. As stated by Goh Chok Tong in 1980, Singapore's "research policies must aim at organising and shifting the direction, composition and quality of research to ensure the marketability of its products".[16] This practice of tying research to product development and, hence, profits and marketability had been the objective behind the product development scheme administered by the EDB. It was also clear that the R&D strategists were concerned chiefly with the "development" side of the R&D equation. This emphasis was in line with the "realistic goals" that Singapore "should not do basic research, either in established technologies or emerging ones, except in individual instances where we have exceptionally talented professionals".[17] They argued that product development "does not require a creative mind, just a knowledgeable scientist doggedly finding new and better ways of doing a particular task".[18] It was also pointed out that Japan's success was strongly based on its frontier efforts in developmental research. Hence, it is fair to conclude that up to the late 1990s there were no clear guidelines or a projected trajectory embedded in a national science policy. Nevertheless, the scientific community was set abuzz with the establishment of the Institute of Molecular and Cell Biology (IMCB) in 1987. It was recommended by Nobel laureate Sydney Brenner. The formation of IMCB signalled a trend towards greater emphasis on basic research in universities. In the new millennium, basic science research "took off" remarkably.

NURTURING SCIENCE BEYOND 2000:
THE BIOMEDICAL WAY

In the early 1990s, Singapore's spending on research actually lagged behind Taiwan and South Korea. But, beginning in the new century, the republic's R&D expenditure surged to $3.2 billion, accounting for 2.1 per cent of its total goods and services produced — on par with the United States and Japan. Biomedical sciences are one of the three niche areas (the other two being interactive digital media and water technologies) which the government had earmarked as key growth areas for the twenty-first century. In the biomedical sector the government forked out significantly more than the private sector.

    In September 2005 the second annual Science and Technology in Society forum was held in Kyoto, attended by more than five hundred scientists and policymakers from over sixty countries. The forum was widely regarded as the scientific equivalent of Davos, the think-tank session of world leaders held annually in Switzerland. One interesting observation made by some of the world's top scientists and policymakers was how the city-state of Singapore was becoming a model for frontier scientific research and how science can provide solutions to problems confronting society — particularly in the field of life sciences.[19] Singapore was seen to have nurtured a "science-friendly" environment marked by fair and transparent regulation, a solid research infrastructure, an expanding talent pool and research-friendly stem cell regulations. It was also noted that the nation had become a regional leader in bird flu research.[20]

Singapore's move into the biomedical sciences (BMS) was the brainchild of Philip Yeo. In his own words, "Passion is what my move into Biomedical Sciences is about. I got into BMS from the pure economic development perspective, to build capabilities in a future-growth sector. To me, BMS is the fourth sector of the economy: Three legs good but four legs better."[21] Undoubtedly, human health and disease is one of the most pressing issues both for the world today and for the future. Spectacular advances have been made in BMS research and medical technologies and these provide opportunities for small newcomers to enter the competitive fray. Singapore's foray into BMS is part of a drive to sharpen the republic's competitive edge and lead its transformation into a knowledge-based, innovation-driven economy. BMS was envisaged to become the fourth pillar of Singapore's manufacturing sector, after electronics, chemicals and engineering (see Fig. 5.1). Although BMS requires extensive research funding and heavy investment in state-of-the-art infrastructure, Singapore's decision to bank on BMS as a growth sector hinges on the thinking that it has several inherent advantages. It has a century of development (including teaching) in medicine, resulting in the excellent healthcare system the people enjoy today. The global burden of diseases is also shifting to Asia because of the importance of the inter-ethnic mix in this part of the world; Singapore has three main Asian ethnic groups (Malays, Indians and Chinese). Finally, Singapore is good at long-term planning and intimate collaboration and coordination between different agencies.

For the best brains in BMS who were willing to re-settle in the city-state, they have been given the freedom and money to pursue their

Figure 5.1
Singapore's Strategy for its Biomedical Industry

BMS Cluster

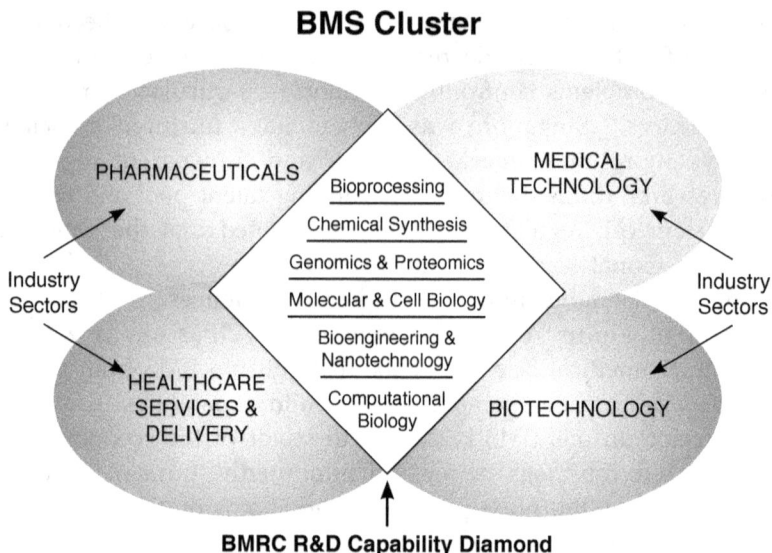

BMRC R&D Capability Diamond

Source: <http://www.asiabiotech.com/publication/apbn/11/english/.../1508_1511.pdf>, p. 1509.

own groundbreaking research areas. Research in BMS and the large pool of scientific talent have all been housed in a new home called the Biopolis. Conceived in 2001, the 1.8 million square feet Biopolis complex consists of seven interconnected blocks, each housing state-of-the-art scientific equipment like electron microscopes, DNA sequencers, X-ray crystallography machines and nuclear magnetic resonance scanners.[22] More than 2,500 scientists and engineers from over seventy countries have been lured to the bio-city. A*Star's — the government agency that drives science and technology development — investment in BMS R&D has grown steadily; from $1.3 billion in 2000–2005, to $2.1 billion in 2006–10, and $2.3 billion for 2011–15.

Singapore's strategy to accelerate the impact of its science policy on economic growth is to attract the best scientific talents to its shores. The carrot is usually large and attractive, particularly for top-notch scientists looking for funding. Singapore's technocrats hope the presence of these scientists will send a positive signal to large MNCs (especially those in the pharmaceutical industry) on the lookout for cutting-edge innovation and, hopefully, motivate them to establish their presence in Singapore. In addition, they could also "pull" Singaporeans to join the scientific community. One of the earliest big "whales" (a term used for talented top foreign scientists) to swim ashore was Edison Liu, who was tasked to start and develop the Genome Institute of Singapore (GIS) in 2001. Under his leadership the facility grew into a major international research institute attracting scientific human capital and research ventures in biomedicine into Singapore. Others soon followed. The most prominent were the world-renowned cancer-geneticist couple, Neal Copeland and Nancy Jenkins, who arrived in 2005. In an interview with *Synergy in Science*, the couple explained their decision: "[We] learned that Singapore was investing billions of dollars into this new campus called Biopolis, which was going to be set up like the NIH intramural programme and be funded directly from the Singapore government. They invited us to set up a lab and offered to give us everything we needed."[23] At the American Association for the Advancement of Science (AAS) meeting in Boston in February 2008, it was reported that dozens of young scientists from the likes of Harvard and Massachusetts Institute of Technology (MIT) had submitted their applications to continue their post-doctoral work in Singapore.[24] More importantly, measures were implemented to expand the local pool of Singaporeans with PhDs to do high-end research. In 2003, A*Star launched a PhD scholarship scheme, targeted at expanding the pool of local researchers in science and engineering by another hundred.[25] In 2006 A*Star disbursed 162 science scholarships and in 2013 it awarded 137 more. Altogether, since 2001, A*Star has disbursed more than 1,200 scholarships to Singaporeans to pursue doctorates, aiming to develop a strong core of local scientists.[26]

What positive gains have been achieved from the investments in the biomedical sciences? And what ails biomedical research in Singapore? One highly visible successful result was the establishment of several top-class biomedical research institutes and consortia by 2010, located in the Biopolis.[27] Many international observers were amazed at the speed and coordination with which these scientific centres were established in the small country. Presumably they could kindle an air of excitement

and curiosity among Singaporean science graduates and, at the same
time, pull in international scientists and researchers. Their presence
and the whole spectrum of research activities in biomedical sciences
could also draw pharmaceutical companies to set up R&D centres
(not just manufacturing facilities) in Singapore. The multiplier effect
would be the creation of jobs and other ancillary services. In September
2006, U.S. pharmaceutical giant Pfizer announced plans to double the
size of its six-year-old clinical trial centre at the Singapore General
Hospital (SGH), its sole trial centre in Asia. Swiss drug maker Lonza
was also attracted to Singapore. Its site is a mammalian cell culture
manufacturing facility for the contract development and production of
biopharmaceutical products. Production started in early 2011. In terms
of economic returns for Singapore, BMS manufacturing output
more than tripled from 2000 to 2009, from $6 billion to $21 billion.
Employment in the biomedical manufacturing sector more than
doubled, from 6,000 to 13,000 over the same period.[28] In the opinion of
Anand Tharmaratnam, senior vice-president and head of Asia-Pacific
for pharmaceutical services giant Quintiles, Singapore has all the
right ingredients to produce a blockbuster drug in the coming years
that would cement the republic's status as a biopharmaceutical hub.[29]
This is because Singapore has "a concentration of money and talent
[and] local government is focussed on making it happen, excellent
regulatory framework and financial governance and intellectual property
protection."

BUREAUCRACY AND THE SCIENTISTS

Historically, a major obstacle to the development of a favourable
environment in Singapore for scientific and technological research was
the limited freedom given to scientists by the authority controlling
funding to research institutes and universities. Essentially, it was a
dilemma of defining the lines between authority and central direction,
on the one hand, and freedom and autonomy on the other. As early
as the 1970s one journalist described the situation starkly: "They [the
scientists] are not allowed to breathe more than four words strung
together about themselves — if they do, the Establishment could fall
on them like a tonne of bricks."[30] Anecdotal evidence of interviews

conducted by the *Straits Times* with scientists and researchers indicated that the bureaucratic, centralized power structure in the universities was something which they could not accept readily.[31] A typical comment made by a scientist is given below:

> In the case of internationally eminent intellectuals, the considerations for an appropriate ambience and scope for freedom will be more important than such material conditions as salaries and so on. It is difficult to see how ideas and the reforms could come from the general academic staff because power is centralised and monopolised. Instead, they will have to come from central administration, or, paradoxically, from the government.[32]

The scientists strongly felt that the involvement of bureaucrats and administrators in research, some of whom had no deep knowledge of the work of their colleagues, should end with the disbursement of funds. Instead they often got themselves inextricably connected with the research projects. The problems of the scientific community were neatly summed up by the journalist:

> But their [the scientists] main complaint still stands — they are not given enough freedom to pursue their own research topics. More specifically, they are unhappy over the emphasis on applied research; that is, if the project is not directly relevant to industry needs, then little support is shown. Not enough attention is paid to the fact that a piece of research has its own merits if the researcher's results are published in international scientific journals and discussed at international conferences, they complained. Some of them admitted that they had been allowed to carry out pure research but they said that it was and is an uphill task getting support for their projects. As a result, there is no truly active research group. And without such a group, it will be hard to attract scientists from the West here, or even Singaporeans who are carrying out world-class research in the West.[33]

While the grievances of the scientists were understandable, they had to recognize that, firstly, Singapore lacks a long scientific tradition and, secondly, the thinking and approach behind its science and technology policy has always been one strongly based on application and pragmatism. It was (and is) all about economics of survival and sustainable growth for the nation. Interestingly, two decades later, similar grievances surfaced despite the fact that basic research was encouraged and funding was easily available. Perhaps the dilemma might never be resolved. On the one hand, Singapore needs expertise in the academic field of the pure sciences in order to produce local science graduates and scientists. On the other hand, the state's pragmatic orientation towards the commercialization of R&D is likely to push pure or basic research into the background.

After a decade of generous funding, successful recruitment of some star scientists and the establishment of several research institutes within the Biopolis, Singapore's science scene was rocked by two unexpected developments as it entered the twenty-first century. The first was the break-up of the eight-year partnership between the Division of Biomedical Sciences, Johns Hopkins in Singapore (DJHS) and A*Star. The second was the government's decision to tighten the criteria for scientists to obtain research funds from taxpayers' money. Both episodes illustrate the tension and mismatch of expectations between the bureaucrats and the scientific community.

In November 1998 the Singapore Government and Johns Hopkins Medicine (JHM) announced final agreements to develop Singapore's first private medical facility combining research and teaching with clinical services, modelled after Hopkins' famed centre in Baltimore. Johns Hopkins was approached because it "fits in perfectly with EDB's vision to develop Singapore into an intellectual hub [and] Johns Hopkins will help to raise standards in medical research and education through collaboration with our local institutions, and also provide world-class medical services to our people, our clients from the region and beyond".[34] Edward Miller, Johns Hopkins Medicine CEO cited several reasons for the agreement with Singapore: "On a more practical level, Singapore has a very impressive and extensive infrastructure already in place. Transportation systems are very adequate. Singapore's per capita income is second only to Japan's for this region, and its citizens tend to be educated. Most importantly, Singapore has expressed a strong commitment to become a regional medical hub and is willing to provide the resources to accomplish this objective."[35] Nearly a decade later the high-end partnership ended on a sour note after A*Star had provided $80 million to set up DJHS and pay for the research and training programmes. Both sides had their stories.[36] Suffice to say, the Johns Hopkins–A*Star controversy underscores the fact that science policy — particularly relating to the funding of research, objectives and the outcomes of funded projects — and the monitoring and evaluation of funded projects is never straightforward. There is the issue of scrutiny and accountability — and the possibility of scientific fraud.[37] And for universities seeking to spread their international wings, the episode brings home the lesson that the promise of external monetary support comes with obligations. Part of the deal required Johns Hopkins to send their very best faculty to Singapore. But it was obvious from the start of the partnership that these are highly sought after individuals who may not have the luxury to lend their expertise for a period of time — and they have the academic freedom not to be involved at all.

The government's decision to tighten the criteria for scientists to obtain research funds from public money resulted in the departure of several of the "branded" foreign-recruited scientists. Since 2010, when the government announced its $16.1 billion R&D kitty, it emphasized that projects needed to have economic value. Public funding of research projects is now more targeted at initiatives aimed at solving problems or developing new materials and devices. As stated in the *Straits Times*, it highlighted a fundamental difference in the way researchers and the funding agencies view a scientist's mission: "Scientists regard the funders' obsession with return on investment as intrusive and counter-productive, while bureaucrats resent scientists the presumption that the rarefied work they do should be permitted maximum leeway."[38] While pure basic research which has no particular use or application in mind still receives public money, the amount set aside is getting smaller. In the opinion of Israeli Nobel laureate for chemistry Ada Yonath, such an approach is short-sighted because "if a scientist is able to do research for pure knowledge, the science may yield unexpected results".[39] The Singaporean in the street now frets and questions the billions spent on esoteric research or what was termed the "scattershot approach" adopted by the scientific community.[40] The departure of the "star" scientists also veiled the contributions of the "anonymous PhDs and research assistants who contribute inestimably to the effort … and are the backbone of the edifice; the stars are the adornment".[41] Applications for research funds are now tied to industrial needs. Inevitably, the more well-known whales left their positions. After ten years Edison Lui left. As explained in one report,

"While funding is famously generous, some scientists here say they are being pressured to get more economic bang for their research buck and that they are increasingly frustrated with the red tape involved in getting hold of such money."[42] Liu suggested that there have been disagreements over the funding of academic versus applied research.[43] Funding agencies were trying to dictate what "the balance between basic and clinical sciences should be, and what optimal technology transfer and commercialization strategies should be", he told the *Straits Times*.[44] In another in-depth interview with the *Straits Times*, Lui added: "there is a strong commitment to science here but there's also a tendency to over-plan, thinking incorrectly that we can predict success in scientific discovery".[45] The shift is now towards translational biomedical research, that is, translating basic research at the "bench" into new diagnostic tests, therapies, medical devices and other technologies that can be used at the "bedsides".[46] The change in direction and emphasis is a clear signal that there is a re-thinking at the highest level. Neal Copeland and Nancy Jenkins, too, left after five years. They explained at length their decision to quit the science scene in Singapore:

> R&D at Biopolis is funded in 5-year cycles — we got there at the beginning of a cycle. When we arrived, they said that they weren't going to assess whether our projects were making money for 25 years; they recognized that biological sciences take time to generate money. But after 4 years, they started thinking about the next cycle. They got impatient: they wanted to make money and their plans changed overnight. They decided that basic researchers should work with pharma to move projects forward, and that was the beginning of the end of hypothesis-driven research at Biopolis. They took away a lot of the budget, and you needed to get it back by writing grants with pharma, that the government would match. And we're old — we've done hypothesis-driven research our whole lives! We weren't willing to do contract research for some pharma company, so we quit on the spot — without another job to go to.[47]

Their views were supported by the eminent biologists David Solter and Barbara Knowles who retired in 2013 after a five-year stint in Singapore. According to Solter there "was a miscalculation in the beginning and the authorities were expecting that the returns would come much faster and when this didn't happen they said people are just sitting on their hands, let's squeeze them a bit".[48] As described by *Nature,* for these famous research scientists "Singapore's salad days are over" and whilst the "move to align scientific objectives with economic reality is understandable … it would be a huge waste if doing so with undue haste and insufficient planning were to destroy Singapore's impressive experiment".[49] While this "impressive experiment" caught the eyes of the international scientific community and, indeed, many were surprised at the scale of funding support for basic research from a small nation, local reactions were less reassuring.

The uncertainties of pouring huge amount of public money into pure basic research were brought to a head when Lee Wei Ling, the director of the National Neuroscience Institute, challenged the wisdom and rationality of Singapore's aggressive push into biomedical research.[50] This was all the more so when the strategy was to attract the "big whales" and letting them decide for themselves what areas of research to engage in. Bearing in mind that Singapore is a small nation with no natural resources, Lee argues that "a more rational approach will be to identify niche areas unique to Singapore['s] population where we have a competitive advantage".[51] She advocates that research efforts could be more focused on diseases prevalent in this region and, more importantly, have direct relevance and benefits to Singapore, such as hepatitis B, strokes and head injuries.[52] On the glowing statistics from the manufacturing activities of the multinational drug firms in Singapore, Lee maintains that they set up shop here "not because of money being thrust into biomedical research, but because of generous government help, good intellectual property (IP) laws that are enforced strictly, and [an] educated, English-speaking workforce, among others".[53] Jackie Ying, executive director of the Institute of Bioengineering and Nanotechnology also shared this view. The professor emphasized the need for "strategic research" that seeks to solve some of the world's bug problems, such as finding a cure to deadly diseases or mitigating the effects of climate change, rather than simply creating academic knowledge.[54] In short, present-day political and economic doctrines advocate that resources be allocated according to predetermined priorities related to their expected benefits, in the shorter or longer term, to national prosperity, security and welfare. "Priority-setting" is a major feature of "steady state" science. [55]

Another thorny issue is that despite the billions being poured into the biomedical sector, the research job opportunities created are usually taken up by foreigners. This is because the city-state does not have the critical mass of PhD holders who are Singaporeans by birth to take up research positions. This high dependency on foreign scientists mirrors the government's pro-MNC industrial policy. In 2003 only 8.2 per cent of the 1,930 researchers (a mere 160) in government research institutes were Singaporeans with PhDs. At the Institute of Bioengineering and Nanotechnology, only one in five researchers is a Singaporean.[56] In addition, there is also a lack of doctors willing to become clinician scientists. In 2004 the National Healthcare Group confirmed that less than 10 per cent of its doctors had taken on a role of clinician scientist.[57] The reasons for this lack of interest are, first, the perception that clinician scientists are worse clinicians than conventional clinicians and, second, that clinician scientists do not have long-term career prospects.[58] The government had planned to double the number of clinician scientists to 160 by 2015.[59] As reported in the *Straits Times*, between 2008 and 2011 the number of citizens and permanent residents in Singapore's science industry fell by 200, according to the latest annual national surveys. But the number of foreign researchers, engineers, technicians and support staff shot up by 4,551 in the same period. By 2011, foreigners made up 30 per cent of the science industry ranks, up from 22 per cent in 2008. This is despite at least 20,000 people per year graduating with science and engineering degrees and diplomas in recent years.[60] One Singaporean scientist working on his doctoral studies in microbiology provided his in-depth views on the need for indigenous scientists:

It is true that Singapore has a very aggressive Science and Technology policy which perhaps make Singapore an exciting and attractive location to attract world-class talents. However, from my point of view, I would say that even with this "aggressiveness" the policies are still not in the favour of Singaporeans. For example, biomedical research in Singapore has been expanding vigorously in recent years, however, there remains a high number of incoming non-Singaporean researchers. I believe that not enough chances are being provided to local talents, and instead (in order to stay on par with the rest of the world), Singapore tends to attract foreign talent to our country in order to "increase" the standards. Sure, some of these world-class talents are really talented, but there exists also many others whom in my opinion are not even better than our own locals. I hope that in the future to come, Singaporeans would be given more chances to "step up" and be a leader of the field. I believe that with aggressiveness, it would be good to the entire Singapore. However, this cannot come at the expense of our own local researchers, but rather a combination of both local and overseas talent would perhaps be the most ideal scenario.[61]

The tension was further heightened by the sensitive issue of Singaporeans being deprived of job opportunities as a result of the government's policy of encouraging the inflow of foreign talent. Some expatriate scientists would eventually contribute to Singapore's growth by becoming Singapore citizens. However, the perception that many "footloose" foreign scientists and researchers use the Singapore experience as a springboard for more challenging and rewarding careers elsewhere is more real than apparent.

On the other hand, there is the argument that today's scientific research and R&D is moving towards what Ziman terms as "transnational collectivization of science" — a situation where "[i]n many fields of science and technology, a major part of the R&D is now organized multinationally".[62] This is particularly so in the case of "big" science projects that are funded by several international organizations from different countries. The reality is that every country in the world (including the United States) is beginning to realize that they can no longer go alone in research. In the case of Singapore, however, the various research projects in the research institutes and universities are supported mainly by the Singapore Government. Ziman argues that "even a relatively small country, such as the Netherlands, Denmark, Switzerland or Australia can still find the resources to maintain a number of world-class research entities. They have come to terms with the fact that their scientific capabilit[ies] are very patchy."[63] Over the last two decades the Singapore Government pressed on to create research institutes and staffed them with scientists of different nationalities. For the BMS industry it created an average of a thousand jobs annually for the period 2000–2005. While this mixture of researchers from all over the world could provide the platform for the sharing of creative ideas and networking, the reality is there is a shortage of local PhD holders. Without a doctoral education, most of Singapore's life sciences graduates are qualified to work only as research assistants. There is also the question of how to motivate young graduates to take on doctorate studies and spend years in a research laboratory whilst many of their peers may already by climbing the corporate ladder and saving enough to buy a car and a house. Until the city-state has a critical mass of indigenous research scientists and technologists, the prospects of nurturing a self-reliant scientific and technological sector is only remotely possible.

Some of the risks mentioned above on Singapore's aggressive foray into biomedical R&D were highlighted in a 2006 World Bank publication.[64] Yusuf and Nabeshima argue that the small city-state faces several challenges. First, it lacks the necessary human capital and material resources. This constraint "reduces the likelihood of anything more than the episodic discovery and makes it hard to think in terms of a continuously replenished pipeline of products".[65] Second, the intense emphasis on the commercialization of research findings "can detract from the necessary attention to basic research that feeds innovation".[66] Third, the heavy dependence on the large pool of foreign scientists and a handful of star scientists creates a certain level of uncertainty and discontinuity because they are not likely to be permanently committed to their roles in Singapore.[67] Fourth, the "lengthy lag between remarkable scientific discovery and eventual practical outcomes" is inevitable and needs a constant flow of financial input and a lot of patience.[68] The Singapore Government is fully aware of these constraints. The biomedical sector is seen as a wealth-generating niche area for the economy for the years ahead. The recent decision to emphasize translational research is part of the overall strategy to entice the world's pharmaceutical giants to set up their biologics plants on the island — and successfully so. In 2013, California-based Amgen agreed to sink in $230 million to start a manufacturing plant in Tuas Biomedical Park. Similarly, Novartis' $500 million investment in a new biologics production plant in Singapore represents a strategic commitment to its growing biologics portfolio. Both companies are among several drug companies to root a biologics production facility — where drugs are produced biologically instead of through chemical synthesis — in Singapore, bringing the sector's fixed asset investment value to $2.4 billion by 2014.

Scientist Edison Lui summarizes the Singapore science scene: "Given all the caveats of a newly-minted system, Singapore has done a remarkable job. Growth has been phenomenal, and the quality of work has been superb. The only thing I worry is over-planning. Research is uncertain and a bit messy. This is not like building up a microchip plant. It's about developing an ecosystem to nurture discovery. You can't predict outcomes, you can only harvest the good that comes."[69] Along the same line, geneticist and president of the Royal Society, Paul Nurse, argues that instead of "ring-fencing and micromanaging" resources, scientific leaders should instead be "educating and inspiring" researchers to work in areas they believe are of particular interest.[70] His comments are part of a long-running debate over whether governmental bureaucrats should "pick winners" or focus on research that could help to boost the economy or society. The Nobel laureate's stand is that too much top-down direction comes from "senior researchers on research council committees" who themselves are not particularly research-active" and hence were not at the "cutting edge" of investigation.[71]

SCIENCE AND SINGAPORE SOCIETY

Did the "big whales" achieve any groundbreaking discovery while in Singapore? Did they leave a legacy which in turn will further spur Singaporean scientists to greater heights? Did Singapore's science policy — visibly represented by the number of research institutes and the presence of international scientists and research engineers all housed in the imposing Biopolis complex — result in greater public interest in science and scientific research? Admittedly, these are questions which will probably receive no conclusive or objective answers. Yet, they are useful to look at because of Singapore's bold and expensive plan to create a scientific haven — or even a utopia — in the "One-North" corridor and they will have strong ramifications for the government's overall strategy of nurturing a scientific culture in Singapore society. While the mobile star scientists did not achieve any groundbreaking discovery during their tenure in Singapore, they did prepare local scientists to assume prominent leadership in the scientific community. This is exemplified by the appointment of local scientist Ng Huck Hui to head the Genome Institute when Edison Lui vacated his position in 2012 and Lam Kok Peng to head the Bioprocessing Technology Institute. It was also reported that scientists in the Genome Institute were "the first in the world to look through the entire complement of 21,000 genes to discover more than 500 candidates that keep ES [embryonic stem] cells in their unchanged state".[72] Scientists at the Institute of Medical Biology (IMB) and Institute of Molecular and Cellular Biology have also discovered a hormone that could aid cardiac repair and provide new therapies for common heart diseases and hypertension.[73]

As put forth by Catherine Waldby, the "Singaporean knowledge economy generally, and its bioeconomy in particular, rely heavily on expatriate expertise, as a way to leaven the allegedly conservative Singaporean scientific culture with the adventurous spirit of global technoscience".[74] The social scientist of biomedicine and life sciences adds: "How does this site [Biopolis] of expert biomedical innovation articulate with the broader Singaporean population, who cannot participate as scientific experts? On what terms are non-scientific citizens, the so-called "heartland Singaporeans", integrated into the promised regenerative economy and in what ways are they valued or devalued?"[75] Singapore citizens are expected to contribute to the growth of Singapore's bioeconomy by participating as tissue donors and research subjects. However, the general perception is that among the city-state's three main ethnic groups (Chinese, Malay and Indian) there is a lower level of willingness to donate blood for genetic research and a lower general awareness of genetic research than among North Americans and Europeans.[76] This lukewarm response from the population to act as a biological resource base to meet the needs of the Biopolis laboratories is not totally unexpected. The explanation could be cultural, but what is certain is that the communication between the scientific community and the masses is poor. There is hardly any public dialogue to educate the people on Singapore's science policy. Even during Singapore's general elections, issues of science and technology are never part of any political debates. In countries with strong scientific traditions, science matters to policy and to the economy.[77] This is not so in the case of Singapore. With the exception of the participation of medical doctors in public forums, the scientists at Biopolis are "trapped" in their ivory towers and have made no systematic attempts to reach out to the masses. It is a real possibility that the Biopolis could turn out to be an exclusive enclave of foreign scientific talent. Such a scenario is not surprising in Singapore where its science policy is largely driven by government-initiated international advisory boards consisting of top foreign scientists and technocrats. The situation motivated the Singapore Academy of Science to openly suggest that they should now have a bigger say in policy, education, research and funding.[78]

Unlike small nations such as Sweden, Israel, Denmark and Japan where science and scientific innovations are very much a component of their national histories, Singapore does not have any traditions that it could anchor on to stimulate an environment for the promotion of science. Even in the United States — purportedly recognized as the most technologically advanced nation in the world and with a long tradition of scientific discoveries — there exists what Chris Mooney and Sheril Kirshenbaum describe as the "science–society gap".[79] They maintain that scientific illiteracy amongst Americans is a serious trend and the scientific community could be more proactive in generating a closer link with the man in the street. Although no empirical studies have been done in Singapore, it is fair to assume that Singaporeans do not despise science. Rather, the people do not have science on their daily radar. While science fiction movies like *Close Encounters of the Third Kind*, *E.T. the Extra-Terrestrial* and *Jurassic Park* were box-office successes in the 1970s and 1980s, they did not result in a craze for things scientific, nor was there a surge in Singaporeans taking up scientific R&D activities. But this was not the case for technological innovations involving digital communication and computer-generated animation. Singaporeans, like the South Koreans, are largely technological geeks, constantly updated on the latest technological gadgets available in the market, as evident by the thousands who flock to technology fairs. Hence, movies like *Transformers*, *Minority Report* and *The Matrix* were popular with techno-savvy Singaporeans because they illustrated the creative use of technological gizmos and computer-generated effects.

The media also plays a part in influencing the public's interest in science and technology. The *Straits Times* is not short of reports and articles relating to science and technology. Each week it provides readers with a few pages on "Science", such as *Think: I'm A Scientist* covering interviews with scientists and researchers, a tabloid on *Body and Mind* on health and medical issues, and *Digital Life* which caters to things technological and digital. A magazine entitled *Asian Scientist* which focuses on Asian scientific R&D news, interviews with scientists and quirky fun science was also launched in early 2014.[80] However, while these efforts to promote science are in the right direction, it is also necessary for the scientific community to be more proactive in bridging the science–society gap with knowledge and understanding of different societal needs. Mooney and Kirshenbaum called them the "renaissance scientists" — scientists who are willing to come out of their ivory towers to bridge the science–society gap with knowledge and an understanding of the different needs of politicians, journalists, and even entertainers.[81] The scientists have to share with the man in the street how science shapes society and culture. As with engineers, there is a need to produce scientists who have a better understanding of other disciplines, who are able to reach out to the rest of society, and who possess essential soft skills. It is heartening that the Singapore Government is bringing science and technology to Pulau Ubin, an island off the northeast of Singapore often considered the last *kampung* (Malay for "village") in Singapore. An integrated laboratory facility — known as the Ubin Living Lab — was built on the island at the end of 2015.[82] Scientists and students will have the opportunity to carry out proper research on-site.

However, it is not surprising that the scientist is still perceived as someone nerdy, encapsulated in his own world of curiosity and researching endlessly to achieve the final goal. One is reminded of the community of scientists, headed by Robert Oppenheimer, working on the "Manhattan Project" at Los Alamos, New Mexico to produce the atomic bomb. What motivated the scientists initially was the belief they were in a race with Nazi Germany to make a nuclear weapon. Although by the end of 1944 it was obvious that Hitler's Germany was effectively defeated, the project continued, in the words of physicist Joseph Roblat (who left the project), because "the most frequent reason given was pure and simple scientific curiosity".[83] Hiroshima and Nagasaki became the "beneficiaries" of this "scientific curiosity". There is also the danger of science being subordinated to politics. Again, gleaning from the pages of history of World War II, the Japanese commander Ishii Shiro and his team of scientists who conducted biological warfare experiments using Chinese subjects in the infamous Unit 731 at Harbin, China were granted immunity from prosecution for war crimes by the Americans in exchange for the technical and scientific information they had gathered. A more recent case is that of the explosion of Japan's Fukushima Daiichi nuclear plant in 2011. Information of the meltdown was deliberately withheld by pro-nuclear scientists who had close ties with the power industry in the country.[84]

The public also reads about how scientists use data selectively in order to, in the words of political scientist Michael Chwe, "make striking new claims".[85] He cited a March 2012 report in *Nature* that scientists Glenn Begley and Lee Ellis could replicate only six out of the fifty-three "landmark" cancer studies, and now scientists worry that many published scientific results are simply not true. In the article, Begley and Ellis commented:

> These results, although disturbing, do not mean that the entire system is flawed. There are many examples of outstanding research that has been rapidly and reliably translated into clinical benefit. In 2011, several new cancer drugs were approved, built on robust preclinical data. However, the inability of industry and clinical trials to validate results from the majority of publications on potential therapeutic targets suggests a general, systemic problem. On speaking with many investigators in academia and industry, we found widespread recognition of this issue.[86]

There was also the recent case of a Japanese study that promised a revolutionary way to create stem cells, published by Japanese researchers Haruko Obokata and Yoshiki Sasai in the January edition of British journal *Nature*. The researchers faced tough questions as Riken Centre for Developmental Biology, the Japanese research institute that sponsored the study, launched a probe over the credibility of the data used to reach the explosive findings. At issue were allegations that the researchers used erroneous image data for the high-profile article.[87] Particularly in biomedical research involving clinical trials, improvements to patients' well-being is at the centre of the research efforts. In view of the pressure to seek funding and to publish for career advancement, in the words of Michael Chwe, scientists may lose their "sense of focus, transparency and urgency".[88] According to a 2012 study by a team of researchers at the University of Washington, the number of fraud cases is on the rise — there has been a tenfold increase in the number of biomedical and life sciences papers retracted since 1975. [89] A wide range of factors have contributed to this trend. At the top of the list is the highly competitive environment for academic research and funding. They conclude that a "[b]etter understanding of the underlying causes for retractions can potentially inform efforts to change the culture of science and to stem a loss of trust in science among the lay public".[90] The situation is all the more sensitive in Singapore where there is strong funding support for scientists and researchers, and promotions of university faculty is, to a large extent, determined by the number of publications and research quantum one is able to obtain.[91] And for the Singapore universities, moving up in the world rankings in scientific publications is a key performance indicator to aim for. Such is the need to play the so-called "numbers game", that journal publication — which may well not have any downstream commercial impact — is very often sought at the expense of good, quality teaching.

In line with the Singapore Government's quest to nurture a scientific culture, science education in schools and tertiary institutions has also undergone changes. Assessment in science and mathematics in schools has shifted from the memorizing of facts and formulae to problem solving of real-life situations. By 2017, secondary schools will offer a Science, Technology, Engineering and Mathematics (STEM) Applied Learning Programme developed by curriculum specialists.[92] The programme is in line with Singapore's push to encourage students and workers to develop special skills that are relevant to industries, rather than just academic knowledge. Since the 1960s the government has emphasized the importance of science and mathematics for the country's industrialization efforts. Hence, till today, Singapore parents have the perception that a science-stream education is the track to take in order for their children to have good careers and even to obtain higher education scholarships. The sciences are seen as more "reputable" and "analytical" than the humanities, which, many parents believe, offer only limited career fields. Such a perception is reinforced by the fact that the majority of Cabinet Ministers — and government scholars, in general — received science-based and engineering-based education. Undoubtedly, Singapore's science and mathematics education are widely recognized as among the best in the world; as proved by the youths' consistent high performance in international tests in the subjects. However, it is too presumptuous to conclude that the trend has had a positive impact on the desire of science graduates to take up lifetime scientific careers and in R&D.

A useful point to note is that while pursuing their undergraduate studies in the sciences, many do not have a deep passion or interest in the subject. They see it as an academic necessity so as to graduate with the degrees.[93] The science-based programmes (Chemistry, Physics, Biological Sciences, Mathematics, Statistics and Pharmacy) are not their priority choice. The majority, particularly the "high-flyers", would opt for courses that are seen as potential money-spinners, such as Law, Business and Medicine. But for those who fail to be allocated places in their first-choice courses, they are usually channelled to the sciences. This linkage of the choice of field of study at university to job prospects is certainly not unique to Singapore. Even in the United States, bright high school graduates would opt for places in law schools that would ensure good economic returns, compared to students on STEM courses who would continue their studies up to the doctoral level.[94] Japan and Taiwan, too, faced the same declining enrolment of science students in universities and a general disinterest of the young in the sciences.[95] But how it is that these Asian nations are still able to give the world the "Sonys", the "Asuses" and the "Samsungs"? While there are many contributing factors, historical traditions and sociocultural attributes are consistently highlighted as the key factors to explain the high level of technological innovations that flood the world markets from these East Asian economies.

Notes

1. S. Dhanabalan, "R&D: Improving Existing Products and Process", *Speech 2*, no. 4 (1978): 53 and *Straits Times*, 18 September 1978. The reference to Japan was made in line with Singapore's admiration for the "Japanese Miracle" and its adoption of the Japanese model of economic development in the 1970s.
2. Sheridan Tatsuno, *Created in Japan: From Imitators to World-Class Innovators* (New York: Harper & Row, 1990), p. 219.

3. Ian Inkster, *Science and Technology in History: An Approach to Industrial Development* (New Brunswick, NJ: Rutgers University Press, 1991), pp. 123–28; Sasaki Chikara, "Science and the Japanese Empire 1868–1945: An Overview", in *Science and Empires: Historical Studies about Scientific Development and European Expansion*, edited by Patrick Petitjean, Catherine Jami and Anne Marie Moulin (Boston: Kluwer Academic, 1992), pp. 243–46; James R. Bartholomew, "Modern Science in Japan: Comparative Perspectives", *Journal of World History* 4, no. 1 (1993): 101–16.

4. Interestingly, although there are ethnic Chinese who have won the prestigious award, they have mainly been living and working in the United States. China has yet to produce a Nobel Prize winner. But with the country's strong push in R&D and a reverse brain-gain of Chinese scientists returning home, it should be a matter of time before China produces a Nobel winner.

5. Tatsuno, *Created in Japan*, p. 220–21.

6. Alun Anderson, "Japanese Academics Bemoan the Cost of Years of Neglect", *Science*, 23 October 1992, pp. 564–82; Yikihiro Hirano, "Public and Private Support of Basic Research in Japan", *Science*, 23 October 1992, pp. 582–83; and Takayuki Matsuo, "Japanese R&D Policy for Techno-Industrial Competitiveness", in *State Policies and Techno-Industrial Innovation*, edited by Ulrich Hilpert (London: Routledge, 1991), pp. 235–59.

7. Teong Eng Siong, Parliamentary Debates Official Report, Singapore, 22 July 1970, col. 140–41. A search was also done on all the parliamentary question and answer sessions for the period 1970 to 1989. Hardly any parliamentary debates on issues relating to science and technology in Singapore came to light across the two decades covered. However, in reality, innovation policymaking is a highly politicized process, especially in its early stages when particular fields of scientific activity are selected for public support.

8. *Straits Times*, 30 June 1983. The physicists were Yang Chen-ning of New York State University, Chau Ling Lie of the Brookhaven National Laboratory, Feng La Hsuan of Drexel University and C.W. Woo of the University of California.

9. Ibid.

10. *Straits Times*, 25 June 1983.

11. Ibid.

12. *Straits Times*, 23 January 1986.

13. *Straits Times*, 27 January 1986.

14. *Straits Times*, 4 February 1987. Professor Yang was part of a panel of eight distinguished scientists invited by the Singapore Government to help to formulate science and technology policies on engineering and the physical sciences.

15. Ibid.

16. *Straits Times*, 5 March 1980.

17. Report of the Economic Committee. In 1984 the government had actually approved a proposal by NUS to set up a $65 million Institute of Molecular and Cell Biology (IMCB) with the express purpose of pursuing basic research, with no hidden commercial objectives. This initial orientation changed over time, mirroring the deeply-embedded philosophy of marketability and profitability of R&D in the country.

18. *Straits Times*, 1 April 1983.

19. *Straits Times*, 9 October 2005.

20. Ibid.

21. Philip Yeo, "Passion Drives", in *Heart Work*, by C.B. Chan (Singapore: Economic Development Board, 2002), p. 300.

22. <http://www.asiabiotech.com/publication/apbn/11/english/.../1508_1511. pdf> (accessed 19 February 2014).

23. <http://www.ncbi.nlm.nih.gov/pmc/articles/pmc> (accessed 25 March 2014).

24. *Straits Times*, 19 March 2008.

25. *Straits Times*, 4 January 2003.

26. *Straits Times*, 17 July 2013.

27. According to the A*Star website, there were eleven biomedical institutes and consortia as of November 2013.

28. *Straits Times*, 27 September 2011.

29. *Straits Times*, 14 May 2014.

30. *Straits Times*, 15 September 1979.

31. The interviews were mainly conducted by the *Straits Times* on 29 August 1983, 1 September 1983 and 16 April 1984

32. Ibid.

33. *Straits Times*, 29 August 1983.

34. <http://www.esgweb1.nts/jhu.edu/press/1998/NOVEMBER/981104.HTM> (accessed 23 March 2014).

35. Ibid.

36. For a full explanation from A*Star, see "It Is Johns Hopkins University Which Has Not Delivered: A*Star", *Straits Times*, 25 July 2006.

37. The case of James Shorvon awakened the Singapore scientific community to the danger of unethical practices. James Shorvon was recruited in 2000 from University College London to direct Singapore's National Neuroscience Institute. But shortly thereafter he became embroiled in a conflict. He was accused by Singapore officials of obtaining neurological information from thirteen patients without consent, recruiting them for his research without proper consent, and changing their medication levels without proper

consent. He was dismissed in 2003 by the institute. The Singapore Medical Council (SMC) found Shorvon guilty of professional misconduct in 2004, after he had returned to the United Kingdom. He was fined and removed from the register of medical practitioners in Singapore. Shorvon has denied emphatically any impropriety. The British General Medical Council (BGMC) became aware of the situation in 2004, and Shorvon, by then in London, sought a UK review to help clear his name. In 2005 the BGMC determined the allegations in Singapore could not be proved beyond a reasonable doubt and halted its inquiry.

38. *Straits Times*, 15 September 2011.
39. *Straits Times*, 15 December 2012.
40. Ibid.
41. Ibid.
42 "Of Mice and Men: Edison Liu Leaves Singapore to Head Jackson Laboratory" <http://www.bio-itworld/news/08/26/11>.
43. Ibid.
44. Ibid.
45. *Straits Times*, 7 September 2011.
46. In October 2006 Professor Edward Holmes became the head of the new Translational and Clinical Sciences Group under A*Star.
47. <http://www.ncbi.nlm.nih.gov/pmc/articles/pmc> (accessed 25 March 2014).
48. *Sunday Times*, 25 August 2013.
49. <http://www.nature.com/nature/journal/v468/n7325/full/468731a.html> (accessed 25 March 2014).
50. *Straits Times*, 4 November 2006. It was reported that the world's first dengue vaccine could be ready by the end of 2015, and that Singapore may be one of the first countries to get it. Developed by drug giant Sanofi Pasteur, once all approval processes have been cleared it will be able to churn out a hundred million doses a year. In 2009, long before the vaccine neared completion, the company invested in a $593 million production plant in France. Guillaume Leroy, who heads the company's dengue vaccine unit, commented that "[i]t was a big risk. But imagine not making the investment, getting the results, and then telling countries they have to wait five more years." This underlines the huge financial commitment and risks in the commercialization of biomedical research. See *Straits Times*, 16 June 2014.
51. Ibid. In the United States, as early as 1967, journalist Daniel Greenberg, in his book *The Politics of Pure Science*, criticized the mindset of scientist who claimed that they must be given full rein to satisfy their curiosity. Greenberg was against the scientists' devotion to pure basic research rather

than in service of any technological application. See Daniel S. Greenberg, *The Politics of Science* (New York: New American Library, 1967).

52. A made-in-Singapore H1N1 flu vaccine is being tested and could hit the market. It would be cheaper and faster to produce than conventional flu vaccines, and could help Singapore with an independent supply, which could be crucial during an outbreak.

53. *Straits Times*, 8 February 2007. In a study conducted on the innovation policies of nations by Harvard don Michael Porter, Singapore achieved top score for its effectiveness in protecting intellectual property, as well as for its support for R&D through tax credits and subsidies. See *Straits Times*, 19 November 2003.

54. *Straits Times*, 13 May 2009. Professor Jackie Ying is often referred to as one of the biggest "whales" lured to Singapore. The Taiwan-born scientist is a chemical engineer by training and has more than 120 patents filed or pending in her name.

55. See John Ziman, *Prometheus Bound: Science in a Dynamic Steady State* (Cambridge: Cambridge University Press, 1994).

56. *Straits Times*, 13 December 2003. An outreach "Young Scientists" programme to schools is a common strategy adopted by most research agencies in Singapore. However, there is no documentation on the effect such programmes had on the number of participants who eventually took up careers in R&D. In addition, the targeted schools are usually elite schools. In her letter to the *Straits Times*, Queenie Tan Khoo Ghee commented that "if we want Singaporeans to fill at least half of the research positions, then it is time to stop ignoring our neighbourhood schools". See *Straits Times*, 19 May 2004.

57. *Straits Times*, 5 April 2004.

58. Manuel Salto-Tellez, Vernon M.S. Oh and E.H. Lee, "How Do We Encourage Clinician Scientists in Singapore?, *Academic Medicine in Singapore* 26, no.11 (2007).

59. <http://news.xin.msn.com/en/singapore/article.aspx?cp-documentid=4398529> (accessed 29 November 2013).

60. *Straits Times*, 1 May 2013. It was also reported that "Singapore is not unique in this respect. A report in science journal *Nature Biotechnology* last December [2012] found many countries have high numbers of foreign scientists. Switzerland, Canada, Australia, the United States, Sweden and Britain had proportions of foreign scientists ranging from 33 to 57 per cent."

61. Email interview with the author, 4 October 2014.

62. Ziman, *Prometheus Bound*, pp. 232 and 235.

63. Ibid., p. 241.

64. Shahid Yusuf and Kaoru Nabeshima, *Postindustrial East Asian Cities: Innovation for Growth* (Washington, DC: World Bank, 2006).
65. Ibid., p. 133.
66. Ibid., p. 134.
67. Ibid., p. 134.
68. Ibid., p. 135.
69. *Straits Times*, 26 May 2013.
70. <http://www.timeshighereducation.co.uk/news/> (accessed 3 December 2013). Sir Paul Nurse was speaking at the Times Higher Education World Academic Summit in Singapore, 2 October 2013.
71. Ibid.
72. *Straits Times*, 11 December 2010.
73. *Straits Times*, 6 December 2013.
74. Catherine Waldby, "Singapore Biopolis: Bare Life in the City State" <http://www.kcl.ac.uk/ssp/departments/> (accessed 5 December 2013).
75. Ibid.
76. In 2002 A*Star formed the Singapore Tissue Network (STN). It is a non-profit, government-supported national tissue and DNA repository. The objective of STN is to provide a Singapore-wide tissue and DNA network to support the development of BMS R&D in Singapore.
77. In the United States, after eight years of enduring George W. Bush's hostility to science and amid fears that the nation could be falling behind in science and innovation, the idea of "ScienceDebate 2008" resonated deeply with the American scientific community.
78. *Straits Times*, 1 June 2014. The academy was founded as early as 1969. It remains an independent body so that it can provide unbiased comments on the Singapore science policy and initiatives.
79. Chris Mooney and Sheril Kirshenbaum, *Unscientific America: How Scientific Illiteracy Threatens Our Future* (New York: Basic Books, 2009).
80. *Straits Times*, 1 January 2014. The magazine was started by Juliana Chan. The first issue focused on biomedical issues, with articles on stem cells, the fight against infectious diseases such as dengue and influenza, and the race to stay ahead of bacteria becoming resistant to antibiotics.
81. Mooney and Kirshenbaum, *Unscientific America*, pp. 125–26.
82. *Straits Times*, 21 June 2015.
83. John Dower, *The Cultures of War: Pearl Harbor, Hiroshima, 9–11, Iraq* (New York: Norton, 2010), p. 253.
84. Lucy Birmingham and David McNeil, *Strong in the Rain: Surviving Japan's Earthquake, Tsunami and Fukushima Nuclear Disaster* (New York: Palgrave Macmillan, 2012), p. 94.

85. Michael Chwe Suk-Young, "Scientific Pride and Prejudice", *Straits Times*, 22 February 2014.
86. *Nature*, 29 March 2012, pp. 531–33.
87. *Straits Times*, 11 March 2014. See also "Japanese Scientist Haruko Obokata Apologises for 'False' Stem Cells" <http://www.dailymail.co.uk/news/article> (accessed 10 April 2014). Haruko Obokata, the lead author, denies the charges despite a tearful apology at a televised press conference. Yoshiki Sasai committed suicide.
88. Chwe, "Scientific Pride and Prejudice".
89. See R. Grant Steen, Alluro Casadeva and Ferric C. Fang, "Why Has the Number of Scientific Retractions Increased?", 8 July 2013 <http://www.plosone.org/article/infor%3Adoi%2F10.1371%2Fjournal.pone.0068397>.
90. Ibid.
91. Scientific misconduct has happened in the case of NUS. In 2012 a former NUS don Alirio Melendez fabricated data in twenty-one papers and in 2014 its former Yong Loo Lin School of Medicine faculty member Anoop Shankar faked his credentials. See *Sunday Times*, 21 September 2014.
92. *Straits Times*, 3 September 2014.
93. This point was highlighted at an informal discussion with pre-service science teachers of the National Institute of Education in July 2013.
94. Daniel S. Greenberg. "The Mythical Scientist Shortage", *Scientist* 17, no. 6 (2003): 68. See also Jerry Mervis, "Studies Suggests Two-Way Street for Science Majors", *Science* 343, no. 6167 <http://www.sciencemag.org/content/343/6167/125.summary> (accessed 19 March 2014).
95. <http://www.nistep.go.jp/achiev/abs/jpn/rep072j/rep072aj.html> (accessed 19 March 2014).

6

SOCIOCULTURAL ATTRIBUTES AND R&D

The impressive economic performance of the East Asian economies since the 1970s has gained not only the attention of economists but increasingly social scientists as well. While not rejecting altogether economic explanations, this latter group of scholars had attempted to link the macroeconomic dynamism with cultural factors inherent in the societal systems of these countries. Though it would be unwise to attribute the so-called "East Asia miracle" solely to the predominance of positive cultural traits, they could, as postulated by Peter Berger, very well serve as a "comparative advantage" in the process of capitalist development.[1]

The nature of technological creativity and innovation is affected by a society's culture and social structure. The specific motives and actions of parties involved with technological change do not crystallize or unfold in a vacuum. Instead, they do so within a background cultural context. The term "culture" here is broadly defined, in the words of Alex Inkeles, as "the grand total of all the objects, ideas, knowledge, institutions, the ways of doing things, habits, behaviour patterns, values and attitudes which each generation in a society receives and passes on — often in altered form — to its successor".[2] These cultural factors interact and influence each other to produce the "cultural system". It is imperative that any account of a country's scientific and technological development be seen against the elements of its overall sociocultural-environmental system.[3] Culture has a profound impact on the innovative capacity of a society. Innovation is a creative process, and the nature of creativity and innovation by which technological progress takes place is affected by the culture and social structure within which that change is occurring. The direction that technological change takes and the ways in which a culture puts scientific and technical knowledge to innovative use are dependent upon the belief systems of the culture, the opportunity and the ability to technologize, the motivation to do so, and the freedom to question and change, if necessary, the established characteristics of the culture. Without these technological imperatives, innovation does not take place.

Several studies, especially the Hofstede Indices or IBM Survey, have shown that the cultural system of a society may either foster or inhibit scientific and technological development.[4] Perhaps the most systematic and scientific study of the relationship between individualistic and collective cultures and innovation potential is that by Geert Hofstede.[5] From the Hofstede study it could be inferred that Singaporeans are law abiding, entrusting the political leaders to run the state and provide the stability and economic well-being. Unlike Westerners, the people generally do not openly say or demand to get things done because of their citizen rights. There is an acceptance that communal interactions are based on unequal relationships between people. The way Singapore society develops also reflects the government's "Shared Values" — key common values that all racial groups and faiths can subscribe to and live by.[6] Outside of these Shared Values, each community can practise its own values as long as they are not in conflict with national ones. The understanding that individuals in societies are not equal is also practised in Japan, South Korea, Taiwan and Hong Kong, where the Confucian legacy is strong. Asian nations, including Singapore, are collectivistic societies, or, as described by Hampden and Trompenaars, communitarian societies which emphasize the importance of the family, clans or organizations.[7]

SOCIAL ENGINEERING OF THE CITY-STATE

The social and political turmoil of the 1960s taught the leaders of Singapore an important lesson. For the small island to survive and succeed it must be ruled with the government overseeing all matters, both public and private. Indeed, it was social engineering at its best, as the whole island was transformed within a short span of time from a communally torn, plural society to a harmonious, multicultural, multi-ethnic one. In an interview with David Lomax of the British Broadcasting Corporation in 1994, Lee Kuan Yew lamented that Singapore society could not be more strictly controlled because "man would be likely to do all the things which satisfies his sensual desires but at great expense to the good of society as a whole".[8] Since the 1960s, campaign after campaign of sloganeering were planned by the government to fine-tune the sociocultural system. In the process, the "all-seeing" bureaucracy has stringently regulated individuals' actions, ranging from chewing bubble gum to flushing the toilet. Even the types of core values to be propagated and ingrained in society have been determined by the government and gazetted as "Shared Values". The assumption taken by the government is that a change in values will produce changes in social practice. This is shown by the ruling party's "constant recourse to propaganda and exhortation as a means of creating or channelling social change and behaviour patterns".[9] As one foreign observer noted, the transformation of Singapore society was done "to an Orwellian extreme of social engineering" and failed to support the generalization that "East Asia's Governments are minimalist".[10]

After nearly five decades of growth, Singapore society is characterized by pervasive consumerism, urbanism and materialism. The people are pressurized to find their own niches because, in the words of Lee Kuan Yew, "Nobody gets a free lunch [and] you have to work for it, and the better you work, the better your lunch".[11] According to one local sociologist, alienation is high in Singapore society as shown by the increasing number of Singaporeans turning to religion and migrating for good.[12] Lee Kuan Yew attested to this new phenomenon:

> There is acute change in East Asia. We are agricultural societies that have industrialized within one or two generations. What happened in the West over 200 years or more is happening here in about

50 years or less. It is all crammed and crushed into a very tight time frame, so there are bound to be dislocation and malfunctions. If you look at the fast-growing countries — Korea, Thailand, Hong Kong, and Singapore, there's been one remarkable phenomenon: the rise of religion.... We are all in the midst of very rapid change and at the same time we are all groping towards a destination which we hope will be identifiable with our past. We have left the past behind and there is an underlying unease that there will be nothing left of us which is part of the old.[13]

According to Lee, this rush for religious solace is "associated with periods of great stress in society".[14] What is also significant is the "underlying unease" that, under the impact of economic growth and technological change, Singapore, like the other NIEs, was fast losing its cultural roots, the moral and ethical base of its forefathers. Hence, there was the need for the government to constantly remind people to return to basics, that is, "the belief in thrift, hard work, filial piety and loyalty in the extended family, and, most of all, the respect for scholarship and learning".[15] In short, historian Frank Gibney maintains that "Lee Kuan Yew had reinvented Confucianism, put it in modern dress, and turned its ancient stress on harmony and unity of the realm into a code of patriotism for his new nation".[16]

To prevent the stagnation and decay of Singapore society, the government also emphasized the ideology of "excellence" and "survival". These concepts have pervaded the whole society, from the national to the grass-roots level, and have become an integral part of the government's rhetoric till today. As expressed by Goh Chok Tong in a public address in 1986,

The key to our long-term survival is the spirit and quality of our people and their leaders. People are important. They matter greatly — as resources for the country, and as individual human beings with their hopes, fears and aspirations.... How we organise ourselves as a State will determine not only our progress but also our very survival as a nation. If we cannot achieve this, the demands on our lives, the degree of danger we will encounter, and the threat to our survival will be greater than you can ever imagine. But if we work with one heart, shared one common vision, then in our lifetime we can be that Nation of Excellence.[17]

The call to become a "Nation of Excellence" so as to ensure national survival reinforced the cultural values propagated by the government. Together they could produce the much-needed cultural ballast to sustain the state and society for the challenges ahead. By the early 1990s, social and economic indicators revealed that "Singapore is today [1993] the most comfortable country in Asia, more comfortable than Japan".[18] In terms of wealth, a 1995 survey by the World Bank ranked Singapore as the eighteenth richest country in the world, with a GNP per capita of US$19,310. In terms of purchasing power, the country was ranked ninth, with a purchasing power per person of US$20,470.[19] By 2012, Singapore was ranked by the World Bank as the fifth richest nation in the world.[20] On both counts, Singapore was ahead of Britain, its former colonial ruler. However, economic statistics are never perfect. While Singapore's GNP per capita figure is high, the country has a long way to go before it catches up with developed countries in various areas, such as its productivity levels, technological innovations or in the quality of intangible benefits such as a lively arts scene. Undoubtedly, the Singapore Government is proud of its achievements. However, the impact of its highly successful social engineering is reflected in two societal trends; namely, the growth and preservation of a *kiasu* culture, and the brain drain of young and skilled professionals

THE *KIASU* ETHOS

What has been the impact of the search for cultural identity and the omnipresent striving for excellence and being Number One in every endeavour within a highly regulated society on the mindsets of Singaporeans? How has this in turn affected the development of science and technology? Singaporeans have developed cultural traits that have constantly dismayed the political leaders because they do not match, in broad terms, with the government's call to build a "creative infrastructure". In more specific terms, these traits run opposed to meeting the objectives of the government's S&T policy and the creation of a technologically innovative society where indigenous technological development could grow and deepen.

One "outstanding" trait of Singaporeans is the *kiasu* spirit, purportedly developed as a result of living in an affluent society where survival depends solely on the ability of each individual to "fan for himself or herself". Singapore society has evolved in such a way that those who cannot follow the route to success are invariably seen as failures who "did not make it". As reported in the *Straits Times*, the typical Singaporean is so "stressed out with striving, pressured by demands to increase his productivity, caught in the rat race, running to stay in the same place [that] he has little time to be kind to himself or generous to others".[21] The term *kiasuism* is derived from the Hokkien dialect and defined as "fear of losing out". The 1997 edition of Australia's *Macquarie Dictionary* defines it as "an obsessive desire for value for money — hailed as a national fixation in Singapore". Its philosophy is summed up in a phrase popularized by a cartoon character, *Mr Kiasu*, in Singlish, the local idiom: "Better grab first, later no more". Extreme *kiasuism* demands Singaporeans to pursue their objectives with single-minded determination to get their money's worth. Embodied in *kiasuism* is a complementary trait in Singaporeans — Singaporeans are known to be *kiasi*, another Hokkien word, which means "afraid to venture". At its worst, *kiasuism* has given Singaporeans an unattractive reputation abroad, prompting the government to extend its annual courtesy campaign to people travelling, studying and working overseas.[22] The aim was to eradicate the image of the "Ugly Singaporean" whose *kiasu* spirit even creates selfishness and dishonesty.

Singaporeans also show an exceptional obsession for money. Indeed, it is not an exaggeration to say that the whole society is money-driven. The government's pragmatic approach to problem solving, often expressed in dollars and cents, has produced an environment in which the flaunting of one's wealth has become a measurement of one's status. As Singapore gets wealthier, competition moves from what the late economist Fred Hirsch called the "material economy" to the "positional economy", where the ultimate objective is the acquisition of limited, "positional goods", such as living in a prime or "choice" residential district, possessing luxury cars, enjoying an "elite" education and occupying a "superior" job, as opposed to basic material goods.[23] Perhaps the most talked about local anecdote is that while the price of cars in Singapore have been touted to be the most expensive in the world, Singaporeans would buy a Mercedes Benz without a second thought; the "three-legged" star is seen as the ultimate symbol of "I made it". As explained by Goh Chok Tong, "it is the more successful, or the elite, who set the norm of social behaviour and the lifestyle for others to aspire to".[24] Not surprisingly, Singaporeans strive frenetically to get rich and live the lifestyle that wealth has brought to them.

Anecdotes abound to indicate the "monetized mentality" of Singaporeans and the search for a good life. Job-hopping has become a common modus operandi for Singaporeans to get a few dollars more. In its *1993 Survey on Manufacturing Operations in Singapore*, the Singapore Manufacturers' Association confirmed that job-hopping has become a habit of Singapore workers. In another 1992/3 survey by the Chicago-based International Survey Research Corporation, Singapore workers were the "most secure but least contented with pay".[25] But the most glaring evidence of Singaporeans' quest for money is speculation activities in shares and properties. Ironically, the share fever was partly triggered by the government itself when it privatized Singapore Telecommunications (SingTel) and made its shares available to all Singaporeans who could now utilize their savings in the Central Provident Fund (CPF) for the purchase of shares and properties. Overnight and for the first time in Singapore, more than 1.4 million Singaporeans became direct shareholders of a giant, national utilities company traded on the Stock Exchange of Singapore. By sending out the "shares" signal, the government tapped on the desire of Singaporeans to earn more money; it knew too well the *kiasu* spirit and herd mentality of Singaporeans would ensure the success of its venture to beef up the capitalization of SingTel. It is not uncommon to find Singaporeans queuing for hours or even days to buy shares and properties, and later trading them to make tidy profits. Some have even mortgaged their homes so they could accumulate more shares. Undergraduates were also caught in the shares fever, with many in the 1970s and 1980s carrying pagers so that their brokers could contact them. Many even applied for bank loans and overdrafts to give them the "spending power".[26] Today, some Singaporeans are even starting young to understand the stock market. The *Straits Times* reported on a twenty-three-year-old "self-taught investor" who gained inspiration from Warren Buffet and developed the passion for money management and dabbling in the markets when he was a child.[27] The "Time is Money" ideology even influenced young Singaporeans to forego opportunities to pursue scholarship education in science and technology in France or Germany and the prospect of completing postgraduate studies in the same fields at the two local universities. In the 1990s, scholarship bodies such as the Public Service Commission (PSC) and the EDB confirmed that they have more awards than takers, the number having dwindled to less than five for each of the two European countries in recent years.[28] This trend continues as a good number of scholarships — particularly in the sciences and engineering — for doctoral studies are being offered to foreign students. To many Singaporeans it is a simple equation between earning money and extra years in full-time studies. In short, it boils down to opportunity cost.

The *kiasu* spirit gives rise to a herd mentality among Singaporeans; everyone goes after the same things and avoids the same things. Basically, no one wants to be different. Young Singaporeans are especially vulnerable to peer pressure when making important decisions. The selection of university courses and subsequent career paths of undergraduates are often influenced by the need to stay as a group and suggestions of seniors who were already "out in the field". Thus, it is not surprising that many (including the brightest) tend to opt first for courses which offer the prospect of earning good money, such as accountancy, law, medicine and business. Science and engineering, often regarded as a dumping ground, is not a popular choice because of limited employment opportunities in the private sector. Tan Su Wen, one of Singapore's brightest (top 15 per cent) in her cohort, explains: "Like any young person, I really did not give much thought to engineering. You just think of an engineer's job as a daily grind, without much reward."[29] Tan eventually enrolled as an engineering student in Nanyang Technological University's "Renaissance Engineering" programme, which offers a combination of liberal arts, business and engineering courses and an internship in innovative companies, such as those in Silicon Valley.[30] While engineering is always in demand given the fact that Singapore is the hub for many multinational organizations, it is not uncommon for a young engineering graduate to follow the general trend of taking a job that does not need engineering knowledge per se but rather an analytical approach which an engineering course provides, such as a forex trader. It is also a trend that a professional engineer would, at one point in his career, sign up for business or related courses so as to climb the management ladder. Both behavioural patterns are attributable to the *kiasu* spirit — the fear of losing out in the rat race and the security of conforming to things or actions popularly done. However, the overarching principle is still "go where the money is" — provided the path is clear and well trodden.

At a time when the government is creating the "second wing" of the economy, that is, an expansion of Singapore's business interests overseas, the *kiasu* syndrome, deterring risk-taking, is seen as the main obstacle to the development of adventurous entrepreneurs. Unlike the bold and adventurous Hong Kong entrepreneurs, their Singapore counterparts, while also money-driven, practise a "no risk, no failure" philosophy. It makes a person overly cautious and wary of failure. While Singapore has no difficulty in producing business entrepreneurs, the country is facing a serious shortage of technological entrepreneurs. This special breed of entrepreneurs requires not only technical knowledge and perseverance but also business and marketing acumen. Since the 1970s the government has lamented that not enough of the country's best and brightest scholars and engineers have been keen to become entrepreneurial technocrats. As expressed by Goh Chok Tong as early as 1978,

> Why have our engineers and other professionals not come forward when there appear to be ample opportunities? Have they lost the drive and courage to take risks like their forefathers did? I think probably it is because the rewards from their professional practices are attractive enough to dissuade them from wanting to embark on some venture with its attendant risks.[31]

In the 1990s (and even today), Singapore grappled with the problem of a lack of indigenous technological entrepreneurs — despite frequent assurances by the government that the country's manufacturing sector is still enjoying healthy growth, thus "dispelling fears that it was losing its attractiveness as an investment centre due to rising costs".[32] For example, manufacturing increased from 16.9 to 29 per cent of GDP (at 1985 market prices) between 1960 and 1990, and the country secured a record $5.8 billion worth of manufacturing investments in 1994. A Member of Parliament summarized the cause of the problem accurately: "If money is not the problem, and technology can be learned, then there remains one last formidable frontier: our mindset. Until we get over this mental hurdle, make things for the world and create an environment for a nation of symbolic-analyst solvers, we will not soon become a developed nation in the 21st century."[33] Strengthening the low prestige of manufacturing in Singapore is the "dearth of local media heroes who have made it rich in manufacturing" and the few successful ones "have attracted less media attention than the non-manufacturing entrepreneurs".[34]

Perhaps peculiar only to Singapore, the technological entrepreneur is likely to be a polytechnic graduate who "is lurking behind the counter of every computer shop".[35] He enters business either because he has been retrenched or feels the need to stay competitively ahead of the graduate engineer. Sim Wong Hoo, the founder of Creative Technology, is one of the many polytechnic graduates who are now managing successful businesses. However, in today's "borderless" world, one is reminded that many ground-breaking technological innovations, such as the smart phone, are the results of a collective effort of teams of engineers, computer programmers, product designers, branding and marketing personnel working together — and, in most cases, working in different parts of the world. Bob McDonald of Procter & Gamble (P&G) explains his company's "Connect & Develop" innovation model:

> We will partner with competitors, consumers, entrepreneurs, academic centers, and inventors; all can offer suggestions through our Web site. Right now, for example, we are working with a supplier whose scientists excel in Chemistry A, while our scientists in the united States excel in Chemistry B.... You have to be comfortable working alongside outside individuals and companies where a common language or culture are not shared or fully understood.[36]

Team innovation and R&D efforts in Singapore were given a big push when the company opened its innovation centre in Singapore in late March 2014, further cementing the republic's position as a regional hub for consumer businesses and R&D. The P&G Singapore Innovation Centre at Biopolis, the company's third in Asia, has been the largest investment in a private research facility here, at S$250 million. The opening comes at a time when demand for consumer goods (such as in the areas of beauty, home care and personal health and grooming) is expanding in the region, supported by population and economic growth. Singapore is already P&G's regional headquarters for the Asia-Pacific. While it is well established that successful R&D work is usually a result of teamwork, the *kiasu* attitude of Singaporeans tends to make them operate as individuals, each guarding zealously their "sphere of interest". Even within Singapore's technology pride, the Science and Technology Park, there is little sharing of information or interaction between scientists and engineers from the various research institutes and companies.[37]

The negative impact of Singapore's cultural system on the development of indigenous technological innovation is also reflected in the attitudes of local firms towards upgrading through measures such as re-training of workers, developing in-house R&D activities and spending money to tap the knowledge and expertise of university research staff. Many companies do not possess the corporate culture to support the growth of creativity and innovativeness of workers. Like all other Singaporeans, the management of these firms are downright pragmatic about their goals, resulting in a focus on how much profit can be made each month given the prevailing business climate. Putting it another way, most firms have a short-term horizon, which invariably means that industrial R&D projects involving long-term commitment of resources with uncertain returns are discouraged or not eagerly pursued. Thus, in terms of industry–university linkages, "assistance provided by University staff is mostly in the form of consultancy with a short time-frame".[38]

In short, Singapore's cultural system discourages initiative and fosters conformity. The state's constant indoctrination of the ideology of survival and excellence has promoted *kiasuism* to the extent that it has created a sort of a dichotomy within the individual and, on a macro level, the cultural system. On the one hand a Singaporean feels a strong desire to operate as a Lone Ranger so that he knows and controls everything. On the other, his herd mentality and "play-safe" attitude tends to drive him towards some form of group integration or teamwork if the pie is good. Invariably, this paradoxical situation creates tension and conflict within the individual and the group. Perhaps as an act of defiance or simply from being fed up with the over-regulated society, thousands of Singaporeans have left the country to seek more meaningful lives overseas.

BRAIN DRAIN

Just why do Singaporeans emigrate from a place touted as "clean and green", safe and orderly, economically and technologically vibrant? Ironically, despite Singapore's high economic growth in the 1970s and 1980s, increasing numbers of skilled professionals have emigrated to the likes of the United States, New Zealand and Australia. Statistics from the Registry of Citizens show that from 1977 to October 1987, 10,916 people became part of the "brain drain" process.[39] The phenomenon of "cashing-out", that is, selling off properties and other assets and living comfortably in an adopted country seems to be the strategy practised by those in their late 30s and early 40s and possessing high skills and drive. Official records show that for the period 1986 to 1988, 85 per cent of Singaporeans who emigrated were between 20 and 49 years of age and with secondary and above education.[40] Some of the key push factors for Singapore's brain drain are the escalating costs of living, especially of housing and owning a car, the perception that the government is too paternalistic and regulates every aspect of social behaviour of its citizens as if they are immature and the breathtaking pace at which one has to work and compete in order to enjoy a quality lifestyle. More than two decades later, the emigration of Singaporeans is still an issue facing the government. Several recent studies suggest that Singapore is an unhappy society. In a study by researchers from the Institute of Policy Studies, it was found that "young Singaporeans had a positive opinion towards working and living abroad, but at the same time were proud of being Singaporeans and of the country. More than a quarter of the sample [of 2,013 respondents] said that they would consider emigrating in the next five years."[41] Gallup polls taken in 2012 found Singapore to be both the least positive nation out of 148 countries surveyed and the least emotional country out of more than 140 countries surveyed.[42] A book titled *Happiness and Wellbeing: A Singaporean Experience*, written by two National University of Singapore Business School professors, found that Singaporeans have grown unhappier over the last ten years.[43] Between 2003 and 2013 the number of overseas Singaporeans increased by 31 per cent, from 157,100 in 2003 to 207,000 in 2013.[44]

Whatever the push factors, political or otherwise, Singaporeans' decisions to leave their home soil have significant implications. It brings to light the question of loyalty and belongingness. The prospective migrant is psychologically prepared to uproot himself and his family because the pros outweigh the cons. But the more ominous implication is that of a steady outflow of skilled talent. The trend indicates that the decades of political authoritarianism have failed to produce a conducive environment for creativity, innovativeness and intellectual freedom. In 1988 the government conceded that "Every Singaporean, especially a skilled and talented person, who decides to leave permanently is a loss to Singapore [and] if nothing is done and the trickle turns into a torrent, the well-being of all Singaporeans will be seriously affected."[45] This sentiment is still applicable today. The departure of Singapore's scientific talents is a worrisome trend.

Scientists are known to be a highly mobile group of professionals. In an international study of the mobility pattern of foreign scientists in sixteen countries, it was found that

> [p]olicy levers appear to be extremely important in attracting scientists to work or study abroad. Regardless of country, opportunities to improve one's future or the availability of outstanding faculty, colleagues or research teams prove the most important reasons for immigration. But policy levers appear to have played little role in pulling returning emigrants back to their home country. For these returnees, and regardless of country, "personal or family reasons" are the most important factor influencing the decision to return. It does not follow, however, that countries have no ability to influence the return decisions of emigrants living abroad. As noted above, emigrant scientists from a handful of countries report that whether or not they return in the future will depend in part on job market conditions.[46]

For some time now the East Asian economies of China, Japan, Taiwan and South Korea have been introducing measures to entice the scientific brains who have left their homelands to come back. The Chinese government is regarded as being among the most assertive in the world in introducing policies to reverse the brain drain of scientific and entrepreneurial talent, as part of its aim of becoming a global economic and science powerhouse.[47] The "Thousand Talents" scheme was launched in 2008 to lure back top talent. The plan was to attract over a period of ten years around two thousand leading researchers who have held professorships or the equivalent in a "renowned" university or research institute abroad, as well as entrepreneurs. Singapore, too, wants to woo home its top scientists working overseas with "The Returning Singaporean Scientists Scheme". Measures such as full funding support and help to set up research laboratories at Singapore's universities are used as "carrots".[48] A Singaporean biomedical engineering scientist based in California expresses his views:

> ...I don't know why the government would not seek out Singaporean talents who have had developed the relevant experience in foreign high tech nations to return and be partners in startups. There are plenty of examples from China and Korea, where successful citizens are encouraged to return to help build the next economy. Rather, the Singapore government is more enamored with so called "foreign experts" who are not citizens. The irony is, I know of and have collaborated with some of these so called celebrities who serve as advisors and directors on boards, who would not be at the top of my list of admirers. What does that say about the Singapore officials who picked them and "manage" them to ensure money is well spent to get the returns? From what I could tell, the yardstick used by most government sponsorship is a lot of grandiose verbiage but nothing specific on details of startup deliverables in the real world.

The public response in the social media on this "brain gain" initiative has largely been negative and cynical with comments like "They [the government] gave away $300+ millions of scholarships to foreigners instead of rewarding to [sic] their own citizens, now need millions to woo them back", "Unfortunately, if we can offer [the Singaporean scientists] benefits and rewards, only bad and greedy people can be drawn back" and "Government used to import cheaper talent [scientists] from China and India but SG scientists [are] head hunted and appreciate[d] by U.S. companies. Good pay, better quality of life. I don't think they will come back."[49]

The lack of a critical mass of indigenous scientists and research engineers is further compounded by the lukewarm attitude of engineers towards R&D.

PERCEPTIONS OF ENGINEERING AND R&D

In Singapore, R&D is not viewed as a profession eagerly pursued by young engineers.[50] The main factors cited by the engineering undergraduates, engineers and technologists who took part in a questionnaire survey in 1993 are the lack of personal interest in R&D, the lack of monetary rewards, slow career advancement, and the long hours of work, which also creates undue stress. The Singapore engineer usually gives himself two to three years of what one research manager termed "shelf-life" as an engineer before making the critical decision whether to stay on or change to a new line of work. This tendency reflects the phenomenon of job-hopping in Singapore, as indicated by the number of job changes by the surveyed engineers and technologists. A few negative traits of the Singapore engineer in the manufacturing sector were also pointed out. Although there is no shortage of creativity, diligence and hard work, the engineer performs well when he has been assigned specific tasks and instructions on how to go about accomplishing them. In most cases, however, when left alone to finish a project, little initiative is being exercised to explore ways of getting a job done. The engineer has to be "spoon-fed" with specific instructions. The Singapore engineer also lacks the patience and determination to see the completion of projects he has been assigned. Related to this cultural attitude is the "down-to-earth" pragmatism practised by Singaporeans, who are too practical minded to indulge in the pure fun of creating something new and lack the desire to find out how and why things work. Two Singaporean senior researchers in the semiconductor industry felt that what is more serious is the fact that, without actually achieving the successful completion of a project, the engineer job-hops to another engineering company, thinking that he has gained sufficient expertise and experience. Their view was also shared by two Taiwanese research scientists recruited by the Singapore Government in the early 1990s to spearhead R&D in their respective fields. According to them, after two years of so-called experience, the engineer feels that he has mastered the knowledge and skills and now aspires to move up into the managerial ranks. However, in the words of one of the scientists, "two or three years of R&D, you are still nothing, you are still not experienced and you want to be a manager. You are still not a researcher because your mind-set is already wrong."

What then can be done to enhance the image of R&D? Back in the early 1990s it was the general consensus that the objective of Singapore's R&D policy was to project the image of a high-technology environment so that more foreign companies could be attracted to invest and sustain the growth of Singapore's manufacturing sector. Hence, the bottom line was that science and technology or R&D was more of an "economic focus" than a "technological focus". As reiterated by one Taiwanese scientist, the problem is that the image of R&D "has been built up for foreigners, to show that Singapore is building up its R&D. But at the grassroot, the people here are not really there yet. Part of people's thinking of R&D is that R&D means Government research institutes, not the commercial world. If you need to go into the next stage, which is more than just the Government institutes, the commercial world has to set up R&D activities, then you would expand into a larger domain and proliferate the potentials of R&D."[51] Echoing what had been said some twenty years ago, a Singaporean biomedical engineering scientist based in California explains:

> My impression is in general there is a huge desire at the institutional level to promote R&D activities in the nation, but behind all that, there always seems to be this economic motivation at both micro and macro level. The government obviously has the incentives to grow the economic base of the nation, but the people are equally incentivized by the financial returns of their investments in technology startup companies. The government is throwing a lot of money into programs, and it has definitely succeeded in attracting foreign partnership in R&D startups (it's free money, why not?), but does this really promote organic growth, or does this simply demonstrate another example of the prowess of Singaporeans in managing money (investment)? In my view, until Singaporeans witness the fruit of these high tech R&D benefiting them in some tangible way, R&D will always remain an academic concept to them.[52]

Finally, are R&D engineers willing to become technological entrepreneurs? Interviews conducted in the mid-1990s indicated the
general view that experienced R&D engineers were not keen to start
up their own businesses. A principal R&D researcher in his early
thirties with an American computer manufacturer did not see himself
leaving his job and becoming an entrepreneur. He found his job both
challenging and rewarding and he saw no reason why he should face
uncertainties and risk in venturing out on his own. He explained that
there is a tendency for experienced researchers in MNCs to remain
where they are because the pay is comfortable for their needs and the
security is there. MNCs "provide stable jobs and hold people back";
but MNCs are also important sources of such people. Moreover, there
are not many success stories of local technological entrepreneurs who
could serve as role models, unlike in the United States. In any case,
technical skill alone cannot guarantee success; it must be combined
with business acumen. In view of these problems, "why take the leap
of faith?" On the other hand, in his opinion, diploma holders are more
willing to face such risks because by doing so there is the possibility
of making it big rather than stagnating as an employee.[53] For others,
personal and family considerations are significant factors that prevent
them from starting their own businesses.

The issue of family constraints was also mentioned by an innovator
who was a recipient of an NSTB Innovator Assistance Scheme to start
commercializing his patent on colour print processing. From his own
experience it would take about ten years of working experience before
someone would be ready to venture into entrepreneurship. But by
then the situation would be complicated by the rising expectations
of the individual and, more importantly, that of his family, which,
in most cases, would deter him from taking unnecessary risks such
as selling or mortgaging his house and pouring his and/or his
wife's savings into a business venture. In the inventor's own words,
"the risks are simply too high". As one of the few who decided to
face such risks, the inventor cautioned that, for successful ventures,
two components — technical knowledge and business acumen — must
be present. More often than not the technological entrepreneur must
find a business partner to team up with.[54] Twenty years later his
view was shared by a marine biologist who played a key role in the
development of Singapore's natural history museum at NUS. He added

that the government could "match-make him with a business partner; otherwise, on his own, just the fear of being cheated would stop him from setting up a company".[55]

A new trend has now been set in place with the government encouraging university staff to spawn high-tech companies as spin-offs from their research efforts. This scheme allows new start-up companies to have direct access to all the facilities and technology within the university, together with early stage administrative support. The scheme was conceived because the government realized that the spin-offs of experienced researchers from MNCs to set up their own ventures had been very limited. While it is true that university researchers have the attributes and ambitions to compete with leaders in their fields, the key process is in the translation of this research into products for the end user. But, in the case of the Singapore research ecosystem, "the lack of market and user base is limiting their understanding of end user needs".[56]

Another factor mentioned by an academic responsible for university–industry linkages is that the cultural values of Singaporeans are such that they tend to operate individually in business. This is because they want to have full control of things and are not willing to employ professional managers to handle administrative or financial matters. Such thinking and behaviour is symbolic of the *kiasu* culture. According to him, research done at MIT shows that technological entrepreneurs' chances of success are greatly enhanced by collective effort; that is, a number of people banded together to sustain the high risks and to pool knowledge and resources. He noted that this concept of teamwork is not rooted in Singapore's cultural system. This explanation was also taken up by a government scholar who was one of the first few Singaporeans to obtain a PhD in Information Technology. He argued that, unlike the environment in Silicon Valley in the United States, there are no supplier-chain effects to produce the network of technology and manpower support if someone decides to venture out on his own. He is left very much on his own, struggling to succeed, like the early migrants in the colonial days.

Today's perceptions of science, engineering and R&D work also attest to the lukewarm attitude of science and engineering graduates towards R&D and the perception that engineering as a profession lacks glamour and career prospects. It does not attract the brightest students.

There are two key reasons. First, a career in engineering has a limited salary and career prospects. Second, engineering as a profession has lost its lustre. Joe Eades of the Institution of Engineers (IES), Singapore gives his view:

> Compared with 30 to 40 years ago, it is a challenge now to get students to choose to study engineering, and to encourage engineering graduates to pursue engineering as a career. This is because the younger generation perceives engineering as a harsh and average-paying job that is limited to construction work.... To alleviate the shortage of engineers, the Institution of Engineers, Singapore (IES), as the national society of engineers, has been working closely with government agencies to appeal to local young talents to join the profession, through National Engineers Day and other activities. We have also encouraged engineers based overseas to return and work in Singapore. In September last year [2013], IES launched the Chartered Engineer Programme to raise the standards of engineering and the profile of engineers. Through this accreditation, we aim to give qualified engineers the salaries they deserve.[57]

The frequent disruptions of train services in recent years brings to light the lack of top-notch engineers with deep and specialized knowledge of railway engineering. For the rail engineers who man Singapore's extensive mass rapid transit rail system, career advancement is limited. Like their counterparts in other sectors, many are likely to seek out careers beyond the engineering field. In an attempt to give a boost to the status of rail engineers, they will now be able to work towards becoming chartered engineers, just like their peers in the fields of aerospace and chemical engineering.[58] *Straits Times'* editor-at-large Han Fook Kwang accurately points out: "The hollowing out of experienced technical staff in Singapore's public sector and the general shortage of engineers nationwide is a serious problem with consequences that might only be beginning to surface."[59]

The chief executive of a leading, home-grown service provider in print management, computer-aided design and drafting (CADD) and building information modelling (BIM), which has about two hundred engineers on its payroll, adds: "Many of the young engineering graduates stayed with the company for less than two years. They prefer more glamorous, non-engineering jobs, such as those in banking and finance."[60] The company's employment policy is to give preference to Singaporean engineers, but even then they have difficulty recruiting fresh (mainly mechanical) engineering graduates, despite frequent participation in career fairs and roadshows. To fill the gap the company has turned to employing foreign engineers (mainly from the Philippines).[61] She speculates that one possible reason why fresh engineers often shun the engineering field and apply for positions in the financial and business sectors is because they do not have a deep passion or interest in the field of study. Not given their priority choices of study, they are being channelled into mechanical engineering. The general apathy towards engineering R&D is also reflected in the sciences domain. It too faces difficulties in attracting young scientists. One Singaporean scientist in microbiology in his thirties explains at length:

> Generally from my own interactions with others, I felt that as the years go by, the number of people keen on doing research is decreasing. In another word, more and more people are leaving research. The main reason which I can think of is because of the lifestyle that most Singaporeans are working. I seriously felt that there is a lack of work-life balance in our current society and because of this coupled with the erratic working hours in some research labs, certain Singaporeans would rather leave research to look for a "8–5" job. I have personally encountered a few of such people in the place where I work. Furthermore, certain Singaporeans themselves have a weak mentality. I have seen people with very strong interest in R&D, but this interest decreased progressively during their PhD years because mainly of all the uncertainties faced during their PhD, citing examples include 1) lack of publications, 2) long working hours, 3) conflicts with supervisor, 4) supervisor is not scientifically capable — with 2) and 4) being the most commonly mentioned reasons. Some Singaporeans do not like R&D also because of the low salaries as compared to other trades and they would rather leave science to look for better paying jobs. In addition, for R&D, the opportunity to be "promoted" is limited. And lastly, from Singaporean students' point-of-view, the lack of scholarship opportunities (and their requirements and bonds) do not entice these students to even apply for these scholarships. So we might even want to ask ourselves, is it because Singaporeans are "too weak" to face certain hardships?[62]

Although expressing his own opinions and perceptions, the micro-biologist did reveal similar thinking to that of scientists and researchers interviewed some twenty years ago. One can conclude that mindset changes or shifts in cultural traits are not easy matters to address.

The engineering profession is also no longer held in high regard by young people or their parents, unlike the "money-making" jobs of being financial analysts, doctors or bankers. One engineer puts it as follows: "There doesn't seem to be any respect for the engineering profession. Everywhere, I read, see and hear about finance and business and such but nothing much about engineering. When have you ever seen a successful engineer being interviewed in the papers or on the television, when have you seen articles highlighting the achievements of engineers and their contribution to our society. Once in a while some media attention is given to engineering not out of respect but out of propaganda."[63] Another engineer added, "why would you want to seek a dull job as an engineer, which offers only a fairly decent salary, not too much, not too little, when you are hearing all around you of bankers and financial managers who are retiring as millionaires in their 40s?"[64] There is also the perception that engineers are "high-class" technicians and technologists, and that there are technicians and technologists who refer to themselves as engineers. However, there are significant differences between the two. Basically, an engineer is the team leader of an engineering team, while technicians and technologists are the doers and implementers. They focus on the practical elements of the job and are the support team for the engineers. Given all the negative vibes about the engineering profession, attempts are being made to improve these perceptions through higher pay packages and professional certification by the IES.[65] Aerospace engineering, computer engineering, information engineering and media, and industrial system engineering graduates are being wooed with higher entry-level salaries. IES is also looking into the process of certifying chartered engineers to recognize the professional competencies they have earned through training and work experience. To attract applicants to the engineering faculties, universities in Singapore have lowered their entry requirements. It is now easier to get into the hard sciences than business studies.

It must be said that the problems and issues relating to engineers and engineering as a university discipline is not peculiar to Singapore.

In a study report on South Korean engineering culture, it was stated that "[d]espite South Korea's enthusiasm for engineering in the past, the same enthusiasm does not seem to be present today.... Recent trends show that many engineering students drop out to pursue more desirable fields, better paying professionals such as those in the medical field."[66] But, the researchers add, the supply of engineers far outstripped the demand from the corporations because Korea's school system and curriculum was designed to produce engineers. The glut of engineers resulted in lower salaries, thus further depressing the outlook for the engineering profession. In the case of Japan, as reported by Martin Fackler in the *New York Times*, the country is running out of engineers.[67] Universities in Japan termed this decline in the number of young people entering engineering and technology-related fields as *rikei banare*, or "flight from science". The shortage is causing rising anxiety about Japan's competitiveness, particularly when China produces some 400,000 engineers every year. Even Germany, the world's powerhouse in engineering and technological innovation, is facing a decline of skilled engineers and now has to fine-tune its immigration laws to recruit foreign engineers.[68] Britain, too, is facing a shortage of engineers. To inspire the next generation of engineers and scientists, the Bloodhound Supersonic Car Project was launched in 2014. The car is designed to go at 1,600 kilometres per hour and aims to set a new land-speed world record. But the people involved have a more important aim — to revive interest in the hard sciences and create the next generation of engineers and scientists. The project is fully supported by Britain's Ministry of Education and students are encouraged to take part in various hands-on activities linked to the project.[69]

All said, within Singapore society a pragmatic approach towards fulfilling one's material needs tends to derail talented science and engineering graduates from pursuing higher degrees. While it is possible to train good researchers with only basic degrees, it is essential for Singapore to have its own pool of native PhDs in science and technology for R&D activities, instead of depending on foreign imports. For the limited number of Singaporeans who decided to pursue their doctoral studies in science and technology, the main driving factor seems to be passion for scientific work in the special area of study. One promising young doctoral scientist explains at length his passion for his research:

> The reasons that drove me to take up a PhD almost four years ago was due to the passion that I have for doing scientific research. I did not really think about doing PhD right after my undergraduate course, however, this passion for PhD was intensified during the one year that I worked as a research officer in the Singapore Immunology Network, which provided me with a very clear picture of what research life is all about. The opportunity to work with renowned researchers led to many moments in which I was scientifically challenged. These made me grow as a researcher and I thoroughly enjoyed how research is carried out through interactions with peers and how we have to design experiments that can help in answering our hypotheses. Even though a PhD life might not be easy, my interest in doing research [in immunology and infectious disease] kept me going for the past three years, and I hope that with my research I can help to understand certain diseases better.[70]

One can sense the microbiologist's passion and enthusiasm for research work and to feel "scientifically challenged" to explore the unknown. Another R&D scientist in biomedical engineering recalls his decision to take up doctoral studies and to pursue a career in R&D:

> At the beginning it was the vanity of getting an advanced degree in a high tech nation, and also knowing it was within reach. That died off very quickly as the drudgery of graduate student life took over. I left my original area of study [Electrical Engineering] and joined the research department of the medical school, thinking this is my way of getting into the medical field without being an MD. That actually worked because I found myself loving the interactions in the hospital environment. Prompted by the example of a colleague who was pursuing his PhD while working in the same department, I decided to follow suit and switched to Biomedical Engineering.... I spent the next 20+ years working in the medical device industry, mostly in R&D. To be honest I hadn't always thought I'd stay in R&D. To be "successful" most of my peers and managers had gone on to pursue corporate executive roles, with or without additional business-related credentials. I was anxious and competitive, and wanted to follow similar paths as well. But it took me many years to realize what makes me thrive in my core is still R&D. It's the thrill of outsmarting others, being a trailblazer that appeals to me.[71]

However, Singapore's S&T planners should recall that a major factor accounting for Taiwan and South Korea's prolific generation of commercially marketable technological innovations is that both economies possess a large pool of indigenous scientists and research engineers, many of whom obtained their PhDs in the United States. These are agents of change who could instil feelings of excitement and challenge in the fields of science and technology and create a technology climate conducive to innovations. Even for industrialized economies like the United States, concerted efforts are still being made to convince larger numbers of young Americans that the rewards of a career in science or engineering are worth the time and effort required. Given the reality that Singaporeans are not particularly obsessed with science or technology, would one say that Singapore is a technologically creative and innovative society?

Notes

1. Peter L. Berger, "An East Asian Development Model?", *Economic News*, 12–23 September 1984.
2. Alex Inkeles, *What is Sociology?* (Englewood Cliffs, NJ: Prentice Hall, 1964), p. 66.
3. See Robert E. McGinn, *Science, Technology and Society* (Englewood Cliffs, NJ: Prentice Hall, 1991), Chapter 4 for a theoretical analysis of a society's sociocultural-environmental system which could foster or inhibit systematic thinking about science and technology and the development of technological innovations.
4. See, for example, Jan Uljin and M. Weggeman, "Toward an Innovation Culture: What are its National, Corporate, Marketing and Engineering Aspects, Some Experimental Evidence", in *The International Handbook of Organizational Culture and Climate*, edited by Cary L. Cooper, Sue Cartwright and P. Christopher Earley (Chichester, NY: Wiley, 2001), pp. 487–517; Cheryl Nakata and L. Sivakumar, "National Culture and New Product Development: An Integrative Review", *Journal of Marketing* 60, no. 1 (1996): 61–72.
5. Geert Hofstede, *Culture's Consequences: International Differences in Work-Related Values* (Beverly Hills: Sage, 1980); Geert Hofstede, *Cultures and Organizations: Software of the Mind* (New York: McGraw Hill, 1991). The four dimensions are Power Distance Index, Uncertainty Avoidance Index, Individualism Index, and Masculinity Index.

6. There are five "Shared Values"; namely, (1) nation before community and society above self; (2) family as the basic unit of society; (3) regard and community support for the individual; (4) consensus instead of contention; (5) racial and religious harmony. The main theme underlying the set of shared values emphasizes communitarian values and reflects Singapore's heritage.

7. See Charles Hampden-Turner and Alfonsus Trompenaars, *The Seven Cultures of Capitalism* (New York: Doubleday, 1993), Chapter 8.

8. Excerpts of the interview were printed in the *Straits Times*, 4 August 1994.

9. John Clammer, "Deconstructing Values: The Establishment of a National Ideology and Its Implications for Singapore's Political Future", in *Singapore Changes Guard: Social, Political and Economic Directions in the 1990s*, edited by Garry Rodan (New York: St Martin's Press, 1993), p. 37.

10. Kim Dae Jung, "Is Culture Destiny? The Myth of Asia's Anti-Democratic Values", *Foreign Affairs* 73, no 6 (1994): 190.

11. Lee Kuan Yew, interview in *TIME*, 2 April 1994.

12. Chiew Seen Kong, "National Identity, Ethnicity and National Issues", in *In Search of Singapore's National Values*, edited by Jon Quah S.T. (Singapore: Times Academic Press, 1990), pp. 66–79.

13. Fareed Zakaria, "Culture is Destiny: A Conversation with Lee Kuan Yew", *Foreign Affairs* 73, no. 2 (1994), p. 118.

14. Ibid.

15. Ibid., p. 114.

16. Frank Gibney, *The Pacific Century* (New York: Scribner's, 1992), p. 272.

17. Goh Chok Tong, *A Nation of Excellence* (Singapore: Ministry of Communications and Information, 1986), p. 11.

18. *Sunday Times*, 3 January 1993.

19. *Straits Times*, 14 January 1995.

20. <http://data.Worldbank.org/indicators/NY.GDP.P> (accessed 7 February 2014).

21. *Straits Times*, 4 October 1990.

22. With the slogan, "Let Courtesy Show, Wherever We Go", the government delivered its message with posters depicting a Singaporean piling a plate high with food from a buffet table, a paper cup being thrown from a tour coach and a bus passenger behind a newspaper while a pregnant woman stood nearby.

23. See Fred Hirsch, *Social Limits to Growth* (Cambridge, MA: Harvard University Press, 1976).

24. Goh, *Nation of Excellence*, p. 5.

25. The survey was reported in the *Straits Times Weekly Edition*, 1 May 1993.

26. *Straits Times*, 20 September 1993; *Straits Times Weekly Edition*, 23 October 1993; *Straits Times*, 7 December 1994.
27. *Straits Times*, 19 October 2014.
28. *Straits Times Weekly Edition*, 9 October 1993.
29. *Straits Times*, 26 March 2014.
30. The thinking behind the "Renaissance Scientist" was first mooted by Samuel C. Florman. His model calls for the training of engineering graduates capable of a broad range of activities, from technology to management to public service. Florman suggests that "[i]f we want to develop renaissance engineers, multi-talented men and women who will participate in the highest councils, we cannot educate them in vocational schools — even scientifically distinguished vocational schools — which is what many of our engineering colleges are becoming." See Samuel Florman, "Engineering and the Concept of the Elite", in *The Bridge* (National Academy of Engineering, Winter 2001).
31. Goh Chok Tong, "Need for Entrepreneurial Technocrats", *Speeches* 2, no. 5 (1978): 61.
32. *Straits Times*, 30 January 1995.
33. *Straits Times*, 27 August 1993.
34. Ibid.
35. Ho Kwon Ping, "Entrepreneurs Need Right Conditions to Grow and Flourish", *Straits Times Weekly Edition*, 13 March 1993.
36. Bob McDonald, "From the Midwest to the Far East", in *Reimagining Japan: The Quest for a Future that Works*, edited by McKinsey & Company (San Francisco: VIZ Media, 2011), p. 253.
37. This point was made by a research scientist of Singalab Pte Ltd in an interview on 2 February 1995. Singalab, Singapore's first commercial R&D company, is situated in the Science Park. While the comments made are dated, recent remarks by an R&D manager to the author still point to a mental mode of company secrecy and confidentiality.
38. Hang C.C., "NUS-Industry R&D Collaboration: An Overview", in *Proceedings of Seminar on NUS–Industry R&D Collaborations: Potential, Resources and Benefits* (National University of Singapore, 1993), p. 13.
39. Lee Boon Yang, *Parliamentary Debates*, Republic of Singapore, Official Report, 11 January 1988, vol. 50, col. 160. Out of the 10,916 people who emigrated, 8,144 renounced their Singapore citizenship and 2,772 had their Singapore citizenship terminated on the ground that they had taken up other citizenship. On the other side of the coin, during the same period, 88,132 people acquired Singapore citizenship and another 67,400 became permanent residents.

40. S. Jayakumar, *Parliamentary Debates*, Republic of Singapore, Official Report, 6 October 1989, vol. 54, col. 659–660.

41. Leong Chan Hoong and Debbie Soon, *A Study of Emigration Attitudes of Young Singaporeans* (Institute of Policy Studies, Working Papers No. 19, March 2011), p. 51. In an interview with the United Press International in 2009, Lee Kuan Yew commented that Singapore is losing 4–5 per cent of the top 30 per cent of its population every year.

42. *Straits Times*, 9 March 2013.

43. See Tambyah Siok Kuan and Tan Soo Jiuan, *Happiness and Wellbeing: The Singaporean Experience* (New York: Routledge, 2013).

44. *Population in Brief 2013* (Department of Statistics, Singapore, 2013), p. 24.

45. *Parliamentary Debates*, 11 January 1988, vol. 50, col. 160.

46. Chiara Franzoni, Giuseppe Scellato and Paula Stephan, *Foreign Born Scientists: Mobility Patterns for Sixteen Countries* (Cambridge, MA: National Bureau of Economic Research, 2012 <http://www.nber.org/papers/w18067> (accessed 24 March 2014).

47. See <http://www.universityworldnews.com/article.php?story> (accessed 24 March 2014). Carrots included huge monetary and other incentives such as assistance with housing and tax-free education allowances for the children of such returnees. Although some three thousand returnees have been recruited in less than five years under the initiative, according to official figures there is concern that it is not bringing researchers back to stay full-time, commit to the long-term development of China's science and technology sector and nurture future local PhD talent. Returnees prefer part-time or visiting research posts in China rather than full-time positions, according to experts. And they are often unwilling to leave tenured positions at major universities in the West.

48. *Straits Times*, 25 October 2013.

49. <http://www.facebook.com/The Straits Times/posts/10151646783737115> (accessed 24 March 2014).

50. The insights into the aspirations and attitudes towards R&D were obtained from the fieldwork conducted in 1993/94 and triangulated with reports in the *Straits Times* and personal interviews conducted by the author in 2014.

51. Interview with the author, April 1994.

52. Email interview with the author, 31 October 2014.

53. Interview with the author, March 1994.

54. Interview with the author, March 1994.

55. Interview with the author, April 1994.

56. Comments by a Singaporean biomedical engineer based in the United States. Email interview with the author, 31 October 2014.

57. *Straits Times*, 10 February 2014.
58. *Straits Times*, 30 May 2015.
59. *Straits Times*, 12 July 2015.
60. Interview with the author, 6 April 2014.
61. The cost of employing foreign engineers is now high because of the levy imposed by the government.
62. Email interview with the author, 4 October 2014.
63. <http://sgforums.com/forums/10/topics/321470> (accessed 25 March 2014).
64. Ibid.
65. *Straits Times*, 28 April 2014.
66. Moses Cho, Mathew Jennings, Vanessa Thompson and Ben Burk, "South Korean Engineering Culture", 29 April 2013 <http://blogs.It.vt.edu/southkoreaengineer> (accessed 25 March 2014).
67. Martin Fackler, "High-Tech Japan Running Out of Engineers", *New York Times*, 17 May 2008 <http://www.nytimes.com/2008/05/17/business/17engineers.html?_r=0&pag> (accessed 25 March 2014).
68 "Germany Fears Decline of Skilled Engineers", 11 August 2006 <http://www.workpermit.com/news/2006_08_11/germany/skilled_engineers_needed.htm> (accessed 25 March 2014).
69. Interestingly, in 1994 a postgraduate engineering student at Nanyang Technological University had created the world's fastest electric car. His request for facilities to test drive it in Singapore was turned down by the Singapore Government. Instead, the Malaysian authorities came to the innovator's rescue and a world record was set at an airport runway in the state of Malacca. The speed recorded was 169.544 kilometres per hour, erasing the previous record of 165.387 set by the Italian, Dario Sassi, in 1992. See *Straits Times*, 23 October 1994.
70. Email interview with the author, 4 October 2014.
71. Email interview with the author, 31 October 2014.

7

TOWARDS A TECHNOLOGICALLY CREATIVE SOCIETY

In 1982, Masanori Moritani of Nomura Research Institute gave a frank assessment of Singapore's ability to develop its own industrial and technological innovations. Based on Japan's successful experience with industrial and technological development, Moritani identified seven cultural traits essential for sustaining high-technology growth.[1] They are diligence, expertise, application ability, quickness and resourcefulness, elaborateness and cleanliness, refinement, and organizing ability. While not doubting that Singaporeans possess the qualities of diligence and quickness and resourcefulness, Moritani had reservations on the remaining five traits, especially the need to develop expertise and organizing ability. Japanese engineers and line workers alike recognized the need to accumulate a high level of knowledge of technology within an enterprise, and thus become "well-informed experts who know in the greatest detail the process of work".[2] This cannot be said of the workers of Singapore because "many people who after working on a job for one or two years, feel that they have mastered the job and want to move on to another job".[3]

Moritani himself downplayed the perception that Japan is a country of groupism, which implies concerted action at the orders of a leader who has absolute power. He clarified that, within a group, each member expresses his view frankly and the leader mediates different opinions and forms a consensus. Thus, the traits of self-restraint and the need to conform do not imply passiveness or meekness. On the contrary, they called for the ability to give constructive and creative suggestions and, at the same time, the ability to tolerate individualism and be ready to compromise to the group's final decision. According to Moritani, this harmonization between the whole and individuals, both at the group and organizational levels, is essential for rapid technological development. Perhaps responding to his observation, the Japanese concept of QCCs was introduced by the government into Singapore's industrial scene in an attempt to stimulate ideas through teamwork. In 1982 about 2,000 QCCs were formed, and by 1988 about 56,000 of them had been introduced.[4] Between 1980 and 1989 there were 703 articles and reports on the QCCs in the *Straits Times*. Particularly in the 1970s and 1980s, Singapore took great pains in learning from her one-time colonial master how to achieve industrial success. In the words of Lee Kuan Yew, "In spite of my experiences during the Japanese occupation and the Japanese traits I had learnt to fear, I now respect and admire them. Their group solidarity, discipline, intelligence, industriousness and willingness to sacrifice for their nation make them a formidable and productive force."[5] Moritani's advice, together with the QCC concept, was taken to heart by the government. A CEO (a former researcher in information technology) of a Singapore-based MNC that specializes in mobile advertising, recalled how "In the 1980s, experimentation was encouraged among small teams of young engineers, infused by the returning scholars from top overseas engineering schools. Interesting work flourished and would have formed the seeds of Singapore's WhatsApp today, had the process continued. Sadly, by the 1990s, small projects were terminated, with engineers pooled together to implement national projects in education and transport."[6] The chance of a technological breakthrough was lost. Since the launch of Singapore's S&T policy in the 1980s and the construction of an elaborate technology infrastructure, the question still remains: Does Singapore possess the prerequisites to be a technologically creative and innovative society?

INNOVATION-LED GROWTH

In his seminal 1990 study on the national competitiveness of nations, Michael Porter argues that Singapore draws its competitive advantages solely from basic factors of production. Singapore was categorized as a "factor-driven" economy. Its indigenous firms compete solely on the basis of price in industries that require little product or process technology or technology that is inexpensive and widely available. Technology is sourced largely from industrialized nations and not created indigenously. More high-end product designs and technologies are provided directly by multinationals that operate production bases on the island. Porter maintains that Singapore, despite the excellent infrastructure and possessing the greatest number of students per capita studying in the United States, "indigenous companies have yet to develop to a significant extent, nor have they been given much emphasis in economic policy" and that the country "is still a foreign production site, not a real home base".[7] According to Porter, for a nation like Singapore to enter into an innovation-driven stage, "[indigenous] firms not only appropriate and improve technology and methods from other nations but *create* them [and] the impetus to innovate, the skills to do so, and the signals that guide its directions must come largely from the private sector."[8] Unfortunately, up to the 1990s Singapore's indigenous firms were mainly providing supportive services to multinationals.

A random sampling of reports in newspaper from the 1980s revealed little public sentiment or excitement about Singapore's so-called high-tech policy strongly promoted as part of its new industrial approach. One report in April 1983 explained why Singaporeans were not keen to commit their time to research in science and technology.[9] First, economic rationality forced a fresh graduate to "thumb down the idea of spending three years doing research, only to find no suitable job awaiting him.... and top Singapore students do not want to spend four years pursuing a doctorate; they [would] rather join banks and multinationals and climb up the corporate ladder as fast as possible". Second, "the Singaporean cultural and social value system does not encourage students to pursue a career in academia because research scientists do not make much money and in a materialistic society like Singapore, that is often a big disincentive". In an interview with the

Straits Times in April 1985, Dr Vincent Yip, then executive director of the Science Council, confirmed that local entrepreneurs were unwilling to risk investing in science and technology projects.[10] He attributed this thinking to the "herd instinct" of businessmen who would readily invest in hotels, real estate, commodities and gold, even though they have no in-depth knowledge of these areas. Others have gained quick financial returns and made their fortunes through such investments. In another May 1986 editorial, it was stressed that,

> while there is some potential for research in MNCs, a more in-depth R&D strategy must rely more, in the long term, on a thriving local business community. We are here, once again, disadvantaged compared with other NICs [Newly Industrializing Countries]. Our business culture is mainly a trading one rather than an industrial one. The other NICs have evolved a full-scale industrial sector, which in striving to compete and grow is constantly in search of new and better manufactures.[11]

In short, by the end of the twentieth century, Singapore was not on the brink of developing an "innovation-driven" economy, despite spending millions on attempts to develop an R&D culture. This spurred the country's economic planners to look hard at pushing the growth trajectory frontier towards sustainable economic growth through innovation. The outcome was the *Report of the Economic Strategies Committee* (ESC) in February 2010.[12] The aim was to establish Singapore as Asia's innovation capital and knowledge hub, as well as a location of choice for commercialization, even if the ideas are not invented in Singapore.

The ESC Report encapsulates the thinking and strategies behind the attainment of three main thrusts of a knowledge-based economy — high skilled people, innovative economy and distinctive global city. The report highlights two crucial issues in creating an innovative economy. First, is the need to attract and develop talent for R&D commercialization. This includes not just research talent but also innovators, technology transfer professionals, patent agents, and start-up mentors. In particular, the report elaborates, is the need to enhance the role of universities in cultivating and training entrepreneurs through seed funding, supporting small-scale innovators and recruiting faculty with entrepreneurial skills as role models. The planners recognized that there are huge gaps along the stages of research, patenting, prototyping and eventual manufacturing of products. After the R&D and product development stages, business development and industry development of the final product are also crucial steps. In most cases inventors will stop at the patenting stage. The most crucial link is to fill the gap of late-stage funding. These funds are for expansion, branding and marketing activities. An R&D director of a biomedical instrument start-up at SimTech, housed within NTU, explains: "This is the biggest headache confronting prospective innovators, the process from patents to commercialization of product. We have inventors in Singapore filing for patents which, strictly speaking, do not generate revenue until they are being commercialized for the mass market."[13] The company is in the final stages of testing its DNA detector equipment and has completed the myriads of procedures of linking up with manufacturers to commercialize the product. Second, is the need to emphasize design-driven innovation and setting up an accreditation system to raise professional design standards through a "Designed in Singapore" certification mark for enterprises. The objective is to enhance Singapore's position as a promising and distinctive design capital in Asia. The issue of product design — and the lack of design engineers — is not new. Back in the 1990s this issue had already been consistently brought to light by entrepreneurs and research engineers. The government is determined to nurture an "innovation-driven" economy.

Scholars have contributed their interpretations of what it means to be technologically creative. As mentioned in Chapter 1, economic historian Joel Mokyr defines technologically creative societies as "those that generated innovations whose benefits dwarfed the costs of invention and development and this created a free lunch".[14] According to Mokyr, for a society to be technologically creative, three conditions must be present. First, there must be a sufficient pool of "ingenious and resourceful innovators" who are willing to bear high risks. Second, economic and social institutions have to encourage potential innovators by providing them with intrinsic and extrinsic rewards. Third, innovation requires "diversity and tolerance" and the society must be prepared to break down the "don't-rock-boat kinds of forces" which impede technological progress.[15] However, Mokyr argues, the desire for stability that pervades in every society could reduce a society to a state of "technological conservatism", that is, "the tendency to adopt a certain technique only because it happened to be used in a previous period".[16] Similarly, Erik Brynjolfsson and Andrew McAfee of MIT argue that the reasons why the United States is capable of creating new ideas and concepts — what they termed as "ideation" — are because the country has a more receptive culture, tolerance in the education system for different kinds of thinking, an active start-up community, great research-based universities, the availability of risk-tolerant financing, a cultural acceptance of failure and respect for the rule of law.[17]

Japan and South Korea are two countries that have technologically creative societies. Within a generation, both East Asian nations rose from the devastations of war to move from being technological imitators to technological innovators — Japan from the Pacific War in 1944 and South Korea from the unfinished Korean War in 1953. In his study of Japan's Tsukuba Science City, Dearing identified three interactive processes which would lead to technological innovations — researchers communicating with each other, collaborating on research projects and working creatively.[18] In a resource-poor society like Japan, it is the people that determine the country's national competitiveness. Scholar Taichi Sakaiya attributes Japan's competitiveness in exporting mass-produced, industrial products to the "culture of diligence and software", reflected in the Japanese appreciation of the value of human effort and their intense obsession for impeccable details.[19] The Japanese learn to avoid the trap of "technological conservatism" because, as explained by prolific inventor Yoshiro Nakamatsu, "I always tell young inventors to forget about money as a prime motivating force ... concentrate on ideas that will benefit mankind. If you do, money will automatically follow."[20] The straight-talking former governor of Tokyo, Ishihara Shintaro added:

> Creativity in Japan is not limited to a scientific or cultural elite. You see it everywhere, among people from all walks of life. Our supremacy in high technology stems from an alert-innovative labour force. Everyone in a company contributes, from top to bottom. One genius is not enough. You need excellent engineers and technicians to take an idea or laboratory discovery to the factory and turn out

quality manufactured goods. The low rate of defective products shows the outstanding level of technical ability in Japan. Excellence in manufacturing bespeaks of a crack work force. [21]

In the case of South Korea, history too played a significant role in germinating a technologically inventive culture. In the sixteenth century, in their wars against the invading Japanese, the Koreans invented the ironclad boat, dubbed the "turtle ship", and the *hwahca*, one of the first pieces of artillery, capable of firing a hundred arrows at the touch of a fuse. Technological progress took off rapidly after 1965 when Japan signed a treaty recognizing an independent South Korea. With it came Japanese funding, access to Japanese industrial know-how and the arrival of Japanese engineers and scientific experts. With the arrival of the Internet in the 1990s, in the words of Myung Oak Kim and Sam Jaffe, "South Korea found its groove [and] by 2004 South Korea had become a technological nirvana".[22]

INDICATORS OF TECHNOLOGICAL CREATIVITY

How should one view the innovation scene in Singapore? Local observers would cite the proud achievements of Singapore's Defence Science Organisation (DSO) National Laboratories, which has a huge pool of scientists and engineers. The defence sector absorbs the largest portion of the annual budget and the city-state is a significant importer of the latest defence technology. Due to its sensitivity, it is unknown to what extent military R&D has created spin-offs for civilian technology with commercial potential. Although measuring "spin-off' has always been difficult because military technology is so diverse, research done in the United States has shown that the diversion of technical talent into military R&D has resulted in scientists and engineers "either conforming to or being socialized in a set of values and procedures that have repeatedly been demonstrated to lead to cost overruns and missed deadlines, patterns that are generally fatal in the civilian sector".[23] Nevertheless, a new trend is now occurring in industrialized countries. Increasingly, technology is moving in the reverse direction, that is, dominance in civil high technology could in turn translate into dominance in military technology.[24] In other words, "spin-ons" are being created due to adaptations of commercial technology to military needs.

Singapore can also boast of its application of technology in water management. It is rightly proud of its indigenous innovation in environmental and water technologies. Singapore had identified water and environment technologies as a key growth sector back in 2006, and the country is now well-placed to take the lead as an R&D base and as a wellspring of water solutions. Through the Environment and Water Industry Programme Office (EWIPO), which spearheads the growth of Singapore's water industry, the National Research Foundation (NRF) has committed $470 million to promote R&D in the water sector. EWIPO, an inter-agency outfit led by the Public Utilities Board (PUB), is spearheading efforts to transform Singapore into a global hydro-hub. By funding promising research projects, the EWIPO aims to foster leading-edge technologies and create a thriving and vibrant research community in Singapore. Today, Singapore's vibrant water ecosystem has a thriving cluster of a hundred international and local water companies and twenty-five research centres. The PUB is actively working with industry to come up with new, innovative ideas that may make a difference to the water world. In the past, buying technology from overseas was viewed as much cheaper, while investing in home-grown research was seen as excessively expensive. No local companies were willing to take up the challenge. But with the global market steadily growing, companies have had to cast their nets wider. The opportunity to make good profits and create more jobs is the motivation behind companies rethinking their "cheap and good" mentality. Today the companies with a global presence — such as STATS ChipPAC, Aromatrix and Hyflux — have built up their expertise in technological systems integration and have learnt to build and improve on existing technologies and adapt them to suit local use.

Singapore has one of the best, if not the best, technology infra-structures in the region. The city-state has successfully projected the image of a high-tech city, with its advanced information technology infrastructure, numerous government-supported research institutes, a well-planned science park and technology "corridor" and the so-called "jewel in the crown" — Fusionpolis. Covering thirty hectares of land in Southwest Singapore, the Fusionopolis cluster is designed to provide an environment conducive to growth in information and communication technologies (ICT), media, physical sciences and engineering industries. The state-of-the-art research facilities promote infinite possibilities in scientific research and technological breakthroughs. Surrounded by convenient and accessible resources such as apartments, food, shopping and entertainment centres and with access to the mass rapid transit system, scientists and researchers could live and think research. However, an observation to note is that while the university-related Science Park and the Fusionpolis are being expanded to cater to more R&D firms, the question as to whether it is a "seedbed" or an "enclave" of innovation has yet to be extensively explored.

Some studies on science parks have shown that "the level of interaction between firms located on science parks and local universities is generally low [and] the choice of a science park location is due as much to the status and prestige effect that these exclusive locations confer, as it is to the perceived benefits in terms of innovation edge".[25] In her comparative study of Silicon Valley and Route 128, Saxenian stresses the importance of social contacts and the socialization processes inherent not just in the research centres and industries themselves but also in the broader local communities to explain the success of Silicon Valley over Route 128.[26] Similarly, Castells and Hall emphasize that "social networks are indeed essential elements in the generation of technological innovations".[27] In the case of the Singapore Science Park, a 2003 empirical study concluded that "the evidence does not support the popular myth of the science park model that the synergies of R&D culture in a place will certainly rise up with a suitable location and an impressive property development, peppered with thick institutions and benefits and incentives [and] that the extent of R&D activities and collaboration among tenant firms tends to be relatively low ... these findings reflect the Park as little more than a form of glorified property development in one of the most outward-oriented global cities".[28] As for the research institutes situated within the park, the study reveals that

> they make up a group of tenants who seem more embedded in the Park than other tenants because of their institutional origin as national research institutes. One reason why these research institutes can be actively involved in R&D is that the Singapore Government funds

them.... While the interviewees described their main activity to be R&D, the "more mundane chores" come in the form of providing testing and inspection services to private firms. This is quite a substantial proportion of their daily operations, but the income from these services "keep them in the blue".[29]

The study also shows that locating next to a university and its research facilities has insignificant impact on the R&D activities of firms located in the park.[30]

There are also statistics that point to the development of a more scientific and innovative Singapore. In an early 1990s study, Eisemon and Davis demonstrated that the scientific output of Singapore's universities had increased dramatically since the late 1970s — from 192 scientific papers in 1977 to 504 in 1987.[31] Another source, the United States–based Institute of Scientific Information, which publishes the journal *Science Watch*, indicated that the output of scientific papers from Singapore increased from 167 in 1981 to 1,220 by 1993.[32] According to the Nature Publishing Index (NPI) released in March 2014, Singapore ranked fifth for scientific research output, and NPI output almost doubled in 2013.[33] Singapore's three main research institutions — NUS, NTU and A*Star — all rank among the Asia-Pacific's top twenty.[34] In the Nature Index 2015 world-rankings, NTU came in at number 40, while NUS was at number 42 and A*Star moved from 133 to 107.[35] The implication of this trend is that basic science research in Singapore — especially in the physical sciences, chemistry, physics, mathematics, and the biomedical sciences of molecular genetics, plant and animal science — is gaining respect in the world scientific community. Similar trends can be seen in the field of engineering. In the latest 2015 QS World University Ranking by subject, NUS and NTU are ranked sixth and seventh, respectively, in the field of electrical and electronic engineering.[36] Even in the field of education, Singapore has done well. The National Institute of Education (NIE), as part of NTU, climbed to tenth position in 2015, from fourteenth in 2014.[37]

The city-state also ranks well in the Global Creativity Index (GCI). Based on the pioneering work of Richard Florida, the GCI evaluates and ranks 82 countries on Technology, Talent and Tolerance, the so-called "3Ts" of economic development.[38] Singapore was ranked eight.

For the second year in a row, Singapore has also been ranked the most innovative country in Asia according to the fifth Global Innovation Index.[39] This is attributed to its well-trained workforce, a robust research community and sophisticated financial markets. However, the report also acknowledges that, "While Singapore has done well in terms of innovation input, scoring first overall, it is placed only 11th on the innovation output sub-index. This means that while Singapore has invested significantly to create the most conducive environment for innovation, the output results of these efforts produced have come in below expectations. In terms of matching innovation input levels with output results, the country ranks only 83rd globally."[40]

Singaporeans, by international standards, are intelligent and well educated. Singapore teenagers are ranked top in the world in problem solving under the Programme for International Assessment (PISA).[41] In the words of Andreas Schleicher, special adviser on education to the Organisation for Economic Cooperation and Development (OECD), "[i]t shows that today's 15-year-olds in Singapore are quick learners, highly inquisitive, able to solve unstructured problems in unfamiliar contexts and highly skilled in generating new insights by observing, exploring and interacting with complex situations."[42] In another OECD report on global quality education rankings, Singapore topped the ranking table.[43] Hong Kong, South Korea, Japan and Taiwan, in this order, made up the next four ranking positions — alluding to Asia on the whole performing better than the West and providing an answer to Kishore Mahbubani's probing question: "Can Asians think?"[44] Despite the success, the government is continually stepping up its efforts in the education system to inculcate a mindset for innovation amongst young Singaporeans. The country's curricula and assessment at the primary and secondary level are designed to allow students to develop skills that can be practically applied in the real world. The establishment of the Singapore Institute of Technology (SIT) and the Singapore University of Technology and Design (SUTD) will also provide more opportunities for tertiary students to develop innovative capabilities through cross-disciplinary and practice-based learning.

Patent statistics are also now widely used as a measure of inventive/ innovative output. Although patents tend to reflect "inventive" rather than "innovative" output, they do provide insight into the creativity and innovativeness of countries. The U.S. Patent and Trade Office said it granted close to 300 patents to Singapore applicants in 2001.[45] Statistics from the World Intellectual Property Organisation (WIPO) indicate that patents filed by Singapore increased from 705 in 2000 to 4,872 in 2012.[46] The Intellectual Property Office of Singapore (IPOS) reported that the number of patents filed increased from 641 in 2004 to 1,143 in 2014 — a 78 per cent jump.[47] Finally, patent statistics from A*Star show that patents awarded doubled, from 451 in 2002 to 934 in 2013.[48] It is difficult, however, to tell the extent to which these patents were eventually turned into commercial products and processes. Two assumptions can be made here. First, the number of patents which were commercialized must be very few and, second, the inventions were not anything near to leading-edge, breakthrough technology. Indeed, many inventions do not immediately enter the stream of commercial or industrial application. Some go through a full gestation period and yet fail to emerge as innovative products, processes or techniques. Even in the United States, some ten thousand new products are invented each year but eighty per cent of them never result in commercially useful products.[49] But must inventors always protect their inventions by patents? A new trend is developing, particularly in the freewheeling, "anything is possible" environments of San Francisco Bay and Silicon Valley. Chris Anderson, founder of 3DRobotics, a drone manufacturing company, explains: "Today, inventors increasingly share their innovations publicly without any patent protection at all. This is what open source, Creative Commons, and all the other alternatives to traditional intellectual property protection do".[50] By sharing their ideas openly, the creators believe they get back more in return than they give away since they are receiving free help and advice in developing their inventions. Creative Commons is one technology platform that helps innovators share their knowledge and creativity with the world. However, such an open and transparent sharing of one's innovation would take time to be ingrained in the *kiasu-kiasi* Singapore society, where publicly sharing an idea with commercial potential is not a norm.

While all the rankings indicate that Singapore's education system is on the right track to grow the manpower capable of facing the challenges of the twenty-first century economy, it must be noted that the city-state is still far from producing top-ranked scientists, inventors, entrepreneurs and trendsetters — people who are given the space and time to dream, to experiment and to bounce back from failures. But, still, there are notable Singaporeans who shine as technological innovators. Creative Technology's Sim Wong Hoo was an early pioneer of the MP3 player. Trek 2000's Henn Tan was the inventor of the thumb drive. Serial entrepreneur Ong Peng Tsin co-founded Match.com, one of the world's most popular dating sites. The government can take heart that the entrepreneurial scene remains lively, with a consistently high Total early-stage Entrepreneurial Activity (TEA) rate that has ranged between 10 and 12 per cent for the past three years (2012–14). In 2006 the TEA rate was just 4.9 per cent.[51] What is unmistakable is that the country has produced quick-thinking, problem-solving and disciplined bureaucrats, technocrats and managers who can sustain the economic competiveness of organizations and the state economy at large. It would be wrong, however, to conclude that Singaporeans lack creativity. Singaporeans have shown their creativity and skill in the planning, development and management of infrastructure construction in areas such as urban renewal, public housing, industrial and science parks, and transportation. Certainly, in the provision of financial, trading and sourcing services, Singaporeans show great ingenuity and resourcefulness.

RISE OF THE SINGAPORE TECHNOPRENEURS

In their book *The New Digital Age*, Eric Schmidt and Jared Cohen stress the inevitable need to understand technology and technological change in a new, hugely connected world.[52] The Internet connects businesses in every nook and corner of the world economy — and also provides a platform to vent seething societal tensions which could even lead to revolutionary changes, as seen in the events of the Arab Spring. The Web-centric world opens up a whole new range of moneymaking opportunities, particularly in the way people communicate, how people are being entertained and in e-commerce. Disruptive technologies of all sorts are constantly being developed by technological entrepreneurs. These digital disruptions are now creeping into mainstream industries, such as education, retail, healthcare, manufacturing, telecommunications, transport, finance, and even in defence.

In recent years there have been Singaporeans who would actually venture out as technopreneurs given the right motivation and incentives. More crucially, they have the savviness to integrate the latest in technological systems and applications into creative innovative products and services. Venture capitalist Scott Anthony of Innosight Ventures suggests some reasons why Singapore is experiencing a start-up surge — a "hospitable environment" to work and live in, a range of grants and related programmes to help start-ups with early development activities, and a spirit of promoting and celebrating entrepreneurialism.[53] With a highly business-friendly governing philosophy and deep talent pool, Singapore is a hotbed for individuals and companies to churn out innovative new products and ideas, which, in an Internet-connected world, could have promises in transforming global business. Such a hotbed seems to be germinating in Block 71 within the Ayer Rajah Industrial Estate. *The Economist* has dubbed it "the world's most tightly packed entrepreneurial ecosystem".[54] It is home to a hundred start-ups, venture capital firms, tech incubators and an accelerator. They include Zimplistic, which makes the world's first automatic chapatti maker, called Rotimatic; Joyful Frog Digital Incubator, Singapore's first tech accelerator; Plug-in@ Blk71, an incubator managed by NUS Enterprise; T-Ware, which makes a therapy jacket for autistic children; and Ohanae, which provides a cloud security solution. Within this start-up ecosystem, investors, entrepreneurs, engineers and software developers are a stone's throw from each other. Anyone with a problem need only ask his neighbours for help. Investors can meet young innovative companies that they may want to fund. Budding entrepreneurs may find technical talent they can hire or with whom they can found new start-ups. However, unlike start-ups in countries like Israel, where they are highly original, not just in terms of business models but also the product–solution fit, Singapore's start-ups tend to delve into modifications or improvements of existing products and processes. It is like a "me-too" set-up. Also, Singapore start-ups typically create solutions for the local market, and then "think globally" only after achieving financial success locally.

What is needed for a more vibrant and sustainable start-up ecosystem is the infusion of a "maker culture"; that is, a technology-based extension of "Do-It Yourself" or DIY culture. The stress should be placed on new and unique applications of technologies and on encouraging invention and prototyping, with a focus on using and learning practical skills and applying them creatively. The maker need not start big. Anderson argues that "today's Maker-style cottage industries sell directly to consumers around the world online on their own websites or through marketplaces like Etsy or eBay [and] they compete on innovation".[55] For Singapore's start-up scene to bloom, it is obvious that there would be a period of gestation, as a culture of technological innovation cannot be created overnight. To sustain this technology climate, more success stories of major innovation efforts that could put Singapore on the R&D map must be forthcoming. And, indeed, there are success stories to tell.

Once seen as Singapore's technology champion, Creative Technology's glory days have passed — a victim of fierce competition and its own strategic misses. Will there be another billion-dollar technology company — or, a "unicorn", to use the geek jargon — in the making? Singapore has other big names, such as Venture Manufacturing, Stats ChipPAC and Teledata Singapore. But they are not "sexy" enough to be tech champions.[56] Most of them make products or implement information technology systems for companies. And, unlike Creative's Sound Blaster, they do not come up with innovative products that dominate the world. A Singaporean biomedical engineering researcher based in the United States commented on this:

> The successful examples of startup companies will serve to motivate more of the same, and this is [where] I believe ... the efforts should be focused ... technologies made in Singapore. I [saw] only a handful of such companies when I searched the startup database in Singapore, and even so, they tend to revolve around consumer type electronics that are more me-toos rather than innovative. Until Singaporeans achieve ... confidence in their own technical abilities, they'll always look to others with envy.

The acquisition of Singapore start-up Zopim — well-known for its live customer support chat widget and described by *TechinAsia* as the "darling of Singapore's start-ups" — by San Francisco's Zendesk for $37 million in March 2014 is a clear testimony to Singapore's capability to produce notable champions in the business of digital information software technology.[57] The company's new owner has filed for a public listing on the New York Stock Exchange, where it hopes to raise US$150 million. Another homegrown "fairy tale" success has been that of Secretlab, the start-up that builds gaming chairs. Its Throne V1 gaming chairs were snapped up at launch and the company broke even within a month. New innovative products — Throne V2 and the premium Omega — were introduced in October 2015, providing gamers and office workers with more choices. There is also the homegrown online retailer Honestbee, which recently expanded its grocery shopping services to Hong Kong and raised US$15 million in funding. In terms of individual technopreneurship success, the outstanding example is that of Tan Chade Meng, a software engineer who was with Google when the company was still an unknown. When Google went public, Tan became an instant multi-millionaire and he is now semi-retired at a relatively young age. One can argue that he was at the right place and the right time. One could also argue that if Singapore has once produced a "Jolly Good Fellow" (the designation on Tan's name card), surely there is the possibility of another in the making.

The search for the next billion-dollar technology champion continues as the government has increased its efforts to nurture technopreneurship and tech start-ups. There are tech start-ups that have been successful enough to be bought over by more established companies and investors. Singapore-based video streaming provider Viki was acquired by the Japanese e-commerce giant Rakuten for S$255 million — believed to be the biggest start-up acquisition in recent years. However, the founders are not Singaporeans, but Viki tapped on the Singapore Government's pro-entrepreneurship support and the strategic location of the city-state.[58] A Singaporean biomedical engineering researcher based in the United States provided his perspective:

> From what I understand, [the Government] is taking two main routes to promote this [start-ups]. On the one hand they're encouraging institutional researchers to create technologies. The gap I see here is these researchers have a hard time finding industry partners, which is what is needed to develop real world products. On the other hand, the industry incubators are made up of opportunists from outside the country … venture companies from the Silicon Valley [who are] more than happy to take the government's money to invest in transplanted start-ups. The [venture capitalists'] motivations are very different than entrepreneurs who have genuine interests in developing their own

ideas. So unless there are startup founders to seek out in the local scene, you'll end up with nothing more than foreign companies moving their base to Singapore for financial reasons.[59]

Indeed, the city-state is seen as a springboard into the region. Foreign start-ups are eyeing Singapore as an Asian hub for their operations in Asia, aiming at largely the Chinese and Indian markets. As part of Singapore's "Smart Nation" initiative, the government openly invites technoprenuers and investors from around the globe to use Singapore as a test bed of urban challenges, such as healthcare, transportation and an ageing population.[60] With the influx of foreign innovators into the Singapore start-up scene, competing for the available funds, the already small number of indigenous start-ups is finding it tough going.

TECHNOLOGICAL START-UP BLUES

It is widely recognized that Singapore is one of the easiest places in the world to start a company or business. In a 2014 study that assessed the attractiveness of doing business for the next five years by the Economist Intelligence Unit (EIU), Singapore emerged as the best place in the world to do business, ahead of perennial rival Hong Kong.[61] One can submit an online application and receive approval within twenty-four hours. It is little wonder then that foreign investors and technopreneurs take advantage of the situation. Singapore is the number one location for start-ups in Southeast Asia, with about forty per cent of all start-up acquisitions in the region taking place in the city-state.[62] Nonstop Games — a gaming start-up launched by four Finnish gaming enthusiasts — set up shop in 2011, and in August 2014 the company was bought over by King Digital Entertainment (developer of the Candy Crush Saga game) for $125 million. While Singaporeans do venture into running their own businesses in services and retail, tech start-ups do not come easily. The government has introduced a range of initiatives, including readily available grants, to create a vibrant start-up ecosystem and, in the process, to motivate Singaporeans to venture into ICT and other technology-related start-ups.[63] But the response has been rather subdued. Why is this so? What is still lacking? A reader commented in the *Straits Times* that there were no high-tech innovators for Singapore's Enterprise 50 Awards 2009.[64] Most of the winning firms are in retail and distribution or engineering services. Several reasons have been put forth to explain the phenomenon.

Though the technopreneurship ecosystem in Singapore has matured considerably over the last few years, there is still some way to go before it can become self-reinforcing and self-sustaining. As in Silicon Valley, the ecosystem should create a virtuous cycle where there are enough entrepreneurs, skills and funding — and for every young company that dies, at least one starts. While the two main universities — NUS and NTU — actively encourage and sprout start-ups, many of these are dependent on continual funding from the university to stay afloat. Although university researchers would like to have their discoveries commercialized, business collaboration between them and industry is often hampered by the thorny issue of intellectual property; that is, the ownership of the fruit of their collaboration. Many of these researchers have a deep passion for their work and, in the words of a Singaporean based in the United States, "have the ambitions and abilities to compete with leaders in their fields [but] the disconnect again is in how to translate these research into end user products. This is true whether you're in the US or elsewhere, but in the case of [the] Singapore research ecosystem, the lack of market and user base is limiting their understanding of end user needs."[65] To circumvent this issue, NTU created NTUitive, a company formed in April 2014 to turn innovative ideas by its start-ups into commercial businesses. It offers mentors with experience in starting and running technology businesses to help the start-ups and spin-offs refine and validate business ideas. The government, too, is linking up with British-based Entrepreneur First to provide lessons on how to be an entrepreneur. The six-month programme is aimed at plugging a gap, as few computer scientists, engineers and software developers make the leap into becoming entrepreneurs.[66]

Nevertheless, there is one perennial barrier to entrepreneurship and the rapid growth of a start-up culture — the risk-averse attitude of Singaporeans.[67] As explained by U.S.-based venture capitalist Ike Lee, founders of start-ups usually have plenty of passion, but their tendency to focus on short-term success rather than long-term strategy means failure is often inevitable.[68] The fear of failure, particularly among the Singaporean youth, is real. This attribute is largely the result of the environment of their upbringing, where parents tend to be protective, or even overprotective, of their children. Success in examinations and in landing a well-paid job brings pride to the family, whilst failure means a loss of "face". Societal pressure to "make it" forces Singaporeans, especially those from the poorer families, to quickly earn a stable wage rather than starting a business that may not guarantee an income for the first few years. An appetite for risk and a tolerance for failure are not part of the Singaporean DNA. University graduates, more often than not, aim to land their first job in MNCs; and for the government scholars, their career paths as technocrats in the Civil Service are already planned. In their study on the entrepreneurial interests of university students in Singapore, Wang and Wong found that while the desire among undergraduates to be "their own boss" is high, many will not actually take the plunge due to inadequate business knowledge and perceived risk.[69] In another study, by Koh and Wong, it was found that the length of formal education reduces the propensity for entrepreneurship, and that the presence of MNCs provides ample opportunities for graduates to find high-paying jobs.[70] For the individuals who are risk-takers and willing to embark on their own business-to-consumers (B2C) ventures, funding is always a critical "make or break" factor.[71] The key common element behind global technology brands like Amazon, YouTube and WhatsApp has been the availability of substantial funding in the pre-revenue or loss-making stage, easily amounting to tens or hundreds of millions, till the point where such firms have over five million users. Clearly, to incubate a successful local B2C brand, it is necessary to have a larger risk appetite and sufficient funding before the revenue starts to flow. But such a shift in the funding mindset of risk-averse Singapore society is not easily come by.

The Singapore technology start-up scene also needs angel investors able to give "wings" to new firms, such as China's Lee Kai–Fu, a high-profile information technology professional and former head of Google China. Lee created Innovation Works in 2009 to act as an incubator for entrepreneurial young Chinese people with innovative business ideas to initiate start-ups. Innovation Works provides them with all-round support, including recruiting people, product manufacturing, management, and financial and legal consultancy.[72] Individuals like Lee could contribute to Singapore's entrepreneurial ecosystem by training and mentoring local talent, providing capital and growing the entrepreneurship community. While in Singapore individuals such as Lee are not easy to come by, small and medium-sized local firms that are keen to adopt innovative growth strategies could seek to be mentored and funded by organizations like Heliconia, a government-funded entity launched in 2010. With government capital of $250 million, Heliconia seeks to invest in promising local firms and nurture them to become globally competitive players.

One critical dampener to the creation of a technologically productive ecosystem in Singapore is the lack of risk-tolerant financing or funding. From 1983 to 1992 the venture capital industry enjoyed rapid growth, from $47.6 million in 1983 to $2,643 million in 1992, indicating that Singapore had been developing into a hub for regional fund management and investment activities. However, unlike countries like Israel and Taiwan, Singapore's venture capital is best considered as supply-pushed; that is, driven by the government rather than demand-pull, as driven by the demand of start-ups and entrepreneurs. Koh and Wong attribute this trend to several factors; namely, the lack of a large base of entrepreneurs, high opportunity costs for people to venture into start-ups and the lack of indigenous R&D activities.[73] While there are angel investors willing to provide seed funds for suitable start-ups, the availability of huge funds at the stage after seed funding and incubation where start-ups are in the early growth stage but in danger of falling off the cliff due to a lack of financing — what investors called the "valley of death" gap — does not come by easily.[74] The decision by Singapore venture capital firm Vertex Venture (which once supported Creative Technology) to create a $100 million fund to help local start-ups in the infocomm technology and healthcare sectors to survive the "valley of death" finance gap is a boon to entrepreneurship.[75] It is also no secret that venture capitalists shy away from Singapore because there is a lack of promising start-ups with potential for global impact. According to angel investor Leslie Loh, there are basic criteria that venture capitalists will look for: innovative and differentiated product, a profitable and scalable market, a committed and passionate leadership and an appropriate risk-return profile.[76] An interesting cultural trait that relates to the requesting of funding support by Singaporeans was also highlighted by the R&D director of a bioengineering start-up. Unlike foreigners, locals are very conservative when it comes to asking for money. More often than not the amount requested is barely sufficient to cover operating and developmental costs. There is also a deep sense of moral obligation to "give back" in return for the financial support. Consequently, the fear of failure and stress imposed on the start-up to succeed is high. He cited the case of a neighbouring start-up run by expatriates who boldly requested substantial funding and explicitly informed the investor that they were not likely to come up with an end product.[77] Indeed, there were cases of local start-ups who garnered funds but failed to deliver on end products.

Pirate3D was often heralded as an exemplary technological innovation start-up by Singaporean technopreneurs. Its "Made-in-Singapore" Buccaneer is touted as one of the world's most affordable 3D printers for home use. The company garnered US$1.5 million in funds from backers from around the world.[78] The locally made 3D printer even managed to get a foothold in the tough Japanese retail market when Yamad-Denki, one of the largest consumer electronics retailer chains in Japan, agreed to carry the printer in two hundred of its stores for demonstration. Unfortunately, Pirate3D has spent the last few years deflecting its commitment to deliver the Buccaneer to its backers. To compound its already weakened image, the company announced in October 2015 that it is discontinuing production of its original product and is attempting to initiate another round of fundraising to make an even better one.[79] The story of Fusion Garage is another popularly cited case of technological start-ups that went awfully wrong. In 2009 it partnered U.S.-based technology blog TechCrunch to develop the long-awaited CrunchPad tablet computer. Despite not having an actual unit, the hardware device was recognized for its potential for Internet surfing. Fusion Garage later pulled out of the collaboration and the CrunchPad was never produced. But Fusion Garage proceeded to announce a new product called the JooJoo tablet and promised backers the production of a fully functional product. Like the Buccaneer, there was a long delay and the JooJoo tablet never saw the light of day. Fusion Garage went into liquidation with reported debts of US$40 million.[80] Some observers would argue that the technopreneurs behind Pirate3D and Fusion Garage are rightly showing their resilience in making comebacks from repeated failures — commonly seen as hallmarks of successful technological ventures. But others would argue that there are moral and business obligations to fulfil, and by not doing so, such companies are sullying the name of all Singapore start-ups.

While the two cases illustrate the uncertainties and risk of technological product innovation, companies and start-ups seeking to create some level of innovation leadership and create new product categories have to break free of their current hardware-centric models and find ways to collaborate with partners, within and outside the organization. Today, the digitization of the electronic industry means that hardware is commoditizing much more quickly than in the past, while software capabilities are becoming more important than hardware engineering ones. Successful and sustainable innovations usually originate in superior customer insights and creative business models rather than technical breakthroughs.

LEARNING FROM SOUTH KOREA

In the early decades after independence, Singapore looked much to Japan for inspiration and strategies for economic growth, especially in setting its technological growth trajectory. In the twenty-first century, perhaps the city-state could look to the once "Hermit Kingdom" — South Korea — for some fresh inspiration. There is much the world can learn from a country that was able to successfully transform itself from a nation of imitators of imported technologies to one defined by innovators, one able to come to dominate the video game industry and to export its *hallyu* culture far and wide.[81] The case of South Korea illustrates the central role of government in creating a sustainable, innovation-led growth pathway. The Korean government takes the initiative to develop policies to push the country's technological frontier out far and wide. After bringing the country to the forefront of cutting edge technology, the Korean government, under the current president Park Guen-hye, is now taking bold and definitive steps to ensure that the twenty-first century becomes known as "Korea's Century". The target is to build a "Creative Economy" through the new ministry, known as the Ministry of Science, ICT and Future Planning, pumping in 3.3 trillion won (S$4 billion) to nurture start-ups over the next three years. In the ministry's website, the "Creative Economy" is described: "The creative asset that combines a creative idea, imagination, and ICT plays a pivotal role in stimulating start-ups. New growth strategies can be mapped out to create many high-quality jobs through the convergence with existing industries, which in turn leads to the emergence of new markets and industries."[82] Riding on its huge success of exporting K-pop culture and entertainment to the world, the South Korean government is now taking up another creative challenge — to export the model the country had successfully used to transform itself into a nation of world-class innovators to the world's developing countries. This is packaged into a knowledge-sharing "wealth kit", a combination of a Samuel Smile's type of self-help read and the Marshall Plan. The topics addressed include funding, the advice of nation-building experts, and strategies. The core component is the advice that all countries should build government-funded research and policy institutes whose sole purpose is to transform the country from Third World to First World status. Such a bold government-led initiative has significant positive multiplier effects, ranging from the establishing of business partnerships between South Korea and other countries to the purchasing by these other countries of Korean products. It is no accident that Google formally opened its first Asian start-up "campus" in Seoul's Gangnam district in May 2015.[83] Euny Hong explains the success of branding and marketing Korean innovations by the Korean government:

> Nearly every Korean triumph … is attributable to this highly paternalistic, mostly benevolent system of what one might call "voluntary coercion". Korea's recent boom in manufacturing, Samsung's success switching from food to semiconductors, the nation's massive Internet infrastructure, and widespread export of pop culture — all of these aspects came about because of the Korean attitude that what's good for the country is good for business and what's good for business is what's good for the individual. Koreans don't see profit as a zero-sum game, to use an economics term — that is no one party has to profit at the expense of the other; everyone can win.[84]

Interestingly, one is reminded that the Singapore Government, too, is widely regarded as paternalistic and benevolent. Some policies were draconic but, in the eyes of the political leaders, were for the good of the people. And it runs the Singapore economy like a "Singapore Incorporated". Singaporeans too were told that through hard work and diligence, everyone can win. The ideology of survival, so strongly ingrained in Singapore society in the early decades of independence, is still a significant driving force behind Singaporeans' quest for economic status, albeit now in a "First World" environment.

All said, by and large, Singaporeans are creative people. There are individuals who have made a name for themselves in the world of the arts, fashion, entertainment and gaming. Creative urban planning, water management and environmental landscaping are also areas where Singapore has attracted a lot of world attention. Notable academics and scientists from all over the world are also attracted to have a teaching or research stint in Singapore's universities. However, to be able to produce someone in the mould of the late Steve Jobs seems remote. And while occasionally there are media reports of local research labelled as "breakthroughs", the reality is that there is still some distance to run before Singapore could claim a podium finish in the world of innovations in science and technology. Yet, like Hong Kong, Singapore is one of the richest countries in the world with huge foreign reserves — thanks to its historical and present role as one of the world's prolific service-brokerage centres.

Notes

1. Masanori Moritani, *Japanese Technology and its Transfer to Singapore*, Working Paper, Policy and Management Research Department (Nomura Research Institute, August 1982). Together with Masao Igarashi, the two experts on Japanese industrial success were invited by the Singapore Government for a dialogue with local entrepreneurs and senior government officials in August 1982. See also *Straits Times*, 9 August 1982 and 27 September 1982.
2. Ibid., p. 3.
3. Ibid., p. 4.
4. Mah Bow Tan, *Parliamentary Debates*, Offical Report, Singapore, 21 March 1989, col. 613.
5. Lee Kuan Yew, *From Third World to First: The Singapore Story 1965–2000* (Singapore: Straits Times Press, 2000), p. 587.
6. <http://www.todayonline.com/voices/what price-innovation-spore> (accessed 7 April 2014).
7. M. Porter, *Competitive Advantage of Nations* (New York: The Free Press, 1990), p. 566.
8. Ibid., pp. 554–55.
9. *Straits Times*, 1 April 1983.
10. *Straits Times*, 22 April 1985

11. *Straits Times*, 9 May 1986.

12. Economic Strategies Committee, *High Skill People, Innovative Economy, Distinctive Global City* (Singapore: Ministry of Trade and Industry, February 2010).

13. Interview with the author, 1 April 2014. See also the *Straits Times*, 19 July 2013 for a report on the start-up.

14. J. Mokyr, *The Lever of Riches: Technological Creativity and Economic Progress* (Oxford: Oxford University Press, 1990), p. 154.

15. Ibid., pp. 11–12.

16. Ibid.

17. Erik Brynjolfsson and Andrew McAfee, *The Second Machine Age: Work, Progress, and Prosperity in a Time of Brilliant Technologies* (New York: Norton, 2014).

18. James W. Dearing, *Growing a Japanese Science City: Communication in Scientific Research* (New York: Routledge, 1995).

19. Taichi Sakaiya, *What is Japan? Contradictions and Transformations*, translated by Steven Karpa (Kodansha International, 1993), pp. 219–29.

20. Angela Jeffs, "Genius at Work", *Asia Magazine*, 1–2 July 1994, p. 12.

21. Shintaro Ishihara, *The Japan That Can Say No*, translated by Frank Baldwin (Simon and Schuster, 1991), pp. 37–38.

22. M.O. Kim and S. Jaffe, "*The New Korea: An Inside Look at South Korea's Economic Rise* (New York: Amacom, 2010), pp. 150–51.

23. Earl H. Kinmonth, "Japanese Engineers and American Myth Makers", *Pacific Affairs* 64, no. 3 (1991): 337.

24. G. Tassey, *Technology Infrastructure Technological Infrastructure Policy: An International Perspective* (Dordrecht: Kluwer Academic, 1996), pp. 244–45.

25. See Doreen Massey, *High-tech Fantasies: Science Parks in Society, Science, and Space* (London: Routledge, 1992); Daniel Felsenstein, "University-related Science Parks – 'Seedbeds' or 'Enclaves' of Innovation?", *Technovation* 12, no. 2 (1994): 93–110.

26. Anna L. Saxenian, *Regional Advantage: Culture and Competition in Silicon Valley and Route 128* (Cambridge, MA: Harvard University Press, 1996).

27. M. Castells and P. Hall, *Technopoles of the World* (London: Routledge, 1994), p. 234.

28. Mae Phillips Su Ann and Henry Yeung Wai-Chung, "A Place for R&D? The Singapore Science Park", *Urban Studies* 40, no. 4 (2003): 710.

29. Ibid., p. 722.

30. Ibid., pp. 723–24.

31. Thomas O. Eisemon and Charles H. Davis, "Universities and Scientific Capacity", *Journal of Asian and African Studies* 27, nos. 1–2 (1992): 68–93.

32. *Straits Times*, 24 August 1994.

33. <http:www.nature.com/press_rleases/media-pitches.html> (accessed 4 April 2015).
34. Ibid.
35. *Straits Times*, 20 June 2015.
36 <http://www.topuniversities.com/university-rankings/university-subject-rankings/2015/eng> (accessed 29 April 2015).
37. Ibid.
38. See Florida, *The Creative Class Revisited* and <http://www.citylab.com/work/2011/10/global-creativity-index/229/>.
39. <http://www.globalinnovationindex.org/content/page/GII-Home>.
40. Ibid.
41. *Straits Times*, 2 April 2014. The top seven nations are all in Asia: Singapore, South Korea, Japan, Macau, Hong Kong, Shanghai and Taipei. However, for the MIT's Andrew McAfee, Singapore's PISA performance does not imply that the education system is good at encouraging this kind of creativity and innovation. See the *Straits Times*, 2 March 2014.
42. Ibid.
43. *Straits Times*, 13 May 2015. The school rankings are based on an amalgamation of international assessments, including the OECD's Pisa tests, the TIMSS test run by U.S.-based academics and TERCE tests in Latin America, putting developed and developing countries in a single scale.
44. See Kishore Mahbubani, *Can Asians Think* (Singapore: Marshall Cavendish, 2009).
45. *Straits Times*, 5 May 2004.
46. <http://www.wipo.int/ipstats/en/statistics/country_profile/countries/sg.html> (accessed 16 April 2014). See also *Straits Times*, 16 August 2012.
47. *Sunday Times*, 21 September 2014.
48. *National R&D Survey of Singapore 2002 and 2013*, Agency for Science, Technology and Research, Singapore.
49. See P.A. Herbig and F. Palumbo, "The Effect of Culture on the Adoption Process", *Technological Forecasting and Social Change*, vol. 46 (1994): 78.
50. Chris Anderson, *Makers: The New Industrial Revolution* (London: Random House, 2012), p. 108.
51. <http://www.gemconsortium.org/country-profile/105>.
52. Eric Schmidt and Jared Cohen, *The New Digital Age: Reshaping the Future of People, Nations and Business* (London: Murray, 2013).
53. See <http://www.straitstimes.com/news/opinion/more-opinion-stories/story/how-singapore became-a-hub-for-tech-start-ups>.
54. See <http://www.economist.com/news/special-report/21593582–what-entrepreneurial-ecosystems-need-to-flourish>.
55. Anderson, *Makers*, pp. 50–51.

56. In the world of high-technology business, "sexy" would be companies like Google, Facebook, Groupon and LinkedIn. They are software players that turn bits and bytes into high-volume, high-margin tech services. They are global brands, highly publicized, and touch consumers worldwide. In June 2014, shares of the semiconductor packaging firm Stats ChipPAC nosedived 10 per cent as the prospect of a takeover fizzled. See the *Straits Times*, 13 June 2014.

57. <http://www.techinasia.com/singapores-zopim-acquired-sendesk/> (accessed 28 April 2014). The Singapore company was started in 2008 by four NUS graduates and came out of beta two years later. The founders struggled in the early going, paying themselves a meagre $410 a month for two years. The company received only about US$400,000 seed funding from the Media Development Authority (MDA), Spring Singapore and NUS Enterprise. Since 2010 its growth has accelerated, becoming one of the most well-used support chat widgets around the world.

58. *Straits Times*, 3 September 2013.

59. Email interview with the author, 31 October 2014.

60. *Straits Times*, 21 April 2015.

61. *Straits Times*, 22 May 2014 and 3 July 2014.

62. *Sunday Times*, 28 September 2014.

63. Government funding Series A (Feasibility Stage), B (Product Development) and C (Product Commercialization) for the various stages of the start-up ventures is generous from such agencies as the National Research Foundation, Spring and the Infocomm Development Authority (IDA).

64. *Straits Times*, 6 November 2009.

65. Email interview with the author, 31 October 2014.

66. *Straits Times*, 21 April 2015.

67. Interestingly, this risk-averse and *kiasi* culture was also exhibited in Singapore's general election in September 2015. Besides other factors, the fear that the opposition was gaining strong ground instigated voters to opt for the safer route; that is, to support the ruling party that has led the country to its "First World" status. There are just too many risks in nurturing a strong opposition presence in Parliament.

68. *Straits Times*, 3 July 2014.

69. C.K. Wang and P.K. Wong, "Entrepreneurial Interest of University Students in Singapore", *Technovation*, vol. 24 (February 2004): 163–72.

70. Winston T.H. Koh and P.K. Wong, "Competing at the Frontier: The Changing Role of Technology Policy in Singapore's Economic Strategy", *Technological Forecasting and Social Change* 72, no. 3 (2005): 255–85.

71. Business-to-Consumers, or B2C, is business or transactions conducted directly between a company and consumers who are the end-users of the

products or services. B2C as a business model differs significantly from the business-to-business model, which refers to commerce between two or more businesses. The term B2C became immensely popular during the dotcom boom of the late 1990s, when it was used mainly to refer to online retailers, as well as other companies that sold products and services to consumers through the Internet. Although numerous B2C companies fell victim to the subsequent dotcom bust as investor interest in the sector dwindled and venture capital funding dried up, B2C leaders such as Amazon.com and Priceline.com survived the shakeout and went on to rank among the most successful companies in the world.

72. *China Daily*, 13 December 2012.
73. Winston T.H. Koh and P.K. Wong, *The Venture Capital Industry in Singapore: A Comparative Study with Taiwan and Israel on the Government's Role*, Working Paper (NUS Entrepreneurship Centre, May 2005), p. 25.
74. Angel investors are usually wealthy people who help entrepreneurs that they believe in to start businesses by funding them.
75. *Straits Times*, 11 January 2014.
76. *Straits Times*, 19 December 2012.
77. Interview with the author, 17 June 2014.
78. *Straits Times*, 14 April 2014. The company was aiming to be listed on the U.S.-based Nasdaq stock exchange by 2015.
79. See <https://en.wikipedia.org/wiki/The_Buccaneer_(3D_printer)> (accessed 30 October 2015) and *Straits Times*, 28 October 2015.
80. *Today*, 15 December 2009 and *Straits Times*, 28 October 2015.
81. For a fascinating account of the rise and rise of K-pop culture in the world, see Euny Hong, *The Birth of Korean Cool: How One Nation is Conquering the World through Pop Culture* (New York: Picador, 2014).
82. <http://english.msip.go.kr/english/wpge/m_74/eng010101.do> (accessed 1 October 2014).
83. *Straits Times*, 9 May 2015.
84. Hong, *Birth of Korean Cool*, p. 249.

8

CONCLUSION
Power of a Service-Brokerage Culture

Singapore's Research, Innovation & Enterprise (RIE) 2015 Plan targets to develop the nation into one of the world's leading research-intensive, innovative and entrepreneurial economies. The Singapore Government will invest $16.1 billion over 2011–15 as part of its RIE$ 2015 plan.[1] This is 20 per cent increase over 2006–10 and demonstrates Singapore's continued commitment to both basic and mission-oriented research for public sector institutions. The city-state is reviewing its science and technology programmes and policies ahead of the 2015 tranche of science funding, which could be up to $20 billion. In 2012 gross expenditure on R&D (GERD) was $7.2 billion, or 2.1 per cent of GDP.[2] This is on par with the GERD figures of small advanced nations such as Israel and Sweden.

Notwithstanding the government's deep commitment to research, innovation and enterprise, Singapore's S&T policy is still highly dependent on foreign inputs. While the government can pump in money to sustain research conducted at the various A*Star institutes and universities, the reality is that it is a huge challenge for the small island nation to achieve scientific and technological self-reliance, as managed by small countries like Israel, Japan, Taiwan and South Korea. Moreover, the transfer and diffusion of scientific and technological knowledge and skills owned by the foreign experts to local Singaporeans is never guaranteed. There is also no critical mass of Singapore-born scientists and research engineers. The number of Singaporeans and permanent resident RSEs actually declined by 1.5 per cent from 21,702 in 2011 to 21,380 in 2012. On the other hand, the number of foreign RSEs grew by 12.2 per cent during the same period.[3] Although the problem can be somewhat alleviated by the "foreign talents" who eventually decide to become Singapore citizens, this pathway could add to the already contentious issue of the government giving away jobs to foreign nationals.[4] Particularly in the biomedical sector, the limited number of Singaporean scientists is also compounded by the problem of Singaporeans generally not being keen to pursue higher degrees and to undertake R&D activities. To top it off, the returns on investment in biomedical R&D is unpredictable. In short, Singapore's aggressive foray into biomedical research could, at best, achieve its aim of luring the big names in pharmaceutical manufacturing to set up shop in Singapore and, in the process, contribute to the national wealth.

Going forward, the city-state will aim to sustain its globally competitive, high-value manufacturing sector at between 20 to 25 per cent of the economy. The shift is now towards complex manufacturing — areas where know-how and intellectual property are crucial, such as nutriceuticals, the design and production of "mission-critical" components such as those in medical devices, and cross disciplinary areas like bioelectronics. However, despite the huge financial outlay and a string of policies to nurture an R&D and technology innovative culture, Singapore has some distance to go before joining the big boys in churning out cutting-edge technological innovations. The city-state is also facing competition from "second-tier" cities in China (particularly Suzhou, Hangzhou, Chengdu and Xian), which are enticing clusters of foreign technology companies to set up R&D facilities there.[5] These cities offer a large pool of relevant talent, lower operating costs and local industrial support. Samsung Electronics opened two research centres in Xian in 2012. While the Singapore Government is pushing hard to develop an indigenous, technologically driven, entrepreneurial sector, there are historical patterns that would continue to influence and ensure the sustainable development of the Singapore economy.

CONTINUATION OF HISTORICAL PATTERNS

In line with Jeffrey Sachs' argument that political institutions alone cannot explain the existence of rich and poor nations in the world, in the case of Singapore, besides the existence of inclusive institutions for all, geography too plays a significant role in explaining its economic success.[6] Indeed, it is the root advantageous factor of Singapore's economic success. The importance of Singapore's geographical location at the crossroads of trade routes in Southeast Asia and the heart of the Malaysia–Indonesia Archipelago is often cited by historians as being critical to the colony's meteoric rise in the nineteenth century. In the fourteenth century, Singapore was already a popular trading node in the Malay–Indonesian archipelago.[7] Economists and geographers have always acknowledged that economic growth is driven by and spread from specific regions, cities or even neighbourhoods. Writing in 1987, Philippe Regnier's explanation for the island's rise to economic eminence centred on its strategic geographical position that enabled her to tap on regional trade.[8] Singapore's strategic location and its connectivity enabled it to connect many parts of Asia, which has put it at a great advantage. Michael Porter, too, has reiterated the importance of Singapore's location in gaining a competitive advantage in the shipping industry.[9] Hence, one development is quite certain — the role of the port will continue to be a significant contributor to the wealth of the city-state, or, as the *Straits Times* accurately describes, "Singapore's port is a microcosm of its economic trajectory over the decades, mirroring ingrained outward impulses and forward-looking strategies, a sine qua non for survival."[10]

The port of Singapore has had a long historical development.[11] As part of the British Empire the port served as a crucial trading and refuelling station for Britain's merchant ships plying the high seas. The port was the pride of the British governors and traders. Since the days of Keppel Harbour, the port had kept pace with technological changes over the years. Indeed, it can be argued that the relentless pursuit of the latest in maritime technology by the Port of Singapore Authority (PSA) has been one of the crucial factors in sustaining the competitiveness of the port. Also significant has been the PSA's efforts to train its staff and to develop their skills in the area of in-house port innovation, and to develop a corporate culture which is conducive to technological change. It has been an indigenous R&D effort to adapt and improve on imported technology to suit local needs.[12] Since the 1980s, several in-house technological innovations have heralded significant success for the port. Portnet, the port's information system that connects the PSA to all its customers and the shipping community was launched in 1987. It gave rise to paperless documentation and improved accuracy and speed of information exchange and transactions. The use of the Computer Integrated Terminal Operations System (CITOS) and the Computer Integrated Marine Operations System (CIMOS) were implemented by the end of the 1980s. CITOS supports the planning, command/control and execution of all container-handling operations, while CIMOS helps to manage and monitor the growing shipping traffic and port activities in the Singapore Strait. In 1997 the Flow-Through Gate system, a fully automated system that identifies container trucks and gives drivers instructions within twenty-five seconds, was introduced. The Remote Crane Operations & Control (RCOC) system, introduced in 2000, enabled the PSA to move away from the conventional yard operations where every yard crane has an operator. The operator only handles the mounting or offloading of containers at the chassis lane. The rest of the action is fully automated by the overhead bridge cranes (OHBC). With RCOC, a sixfold increase in productivity has been achieved.[13] In short, the PSA is an unparalleled example of an indigenous organization making a successful transition from "imitators to innovators".

Technological innovations have given the port unsurpassed connectivity with other ports around the world. The Singapore Port and the maritime industry as a whole were given a strong boost with the formation of the Maritime and Port Authority of Singapore (MPA) on 2 February 1996. The mission of the MPA is to develop Singapore as a premier global hub port and international maritime centre and to advance and safeguard Singapore's strategic maritime interests. As part of its job to develop Singapore as a premier global hub port and maritime centre, the MPA supports investments in R&D. With the help of the $150 million Maritime Innovation and Technology Fund, the MPA has built up maritime R&D capabilities in many areas, such as automation, simulation and modelling, data analytics tools, and ideas and strategies to meet environmental rules and reduce energy costs.

Today, despite facing increasing competition from neighbouring ports, particularly Malaysia's Port of Tanjung Pelepas in Johor, the PSA is able to hold its ground as one of the world's busiest ports. Two new terminals were added to the port facilities at Pasir Panjang in June 2015 and will add fifteen million TEUs (twenty-foot equivalent units) to Singapore's handling capacity. This will boost Singapore's container throughput by forty per cent to fifty million TEUs every year. Besides being able to handle the megaships of the future, the new terminals will also have a container yard with automated rail-mounted gantry cranes. These cranes stack containers with the help of computers, sensors and cameras. They are electrically powered and have zero emissions. The Singapore port has consistently clinched the top spots on the rankings of global shipping centres.[14]

Taking advantage of its unique geographical position, the city-state, since the nineteenth century, has developed a strong "middleman", or comprador, role in the region. Today, after nearly two hundred years of its modern history, the strategic location of Singapore is still seen by international investors and multinationals as a "pull" factor to set up their regional headquarters here. During the nineteenth century and the decades before 1940, the strategic location of the island attracted a constant inflow of people from Asia, particularly from southern China and India. It was the centre of the Chinese diaspora to Nanyang, or the "Southern Seas". These were the pioneering builders of modern Singapore. This historical role of Singapore is still actively re-enacted with the migration of international talent from all over the world, motivated by the government's "open-arms" immigration policy. The argument that today's New Economy does not require the knowledge worker to uproot him or herself in order to settle in a new location is not completely convincing. "When the world is flat", as Thomas Friedman argues, "you can innovate without having to emigrate".[15] Technological advances have led to the demise of distance. However, the explosive growth of cities and urban centres worldwide is a strong testimony that those with the skills to market and the financial power to invest will continue to seek out the most appropriate and conducive location to match their economic and social expectations. Hence, what is certain in the decades ahead is that the trading and brokerage culture that was nurtured during the colonial era will continue to impact the wealth-making opportunities not only of Singaporeans but also foreigners who are attracted to the "Smart Nation".

Stephen Hill maintains that cultures are not only resilient, but that they may freeze. By freezing of culture, Hill refers to the situation whereby "the whole inter-connected fabric of meanings, knowledge and actions of the society (or organization) become institutionalized or habituated into a coherent way of doing and interpreting things and thereafter changes with glacial slowness".[16] It is argued here that Singapore's comprador trading and brokerage role has been preserved and, indeed, strengthened and modernized through time. One factor that has contributed to the preservation and expansion of trading and brokering activities is that Singapore, since its colonial days, has been a transnational overseas Chinese business network. The island's geographical position, its excellent telecommunications infrastructure, and a stable political environment have motivated many large Chinese business families in the region to make Singapore their base to develop their commercial and financial activities. Notable examples have included Robin Loh from Indonesia, the Kwek family heading the Hong Leong financial group, banker Khoo Teck Puat, Ng Teng Fong and Malaysia's Kuok family. In his interpretation of history through an analysis of the roles of three castes — the commercial and competitive merchant, the aristocratic and militaristic soldier and the bureaucratic sage — David Priestland describes the merchant as someone who

> is Janus-faced: with his flexibilities, love of networking, willingness to trade with all regardless of class, ethnicity and religion, he shows his "soft" tolerance and liberal face. But he also has a much "harder", more moralistic aspect, apparent when in conflict with others. And so, while his love of efficiency and innovation has undoubtedly helped to enrich mankind as a whole, the merchant's interest in the highest

profit in the quickest time is sometimes difficult to align with the broadest interest of particular communities...[17]

Collectively, the multi-ethnic merchants of Singapore society symbolize the success of hard work, thrift and perseverance reminiscent of the pioneering nineteenth century compradors and the business icons of the 1950s and 1960s. The attraction of Singapore for Chinese capital and the close *guanxi* of Chinese business circles have sustained the role of the city-state and the local bourgeoisie as an intermediary in regional transactions. The accumulation of wealth in individual and family businesses is achieved not through the input of scientific knowledge but through business acumen, catching the right opportunities and plenty of luck.

THE CONTINUAL IMPORTANCE OF THE BROKERAGE-SERVICES SECTOR

Like Hong Kong, the growth engine of Singapore has been the services sector. The sector provides jobs to 80 per cent of 3.03 million workers and employees, and it creates over 70 per cent of GDP. Interestingly, Hong Kong's expenditure on R&D is miniscule compared to that of Singapore. In 2012, Hong Kong's GERD was only 0.73 per cent and it had only 25,264 RSEs.[18] Despite its negligible R&D scene, Hong Kong remains a vibrant economy, supported by myriads of enterprising small and medium companies and its strong financial sector. Forcing Singapore to run a hard race, Hong Kong has also become an international hub for business, trade and finance, with importers keen to access the large hinterland of China. According to the Monetary Authority of Singapore (MAS) in its half-yearly Macroeconomic Review, activity in the services sector will continue to play an increasing role in the economy. The services sector accounted for more than two-thirds (about 72 per cent) of output in 2013.[19] Other than shipping, logistics and storage, banking, finance and insurance make up a large part of the economy. The MAS noted that the country's comparative advantage has been in the provision of "modern services", such as finance and insurance, telecoms and other business services, which grew from 35 to 40 per cent of total services exports between 2003 and 2013.[20]

Another contributor to the rising importance of services exports has been the shift towards a more services-based manufacturing sector, where firms are increasingly providing services that complement the goods they produce.

Singapore's current premier status as the "Switzerland of Asia" and as one of the main financial centres in the world is the result of a decision by the government in the 1960s. The foundation for Singapore's core competencies in trading and services was laid as early as 1968, when the government created the Asian Dollar Market to channel funds for economic development in the region.[21] By 1994, Singapore was the world's fourth-largest foreign exchange trading centre in Asia for trading of international currencies. In the words of Lee Kuan Yew, the task of government is to "emulate the best attributes of the major financial centres — safe haven of Zurich; dynamism of the futures exchanges of Chicago; and the inventiveness of New York and London".[22] Howard Davies, a professor at Sciences Po in Paris, writes, "Hong Kong and Singapore have played their cards astutely. The combination of an Asian market with strong Chinese connections and a system of English law and property rights continues to provide a powerful competitive advantage. This is especially true in fund management. Chinese firms may increasingly raise capital in Shanghai, but wealthy Chinese with money to invest like to hold it in financial centres that are perceived as safe and non-political".[23] Singapore, with its excellent information technology infrastructure, is seen as the springboard for Chinese firms wishing to expand their international influence. In this respect, the Singapore Government has actively played its traditional comprador role to attract Chinese firms and their investments.[24] In October 2014 the Singapore dollar joined the exclusive club of currencies allowed to trade directly with the Chinese yuan. This milestone move was unequivocal recognition of Singapore's role in the internationalization of the yuan and boosted the republic's status as a global financial centre. As the world's second-largest yuan trading hub (after Hong Kong), Singapore attracts China's top entrepreneurs to sink their money in the city-state. Efforts are being made to build up the necessary critical mass of financial analysts, fund managers and investment bankers in order to enhance the country's expertise in fund raising, asset and financial management.

As a global financial hub, Singapore is also well positioned to tap on the rapidly growing use of technology in developing financial innovations, particularly in Africa and Asia's financial markets. Popularly known as fintech, financial technology is a line of business based on using software technology to provide financial services. Fintech companies are generally start-ups founded with the purpose of disrupting incumbent financial systems and corporations that rely less on software.[25] Fintech venture capitalist Vladislav Solodkiy explains his reasons for believing that Singapore is the best place in the world for financial innovation.[26] Singapore markets itself as a "lab" or "test-bed" for entrepreneurs to innovate and commercialize their ideas within a business-friendly environment, topped with stringent intellectual property rights and transparency of financial processes. A $225 million initiative to help financial firms to set up innovation labs and to fund infrastructure to deliver fintech services was launched by the government in June 2015. It is part of the Financial Sector Technology & Innovation (FSTI) scheme aimed at establishing Singapore as a smart financial centre, which is in turn part of the government's "Smart Nation" initiative.[27]

To compete effectively in high-technology competition, Singapore needs to produce more of what Robert Reich terms the "symbolic-analytical solver", notable for their "quality, originality, cleverness, and, occasionally, speed which they solve, identify, or broker new problems".[28] Bill Gates, Jack Ma and the late Steve Jobs are some of the outstanding strategic brokers. Besides the research scientists and professional engineers, also included are investment and financial brokers, consultants, real estate developers, and others who have the ability to "efficiently deploy resources or shift financial assets, or otherwise save time and energy".[29] While Singapore is still hoping to produce a Jack Ma or Steve Jobs, the city-state is certainly not short of symbolic analysts in the increasingly sophisticated and specialized services sector — financial planning, investment banking, logistics, forex trading, advertising, taxation and accounting consulting, legal services in intellectual property, communication and information systems and market research. R&D in the services sector is geared more towards systematizing the delivery process and introducing new technology to enhance productivity. This, too, is an indication of the city-state's efforts in achieving innovation-led growth. As explained by Porter, "Competitive success in the multiple business category and sophisticated general business services is a sign of achieving truly innovation-driven competitive advantage."[30]

Singapore today is still a nation of traders, middlemen and brokers. There are many success stories of Singaporeans gaining much personal wealth through their brokering roles. The use of the so-called "hard sciences" was never a critical component in the growth of these home-grown, largely Chinese-dominated conglomerates, such as the *keiretsu*-type of network of companies established by the late banker Tan Chin Tuan.[31] Journalist Lee Su Shyan writes: "One look at Singapore's league tables of the wealthy and it is clear that this is a nation where creativity and innovation take a back seat to bricks and mortar".[32] The majority of the wealth of Singapore's thirty-two billionaires — and that of the more than 1,300 ultra-rich, with more than US$30 million in net assets (in 2014) — is derived from property and business and financial investments.[33] The number of these self-made wealthy individuals would have been greater if not for the softening of the real estate market and underperforming Asian equities in recent years. They are the icons of Singapore's economic success and are seen by many as benchmarks to aim for. They are the entrepreneurs who created their business empires without resorting to R&D. Only now, in the twenty-first century, are innovations in the form of technological advances in information and communication technologies being actively harnessed to enhance the profitability of their businesses and, in general, the productivity of Singapore's financial and brokerage services sector. Like in Hong Kong, Singapore does have a large pool of home-grown entrepreneurs operating small and medium-sized enterprises. These entrepreneurs, however, are active in every sector except for high-end manufacturing, which requires the input of significant scientific and technological knowledge and skills. An empirical study conducted by Lee and Low on the development of local entrepreneurship in Singapore concluded that while Singapore is not short of entrepreneurs, a majority of them move into commerce and services rather than industry.[34] Rather than inventing things, such people are continuously engaged in managing ideas creatively and meeting peoples' needs.

GOING FORWARD

Singapore is currently shifting towards innovation-led growth. It has generous public funding for basic scientific research conducted in Fusionpolis and the world-class universities. It has a range of policies to nurture an entrepreneurial and start-up culture. It has achieved top rankings in many areas, from economic performance, competitiveness and business environment to quality lifestyles for expatriates.[35] In manufacturing, the shift has been towards very niche, high value-added sectors, such as precision engineering, transport engineering, aerospace, and marine and offshore engineering. For the IT industry, change has come in the shape of a fundamental shift from legacy software and hardware systems to cloud computing, mobile computing and "clean tech". Local manufacturers are encouraged to be innovative, even though the Singapore Manufacturing Federation highlighted a survey which shows that only six per cent of 250 manufacturing firms polled had reinvented aspects of their operations to generate greater value.[36]

To move up the innovation ladder in the decades ahead, the government has announced its strategy will shift from "value-adding" to "value-creating".[37] Essentially, this means moving from merely imitating and improving on existing products and services to reinventing and creating new products and services. Instead of contending with "Made in Singapore", the drive is towards "Create in Singapore". The Japanese and the South Koreans (and, to a certain extent, the Taiwanese) have successfully made the leap — from imitators to innovators. Can Singapore do it too?

There is still some way to go for Singapore to develop a technologically innovative and self-reliant economy. This is due to a complexity of factors. To local manufacturers, instead of nurturing deep technical skills of workers, to innovate and increase productivity usually implies replacing old machinery with the latest technologies. But buying the latest equipment is one thing; having the capacity to maintain and troubleshoot issues with this technology is quite another. It is not surprising that companies need to request technical assistance from the equipment manufacturers to handle breakdowns, because local engineers do not have the capacity to do so. While there is an increasing trend towards reverse engineering, unlike in South Korea the aim is more towards copying and producing similar and cheaper products, not in innovating and producing better products. There is also the lack of a critical mass of indigenous scientists, research engineers, technological entrepreneurs and expert personnel able to advise and complete the tedious transactions of the invention–innovation–commercialization cycle of product development. The limited talent pool for the knowledge-based economy is compounded by the diminishing attractiveness of Singapore as a regional education hub, due to the increasing costs of attending higher education and the priority of the labour market to employ Singapore citizens. It is becoming more difficult for those foreign students who enjoyed subsidized university fees to find employment in order to serve their three-year bonds to work in Singapore after graduation.

There is also the continual attraction of a lucrative service-brokerage sector that lures away science and engineering graduates. This is because the motivations of Singaporeans are too deeply rooted in the culture and history of the city-state. Like it or not, the majority of pragmatic Singaporeans aim for economic stability, and not at delving into such uncertainties as exist in R&D activities, hoping for technological breakthroughs. The dream of the 5Cs (cash, car, condominium, credit card and country club) in Singapore is still very applicable. The pragmatic society also promotes the practices that, first, "it is better to work on something which has the backing of the government and which can guarantee some gains", and second, "to wait until someone has done it before joining in". Such risk-averse or "play-safe" attitudes are a reflection of the *kiasu-kiasi* spirit which has caused "the withering away of Singaporean creativity".[38]

While there is a need to upgrade the skills of Singaporeans to handle the challenges of a technologically advanced economy, in the decades ahead, Singapore's growth strategy will be to continue to tap on its historical strengths and the cultural attributes of its people. The economic planners are right to forge ahead in making Singapore a leading global financial and business and logistics hub that connects the global and Asian business communities. This is Singapore's modern comprador role writ large. And, in Temasek Holdings, Singapore has its own brokering and investment house and a major player in international investing, jostling with Hong Kong tycoons, Arab sheikhs and other big players. It recently announced that it will pump $857 million into Vertex Venture Holdings, Singapore's largest and oldest venture capital firm, so that it can be a global player.[39] The infusion of funds will allow Vertex Venture Holdings to invest in start-ups in the hot seats of innovation and technological disruption — the United States, Israel and China — after having been mainly focused on Singapore. There are also many successful local companies who perform the middleman role, as an interface between the downstream customer and the upstream supplier, sourcing for materials and services required by the customer from nooks and corners of the world. The city-state aims to become an innovation centre for multinationals, the base for global players seeking to tap into opportunities offered by a rising Asia, and for Asian enterprises looking to expand beyond their home markets. Tapping on its geographical position and its pro-business environment, more firms across diverse sectors — from pharmaceuticals and manufacturing to consumer goods and marketing — are moving their core operations to the region and catering to Asian markets. Singapore can serve as a vital nerve centre where ideas for new products and services can be born, tested and eventually commercialized for sale in the region and around the world.

To support Singapore's innovation-driven growth, the educated Singaporean has the intelligence, values and attributes to become Reich's "symbolic analysts and brokers" and Florida's "creative class" in business and trade. They need not be technological experts. The real value these people add to the economy derives instead from their creativity — their insights into what can be done in a particular medium (such as software, music, entertainment, physics, etc.), what can be done for a particular market and how best to organize work. They are what Robert Reich terms as the "geeks" and "shrinks" of today's knowledge economy — the "masters of innovation, and innovation lies at the heart of the new economy".[40] And the Singapore Government is creating a "creative place" for its creative class to grow and flourish. The highly urbanized city-state aims to showcase an ecosystem that invests in and harnesses talent and attracts and energizes new entrants to the creative class. As suggested by the late Lee Kuan Yew, Singapore can have its "little bohemias" where the stifling sense of discipline and order can give way to creative chaos so as to generate innovation, stimulate entrepreneurship and ultimately spawn its own Silicon Valley.[41] Critics will argue that it is not going to be easy for Singapore to clone a Richard Florida's type of creative functional city after decades of social engineering by the government. Clearly, to nurture the growth of a "Creative Singapore" where all Singaporeans are creative people, the starting point of the journey has to be its education system. Singapore's brand of education has often been cited as a high-performing system, producing students who excel in international tests. But despite all the accolades, the system is still largely perceived as one that stifles creativity — even at the preschool level. The important development, however, is that the government is moving towards achieving its aspiration of making the city-state a place where people can generate creative ideas and put them into use. The Dutch sociologist best known for her work on globalization, Saskia Sessen, has earmarked Singapore as one of the world's top three niche global cities that offer specialized knowledge for the global world — notably port management and financial services — and where people from all over the world choose to come to live and work.[42]

It would be an interesting case study of whether a small nation, devoid of any natural resources and historically developed as a trading port and brokerage hub, is able to morph into a nation of scientific and technological innovators. Singapore's investment-driven economy has successfully attracted high-tech companies to set up shop in the country. What remains to be seen is the outcome of Singapore's highly proactive R&D policy that aims at achieving indigenous innovation-driven economic growth. While the impact of historical antecedents might soften as time passes, history and culture are significant factors for Singapore's leaders to consider in the nation's quest for technological creativity. While historically Singapore is not known as an engineering powerhouse, in the same way as it is recognized as a global brokerage and financial centre, the nation's early ventures in port management, oil refinery and water management in the twentieth century laid a strong foundation for the city-state's current technological prowess in these fields. In the words of the late Lee Kuan Yew, "[i]t takes more than one generation for the political, economic, social and cultural implications of policies to work themselves out".[43] It has taken one generation for the city-state to transform itself from "The Third World to the First". Perhaps, the same would be needed for Singapore to be transformed from a nation of traders to a nation of technological innovators.

Notes

1. <http://www.nrf.gov.sg/media-resources/publications/research-innovation-enterprise-2015> (accessed 10 June 2015). The government will be sustaining its commitment to research, innovation and enterprise, and will invest $19 billion for the RIE2020 Plan between 2016 and 2020.
2. *National Survey of R&D in Singapore 2012* (Singapore: Agency for Science, Technology and Research, December 2013), p. 1.
3. Ibid., p. 8.
4. The issue of the rising proportion of foreigners in the city-state — including academics in the local universities — is becoming highly political. Some Singaporean academics are talking of an "imbalance" being caused by hiring many international academics and researchers, particularly into "sensitive" departments like political science and mass communication. And some young Singaporean doctoral students and faculty members fear they are being passed over for academic jobs and promotions in favour of professors from abroad.
5. *China Daily Asia Weekly*, 29 May – 4 June 2015.
6. J.D. Sachs, "Government, Geography, and Growth: The True Drivers of Economic Development", *Foreign Affairs* 92, no. 5 (2012): 142–50.
7. See Kwa Chong Guan, *Locating Singapore on the Maritime Silk Road: Evidence from Maritime Archaeology, Ninth to early Nineteenth Centuries* (Singapore: Institute of Southeast Asian Studies, 2012).
8. P. Regnier, *Singapore: City-State in South-East Asia*, translated by Christopher Hurst (Honolulu: University of Hawai'i Press, 1987), p. 39. It was geography that influenced Stamford Raffles to land on the island in January 1819. It was due to geography in the form of a sheltered deep-water harbour at the southern end of the island that was transformed and eventually became the famous port of call for the world's shipping lines. This coastal site offered deep-water berthing and better servicing facilities for larger vessels.
9. M. Porter, *Competitive Advantage of Nations* (New York: The Free Press, 1999), p. 256.
10. *Straits Times*, 4 July 2015.
11. See Goh Chor Boon, *Technology and Entrepot Colonialism in Singapore, 1819–1940* (Singapore: Institute of Southeast Asian Studies, 2013), Chapter 3, for a discussion on maritime technology and development of the port.

12. See Tan Yam Hua, Gertrude, "Technological Change and Development: A History of the Port of Singapore Authority from 1964–1990" (Honours thesis, Nanyang Technological University, 1966), for a study of how management and staff perceived technological change.

13. <http://www.singaporepsa.com/our-commitment/innovation> (accessed 30 April 2014).

14. See *Straits Times*, 15 September 2015. Singapore clinched the top spot on an index of global shipping centres for the second year in a row. The International Shipping Centre Development Index ranks the performances of forty-six major ports. London took second place and Hong Kong was third.

15. See Thomas Friedman, *The World is Flat* (New York: Farrar, Straus and Giroux, 2005).

16. Stephen Hill, "Creativity and Capture: The Social Architecture of Technological Innovation in Australia", *Verbatim Report: Contemporary Australian Speeches on Vital Issue* 1, no. 5 (1992): 162.

17. David Priestland, *Merchant, Soldier, Sage: A New History of Power* (London: Penguin Books, 2012), pp. 6–7.

18. <http:www.censtad.gov.hk/hkstat/sub/so120.jsp> (accessed 15 July 2014).

19. <http://www.enterpriseone.gov.sg and http://www.tradingeconomics.com/singapore/gdp-growth-annual> (accessed 7 August 2014).

20. *Straits Times*, 20 October 2014.

21. Lee Kuan Yew, *From Third World to First: The Singapore Story 1965–2000* (Singapore: Straits Times Press, 2000), Chapter 5.

22. *Sunday Times*, 25 September 1994.

23. *Straits Times*, 18 April 2014.

24. The annual Future China Global Forum is a significant channel initiated to foster China–Singapore business ties.

25. Bill Gates commented that digital or mobile banking is likely to take-off rapidly in countries such as South Africa, where a good proportion of the people do not use banks or banking institutions ("unbanked" people). While people in Singapore largely use their banks for financial transactions, mobile operators are already teaming up with banks to launch fintech services. Singtel has partnered Standard Chartered to launch the new mWallet Dash. See <http://e27.co/singtel-stanchart-make-dash-m-commerce-20140603> (accessed 10 June 2015).

26. Vladislav Solodkiy, "Ten Teasons Why Singapore Is the Next Big City for Fintech" <http://www.technasia.com.talk/lifesreda-emigrussia-inspirasia/> (accessed 10 June 2015).

27. *Straits Times*, 30 June 2015.

28. Robert Reich, *The Work of Nations* (New York: Vintage Books, 1992), pp. 177–78.

29. Ibid.

30. Porter, *Competitive Advantage of Nations*, p. 563.

31. See Grace Loh, Goh Chor Boon and Tan Teng Lan, *Building Bridges, Carving Niches* (Singapore: Oxford University Press, 2000), Chapter 7.

32. *Straits Times*, 2 April 2014.

33. *Straits Times*, 19 September 2014 and 20 November 2014. Singapore ranked fifth in Asia in terms of the number of billionaires in the population, behind leader China with 190 mega-wealthy, then followed by India, Hong Kong and Japan.

34. Lee Tsao Yuan and Linda Low, *Local Entrepreneurship in Singapore, Private and State* (Singapore: Times Academic Press, Institute of Policy Studies, 1990).

35. For a list of accolades pegged to the Singapore brand, see <http://www.edb.gov.sg/content/edb/en/why-singapore/about-singapore/facts-and-ranking...>.

36. *Straits Times*, 9 October 2014.

37. *Straits Times*, 29 October 2015.

38. David Chan Kum Wah, "Kiasuism and the Withering away of Singaporean Creativity", in *Singapore: Reflective Essays*, edited by Derek Da Cunha (Singapore: Institute of Southeast Asian Studies, 1994), p. 71.

39. *Straits Times*, 3 October 2015.

40. Robert Reich, *The Future of Success* (New York: Knoff, 2001), p. 68.

41. Kevin Hamlin, "Remaking Singapore", *Institutional Investor*, 7 June 2002.

42. *Straits Times*, 7 September 2015. The other two global cities on Sessen's list are Dubai and Hong Kong. See also the HSBC Expat Explorer survey report in the *Straits Times*, 23 September 2015, in which the majority of the 21,950 expats from the thirty-nine countries surveyed voted Singapore as the best place in the world to live and work.

43. Lee, *From Third World to First*, p. 597.

BIBLIOGRAPHY

Abramovitz, M. "Catching Up, Forging Ahead, and Falling Behind". *Journal of Economic History* 46, no. 2 (1986): 385–406.

Acemoglu, D. and J. Robinson. *Why Nations Fail: The Origin of Power, Prosperity and Poverty*. London: Profile Books, 2013.

Ahmed, A. "The Role of the Capital Goods Sector in Small, Open Economies". *Journal of Contemporary Asia* 24, no. 3 (1994).

Ali, A. *Malaysia Industrialization: The Quest for Technology*. Singapore: Oxford University Press, 1992.

Amin, S. *Neocolonialism in West Africa*. Harmondsworth: Penguin, 1973.

Amsden, A.M. *Asia's Next Giant: South Korea and Late Industrialisation*. New York: Oxford University Press, 1989.

———. *The Rise of 'The Rest': Challenges to the West from Late-Industrializing Economies*. New York: Oxford University Press, 2001.

Anderson, A. "Japanese Academics Bemoan the Cost of Years of Neglect". *Science*, 23 October 1992, pp. 564–82.

Anderson, C. *Makers: The New Industrial Revolution*. London: Random House, 2012.

Bartholomew, J.R. "Modern Science in Japan: Comparative Perspectives". *Journal of World History* 4, no. 1 (1993): 101–16.

Bello, W. "The Spread and Impact of Export-Oriented Industrialisation in the Pacific Rim". *Third World Economics*, 16–18 November 1991.

Berger, P.L. "An East Asian Development Model?" *Economic News*, 12–23 September 1984.

Bernard, M. and J. Ravenhill. "Beyond Product Cycles and Flying Geese: Regionalisation, Hierarchy and Industrialisation of East Asia". *World Politics* 47 (1995): 171–209.

Birmingham L. and D. McNeil. *Strong in the Rain: Surviving Japan's Earthquake, Tsunami and Fukushima Nuclear Disaster*. New York: Palgrave Macmillan, 2012.

Bloom, M.H. "Globalization and the Korean Electronics Industry". *Pacific Review* 6, no. 2 (1993).

Booth, A. "Did It Really Help to be a Japanese Colony? East Asian Economic Performance in Historical Perspective". Asia Research Institute Working Paper Series, no. 43. National University of Singapore, June 2005.

Brynjolfsson. E., and A. McAfee. *The Second Machine Age: Work, Progress, and Prosperity in a Time of Brilliant Technologies*. New York: Norton, 2014.

Buchanan, I. *Singapore in South East Asia: An Economic and Political Appraisal*. London: Bell, 1972.

Carnoy, M., M. Castells, S. Cohen and F.H. Cardoso. *The New Global Economy in the Information Age: Reflections on Our World*. Pennsylvania: Penn State University Press, 1993.

Castells, M. and P. Hall. *Technopoles of the World*. London: Routledge, 1994.

Chan, C.B. *Heart Work*. Singapore: Economic Development Board, 2002.

Chan, H.C. *Singapore: The Politics of Survival 1965–67*. Singapore: Oxford University Press, 1971.

Chen E.K.Y. *Multinational Corporations, Technology and Employment*. Hong Kong: Macmillan, 1983.

Chng M.K., ed. *Effective Mechanisms for the Enhancement of Technology and Skills in Singapore*. Singapore: ASEAN Secretariat, 1986.

Clark, N. "The Multinational Corporation: The Transfer of Technology and Dependence". *Development and Change* 6, no. 1 (1975).

Cooper, C.L., S. Cartwright and P.C. Earley, eds. *The International Handbook of Organizational Culture and Climate*. Chichester, NY: Wiley, 2001.

Cunha, D., ed. *Debating Singapore: Reflective Essays*. Singapore: Institute of Southeast Asian Studies, 1994.

Dahlman, C.J. and L.E. Westphal. "The Meaning of Technological Mastery in Relation to Transfer of Technology". *Annals of the American Academy of Political and Social Sciences* 458 (November 1981).

Dearing, J.W. *Growing a Japanese Science City: Communication in Scientific Research*. New York: Routledge, 1995.

Dixon, C. *South East Asia in the World Economy*. Cambridge: Cambridge University Press, 1991.

Douglas, S.J. "Some Thoughts on the Question: "How Do New Things Happen?" *Technology and Culture* 51, no. 2 (2010): 293–304.

Dower, J. *The Cultures of War: Pearl Harbor, Hiroshima, 9–11, Iraq* (New York: Norton, 2010).

———. *Ways of Forgetting, Ways of Remembering: Japan in the Modern World*. New York: The New Press, 2012.

Economic Development Board. *Growing With Enterprise: A National Effort*. Singapore, 1993.

Economic Planning Committee. *The Strategic Plan: Towards a Developed Nation*. Singapore: Ministry of Trade and Industry, 1991.

Economic Review Committee. *New Challenges, Fresh Goal — Towards a Dynamic Global City*. Singapore: Ministry of Trade and Industry, 2003.

Economic Strategies Committee. *Report of the Economic Strategies Committee*. Singapore: Ministry of Trade and Industry, February 2000.

———. *High Skill People, Innovative Economy, Distinctive Global City*. Singapore: Ministry of Trade and Industry, February 2010.

Eisemon, T.O. and C.H. Davis. "Universities and Scientific Capacity". *Journal of Asian and African Studies* 27, nos. 1–2 (1992): 68–93.

Ernst, D. and D. O'Connor. *Technology and Global Competition: The Challenge for Newly-Industrialising Economies*. OECD, 1989.

Etzkowitz, H. *The Triple Helix: University-Industry-Government Innovation in Action*. New York: Routledge, 2008.

———. "StartX and the Paradox of Success: Filling the Gap in Stanford's Entrepreneurial Culture". *Social Sciences Information* 52, no. 4 (2013): 605–37.

Far Eastern Economic Review. *Asia Year Book 1979*.

Felsenstein, D. "University-related Science Parks — 'Seedbeds' or 'Enclaves' of Innovation?" *Technovation* 12, no. 2 (1994): 93–110.

Florida, R. *The Rise of the Creative Class Revisited*. New York: Basic Books, 2013.

Florman, S. "Engineering and the Concept of the Elite". *The Bridge*. National Academy of Engineering. Winter 2001.

Fong, S.C. *The PAP Story: The Pioneering Years, November 1954 — April 1968*. Singapore: Times Periodicals, 1979.

Frank, A.G. *Capitalism and Underdevelopment in Latin America*. New York: Monthly Press Review, 1967.

———. "Global Crisis and Transformation". *Development and Change* 14 (1984): 323–46.

Fransman, M. *Technology and Economic Development*. Brighton, Sussex: Wheatsheaf, 1986.

Friedman, T. *The World is Flat*. New York: Farrar, Straus and Giroux, 2005.

Fuess, H., ed. *The Japanese Empire in East Asia and Its Postwar Legacy*. Munich: Ludicium, 1988.

Gereffi, G. and D.L. Wyman, eds. *Manufacturing Miracles: Paths of Industrialization in Latin America and East Asia*. Princeton, NJ: Princeton University Press, 1990.

Gibney, F. *The Pacific Century*. New York: Scribner, 1992.

Glaeser, E. *The Triumph of the City: How Our Greatest Invention Makes Us Richer, Smarter, Greener, Healthier and Happier*. New York: Macmillan, 2011.

Goh C.B. "Science and Technology in Singapore: The Mindset of the Engineering Undergraduate". *Asia Pacific Journal of Education* 18, no. 1 (1998) 7–24.

──────. *Technology and Entrepot Colonialism in Singapore, 1819–1940* (Singapore: Institute of Southeast Asian Studies, 2013).

Goh, C.T. *Nation of Excellence*. Singapore: Information Division, Ministry of Communications & Information, 1987.

Goh. K.S. *The Economics of Modernization*. Singapore: Asia Pacific Press, 1972.

Greenberg, D.S. *The Politics of Science*. New York: New American Library, 1967.

──────. "The Mythical Scientist Shortage". *Scientist* 17, no. 6 (2003).

Haden, C.R. and J.R. Brink, eds. *Innovative Models for University Research*. Amsterdam: North-Holland, 1992.

Hafiz, M. *Multinationals and the Growth of the Singapore Economy*. London: Croom Helm, 1986.

Haggard, S., D. Kang and C.-I. Moon. "Japanese Colonialism and Korean Development: A Critique". *World Development* 25, no. 6 (1997): 867–81.

Hakam, A.H. "Deliberate Restructuring in the Newly Industrializing Countries of Asia — The Case of Singapore". In *East Asia*, vol. 3. Frankfurt: Campus, 1985.

Hakam, A.N. and Z.-Y. Chang. "Patterns of Technology Transfer in Singapore: The Case of the Electronics and Computer Industry". *International Journal of Technology Management* 13, nos. 1–2 (1988).

Hamlin, K. "Remaking Singapore". *Institutional Investor*, 7 June 2002.

Hampden-Turner, C. and A. Trompenaars. *The Seven Cultures of Capitalism*. New York: Doubleday, 1993.

Hang, C.C. "NUS-Industry R&D Collaboration: An Overview". *Proceedings of Seminar on NUS-Industry R&D Collaborations: Potential, Resources and Benefits*. National University of Singapore, 1993.

Hayashi, T., ed. *The Japanese Experience in Technology: From Transfer to Self-Reliance*. Tokyo: United Nations University Press, 1990.

Heitger, B. "Comparative Economic Growth: Catching Up in East Asia". *ASEAN Economic Bulletin* 10, no. 1 (1993): 68–74.

Herbig, P.A. and F. Palumbo. "The Effect of Culture on the Adoption Process". *Technological Forecasting and Social Change* 46 (1994): 71–101.

Hill, H. and Pang E.F. "Technology Exports from a Small, Very Open NIC: The Case of Singapore". Working Papers in Trade and Development. Australian National University, August 1989.

Hill, S. "Creativity and Capture: The Social Architecture of Technological Innovation in Australia". *The Verbatim Report: Contemporary Australian Speeches on Vital Issue* 1, no. 5 (1992): 161–69.

Hilpert, U., ed. *State Policies and Techno-Industrial Innovation*. London: Routledge, 1991.

Hing, A.Y. "Automation and New Work Patterns: Cases from Singapore's Electronics Industry Work". *Employment & Society*, vol. 9 (June 1995): 309–27.

Hirano, Y. "Public and Private Support of Basic Research in Japan". *Science*, 23 October 1992, pp. 582–83.

Hirsch, F. *Social Limits to Growth*. Cambridge, MA: Harvard University Press, 1976.

Hobday, M. "Technological Learning in Singapore: A Test Case of Leapfrogging". *Journal of Development Studies* 30, no. 30 (1994): 831–58,

Hofheinz, R. and K. Calder. *The Eastasia Edge*. New York: Basic Books, 1982.

Hofstede, G. *Culture's Consequences: International Differences in Work-Related Values*. Beverly Hills: Sage, 1980.

———. *Cultures and Organizations: Software of the Mind*. New York: McGraw Hill, 1991.

Hong, E. *The Birth of Korean Cool: How One Nation is Conquering the World through Pop Culture*. New York: Picador, 2014.

Inkeles, A. *What Is Sociology?* Englewood Cliffs, NJ: Prentice-Hall, 1964.

Inkster, I. *Science and Technology in History: An Approach to Industrial Development*. New Brunswick, NJ: Rutgers University Press, 1991.

Ishihara, S. *The Japan That Can Say No*. Translated by Frank Baldwin. Simon and Schuster, 1991.

Jacobs, J. *The Economy of Cities*. New York: Random House, 1969.

Jeffs, A. "Genius at Work", *Asia Magazine*, 1–2 July 1994.

Johnson, C. "Political Institutions and Economic Performance: The Government-Business Relationship in Japan, South Korea and Taiwan". In *Asian Economic Development: Present and Future*, by R.A. Scalapino et al. Berkeley: Institute of East Asian Studies, 1985.

Kennedy, P. *The Rise and Fall of British Naval Mastery*. London: Fontana, 1991.

———. *Engineers of Victory: The Problem Solvers Who Turned the Tide in the Second World War*. New York: Random House, 2013.

Kim, D.J. "Is Culture Destiny? The Myth of Asia's Anti-Democratic Values". *Foreign Affairs* 73, no. 6 (1994): 189–94.

Kim, L. *Imitation to Innovation: The Dynamics of Korea's Technological Learning* (Boston: Harvard Business School Press, 1997).

———. "Crisis Construction and Organizational Learning: Capability Building in Catching-Up at Hyundai Motor". *Organization Science* 9, no. 4 (1998).

Kim, M.O. and S. Jaffe. *The New Korea: An Inside Look at South Korea's Economic Rise*. New York: Amacom, 2010.

Kinmonth, E.H. "Japanese Engineers and American Myth Makers". *Pacific Affairs* 64, no. 3 (1991): 328–50.

Koh, W.T.H. and Wong P.K. *The Venture Capital Industry in Singapore: A Comparative Study with Taiwan and Israel on the Government's Role*. Working Paper. NUS Entrepreneurship Centre, May 2005.

———. "Competing at the Frontier: The Changing Role of Technology Policy in Singapore's Economic Strategy". *Technological Forecasting and Social Change* 72, no. 3 (2005): 255–85.

Kohli, A. *State-Directed Development: Political Power and Industrialization in the Global Periphery*. Cambridge: Cambridge University Press, 2004.

Kosaka, M., ed. *Japan's Choices: New Globalism and Cultural Orientations in an Industrial State*. London: Pinter, 1989.

Krause, L.B., Koh A.T and Lee. T.Y. *The Singapore Economy Reconsidered*. Singapore: Institute of Southeast Asian Studies, 1987.

Krugman, P. "The Myth of Asia's Miracle". *Foreign Affairs* 73, no. 6 (1994).

Kunio, Y. *The Rise of Ersatz Capitalism in South-East Asia*. Singapore: Oxford University Press, 1988.

Kwa C.G. *Locating Singapore on the Maritime Silk Road: Evidence from Maritime Archaeology, Ninth to early Nineteenth Centuries*. Singapore: Institute of Southeast Asian Studies, 2012.

Lee S.K., C.B. Goh, B. Fredriksen and J.P. Tan, eds. *Toward a Better Future: Education and Training for Economic Development in Singapore since 1965*. Washington, DC: World Bank, 2008.

Lee T.Y. and Linda Low. *Local Entrepreneurship in Singapore, Private and State*. Singapore: Times Academic Press/Institute of Policy Studies, 1990.

Lee, K.Y. *From Third World to First: The Singapore Story 1965–2000*. Singapore: Straits Times Press, 2000.

Lee, S.A. *Industrialization in Singapore*. Camberwell, Australia: Longman, 1973.

Leong, C.H. and D. Soon. *A Study of Emigration Attitudes of Young Singaporeans*, Working Papers no. 19. Institute of Policy Studies, March 2011.

Lim C.Y. and P.J. Lloyd., eds. *Singapore Resources and Growth*. Singapore: Oxford University Press, 1986.

Lim, J.J. "Bold Internal Decisions, Emphatic External Outlook". *Southeast Asian Affairs 1980*, edited by Leo Suryadinata. Singapore: Institute of Southeast Asian Studies, 1980.

Lim, L.Y.C. "Multinational Firms and Manufacturing for Export in Less Developed Countries: The Case of Malaysia and Singapore". PhD dissertation, University of Michigan, 1978.

Lindsey, C.W. "Transfer of Technology to the ASEAN Region by U.S. Transnational Corporations". *ASEAN Economic Bulletin* 3, no. 2 (1986).

Loh, G., Goh C.B. and Tan T.L. *Building Bridges, Carving Niches.* Singapore: Oxford University Press, 2000.

Mae, P.S.A. and H.W.C. Yeung. "A Place for R&D? The Singapore Science Park". *Urban Studies* 40, no. 4 (2003): 707–32.

Mahbubani, K. *Can Asians Think.* Singapore: Marshall Cavendish, 2009.

Massey, D. *High-tech Fantasies: Science Parks in Society, Science, and Space.* London: Routledge, 1992.

McGinn, R.E. *Science, Technology and Society.* Englewood Cliffs: Prentice Hall, 1991.

McKinsey & Company, ed. *Reimagining Japan: The Quest for a Future that Works.* San Francisco: VIZ Media, 2011.

Ministry of Trade and Industry. *Strategic Economic Plan.* Singapore: Ministry of Trade and Industry, 1991.

Mokyr, J. *The Lever of Riches: Technological Creativity and Economic Progress.* Oxford: Oxford University Press, 1990.

Mooney, C. and S. Kirshenbaum. *Unscientific America: How Scientific Illiteracy Threatens Our Future.* New York, Basic Books, 2009.

Morishima, M. *Why has Japan succeeded? Western Technology and the Japanese Ethos.* London: Cambridge University Press, 1982.

Morita, A. *Made in Japan: Akio Morita and Sony.* London: Collins, 1987.

Moritani, M. *Japanese Technology and its Transfer to Singapore.* Working Paper. Policy and Management Research Department, Nomura Research Institute, August 1982.

Myers, R.H. and M.R. Peattie, eds. *The Japanese Colonial Empire.* Princeton, NJ: Princeton University Press, 1984.

Nakata, C. and L. Sivakumar. "National Culture and New Product Development: An Integrative Review". *Journal of Marketing* 60, no. 1 (1996): 61–72.

National Survey of R&D in Singapore 2002. Singapore: Agency for Science, Technology and Research, December 2003.

National Survey of R&D in Singapore 2012. Singapore: Agency for Science, Technology and Research, December 2013.

Ng C.Y., R. Hirono and R.Y. Siy, Jr., eds. *Effective Mechanisms for the Enhancement of Technology and Skills in ASEAN: An Overview.* Singapore: Institute of Southeast Asian Studies, 1986.

Ozawa, T. "The (Japan-Born) 'Flying Geese' Theory of Economic Development Revisited — and Reformulated from a Structuralist Perspective. Columbia Business School Working Paper Series, no. 291. Columbia University in the City of New York, 2010.

Pang, E.F. *Foreign Investment and the State in a Newly-Industrializing Country: The Experience of Singapore.* East Asia, vol. 3. Frankfurt: Campus, 1985.

Petitjean, P., C. Jami and A.M. Moulin, eds. *Science and Empires: Historical Studies about Scientific Development and European* Expansion. Boston: Kluwer Academic, 1992.

Porter M. *Competitive Advantage of Nations*. New York: The Free Press, 1990.

Portnoff, A. *Pathways to Innovation*, translated by Ann Johnson. Paris: Futuribles Perspectives, 2003.

Priestland, D. *Merchant, Soldier, Sage: A New History of Power*. London: Penguin Books, 2012.

Puthucheary, J.J. *Ownership and Control in the Malayan Economy*. Singapore: Eastern Universities Press, 1960; repr., Kuala Lumpur: University of Malaya Co-Operative Bookshop, 1979.

Quah, S.T., ed. *In Search of Singapore's National Values*. Singapore: Times Academic Press, 1990.

Regnier, P. *Singapore: City-State in South-East Asia,* translated by Christopher Hurst. Honolulu: University of Hawai'i Press, 1987.

Reich, R. *The Work of Nations*. New York: Vintage Books, 1992.

———. *The Future of Success*. New York: Knoff, 2001.

Rodan, G., ed. *Singapore Changes Guard: Social, Political and Economic Directions in the 1990s*. New York: St Martin's Press, 1993.

———. *The Political Economy of Singapore's Industrialization*. Kuala Lumpur: Forum Press, 1991.

Romjin, H.A. and M.C.J. Caniëls. "Pathways of Technological Change in Developing Countries: Review and New Agenda". *Development Policy Review* 29, no. 3 (2011): 359–80.

Rosenberg, N. *Perspective on Technology*. Cambridge: Cambridge University Press, 1976.

Sachs, J.D. "Government, Geography, and Growth: The True Drivers of Economic Development". *Foreign Affairs* 92, no. 5 (2012).

Sahal, D., ed. *The Transfer and Utilization of Technical* Knowledge. Lexington, MA: Lexington Books, 1980.

Sakaiya, T. *What Is Japan? Contradictions and Transformations*, translated by Steven Karpa. Tokyo: Kodansha International, 1993.

Salto-Tellez, M., V.M.S. Oh and E.H. Lee. "How do we Encourage Clinician Scientists in Singapore? *Academic Medicine in Singapore* 26, no. 11 (2007).

Saxenian, A.L. *Regional Advantage: Culture and Competition in Silicon Valley and Route 128*. Cambridge, MA: Harvard University Press, 1996.

Scalapino, R., S. Sato and J. Wanandi, eds. *Asian Economic Development: Present and Future*. Berkeley: Institute of East Asian Studies, 1985.

Schmidt. E. and J. Cohen. *The New Digital Age: Reshaping the Future of People, Nations and Business*. London: Murray, 2013.

Schnaars, S.P. *Managing Imitation Strategies: How Later Entrants Seize Markets from Pioneers*. New York: The Free Press, 1994.

Schumpeter, J.A. *Capitalism, Socialism, and Democracy*, 6th ed. London: Routledge, 2010.

Shimizu, T. "Technology Transfer and Dynamism in Technology Education in Japan". In *Technology Culture and Development*, edited by Ungku A. Aziz. International Symposium at the University of Malaya, December 1983.

Suzuki, T.-M. *The Technological Transformation of Japan from the Seventeenth to the Twenty-first Century*. Cambridge: Cambridge University Press, 1994.

Tai, H.-C. *Confucianism and Economic Development: An Oriental Alternative?* Washington, DC: The Washington Institute Press, 1989.

Tambyah, S.K. and Tan S.J. *Happiness and Wellbeing: The Singaporean Experience*. Abingdon: Routledge, 2013.

Tan. G.Y.H. "Technological Change and Development: A History of the Port of Singapore Authority from 1964–1990". Honours thesis, Nanyang Technological University, 1966.

Tassey, G. *Technology Infrastructure Technological Infrastructure Policy: An International Perspective*. Dordrecht: Kluwer Academic, 1996.

Tatsuno, S. *Created in Japan: From Imitators to World-Class innovators*. New York: Harper & Row, 1990.

Tessitore, J. and S. Woolfson, eds. *The Asian Development Model and the Carribean Basin Model Institute*. New York: Council on Religious and International Affairs, 1985.

Thurow, L.C. *Head to Head: The Coming Economic Battle among Japan, Europe, and America*. New York: Morrow, 1992.

Ting, W.L. *Business and Technological Dynamics in Newly Industrializing Asia*. Westport: Quorum Books, 1985.

Turnbull, M. *History of Singapore, 1819–1988*. Singapore: Oxford University Press, 1989.

Vogel, E. *The Four Little Dragons: The Spread of Industrialisation in East Asia*. Cambridge: Harvard University Press, 1991.

Wang, C.K. and P.K. Wong. "Entrepreneurial Interest of University Students in Singapore". *Technovation*, vol. 24 (February 2004): 163–72.

Walsh, V. *Technology and the Economy: The Key Relationships*. Parish: OECD, 1992.

Westphal, L., E. Kim and C. Dahlman. *Reflections on Korea's Acquisition of Technological Capability*, DRD Discussion Paper 77. Washington, DC: World Bank, 1984.

Williamson, J. and C. Milner. *The World Economy: A Textbook in International Economics*. New York: New York University Press, 1991.

Wong, Poh Kam. *National Innovation Systems for Rapid Technological Catch–Up: An Analytical Framework and a Comparative Analysis of Korea, Taiwan and Singapore*. Paper presented at the DRUID Summer Conference on National Innovation Systems, Industrial Dynamics and Innovation Policy, Rebild, Denmark, 9–12 June 1999.

———. "Commercialising Biomedical Science in a Rapidly Changing "Triple Helix" Nexus: The Experience of the National University of Singapore". *Journal of Technology Transfer* 32, no. 4 (2007): 367–95.

You, Poh Seng and Lim C.Y., eds. *The Singapore Economy*. Singapore: Eastern University Press, 1971.

Young, A. "A Tale of Two Cities: Factor Accumulation and Technical Change in Hong Kong and Singapore". In *NBER Macroeconomics Annual 1992*. Massachusetts Institute of Technology Press, 1992.

Yusuf, S. and K. Nabeshima. *Postindustrial East Asian Cities: Innovation for Growth*. Washington, DC: World Bank, 2006.

Zakaria, F. "Culture is Destiny: A Conversation with Lee Kuan Yew". *Foreign Affairs* 73, no. 2 (1994): 109–26.

Ziman, J. *Prometheus Bound: Science in a Dynamic Steady State*. Cambridge: Cambridge University Press, 1994.

Official Reports

Colony of Singapore. Annual Report. 1965.

———. The United Nations Report on Singapore. 1961.

Department of Statistics. Yearbook of Statistics. 1986 and 1989.

Economic Development Board. Annual Report. 1972 and 1980.

Gilmour, A. Official Letters, 1931–1956, Mss. Ind. Ocn. s. 154.

Government Printing Office. Singapore Year Book 1969.

Parliament of Singapore, Official Reports – Parliamentary Debates, various years.

Singapore. Census of Industrial Production, 1959 to 1969.

INDEX

About the Author

GOH CHOR BOON is currently the Associate Dean at the National Institute of Education (NIE) International. He is the author of *Technology and Entrepot Colonialism in Singapore, 1819–1940.*